Rave Reviews for *Guerrilla Trade Show Selling*

"Here is everything you'll need: Who to call, what to do, where to go, what to avoid. This is the most comprehensive and practical book on trade show selling I've ever seen."

Jim Cathcart, CSP, CPAE
Past President, National Speakers Association
Author, *Relationship Selling*

"The work is a comprehensive primer for newbies and wannabes, as well as a useful reference for the experienced exhibitor and show manager."

R. William Taylor, CAE
President, American Society of Association Executives

"The information is presented in a dynamic, professional, easy-to-use format. I heartily recommend it to anyone who wants to get the most from their first, or five thousandth, trade show experience."

Corrie Shaw
Corporate Communications Manager, AT&T Capital Corporation

"This book is long overdue in the industry. For the beginner, it offers no-nonsense information to jump-start a career. And for those already in the industry, the information is a refresher course with new and innovative ideas. I'm looking forward to recommending it to readers and ad~~vertisers~~ ~~and will refer to it~~ frequently. It should be on the shelf ~~~~ side *Exhibitor Times*, of course."

.M. Demetros
Exhibitor Times

D0973443

"I have spent many l   trade shows. Finally, *Guerrilla Trade ~~Show Selling~~* has shown me and my staff how to do it right. I only wish I had it ten years ago!"

Jack Canfield
Coauthor, *New York Times* #1 Bestseller, *Chicken Soup for the Soul*

"A powerful survival guidebook for every serious exhibitor."

Susan A. Friedmann
Author, *Exhibiting at Tradeshows: Tips & Techniques for Success*

"Incredible!!! You have done it again!! Having been involved in trade shows for 28 years—you have produced a revolutionary guide to peak performance results for your trade show investment!"

Naomi Rhode, CSP, CPAE
Past President, National Speakers Association
Vice President, Smart Practice, Inc.

"A great overview for the trade show marketer. You put the 'guerrilla' to work on every page." **Jane Lorimer**
Past President, Trade Show Bureau
Principal, Lorimer Consulting Group

"The fast-attacking Guerrilla Group strikes again . . . with their highly readable, clear-as-a-bell *Guerrilla Trade Show Selling*. If you're into exhibits and displays and selling in critical trade shows, you *must* have this thorough, accurate, and comprehensive blockbuster of a guide!" **Nick Carter**
Vice President, Communications Research, Nightingale Conant

"When it comes to guerrilla tactics for trade show business growth, this book has it all wrapped up. Prepare to do battle!" **Thomas Winninger**
Past President, National Speakers Association
Founder & CEO, Winninger Institute for Market Strategy
Author, *Price Wars*

"The techniques in your book can make companies hundreds of thousands of dollars if they implement them at shows. After reviewing your manuscript, I immediately thought of exhibitors who have made every mistake that you caution against, specifically 'That's the way we've always done it!!!' " **Alan J. Huber**, CFP
President, Life & Health Product EXPO (The Insurance Trade Show)

"*Guerrilla Trade Show Selling* hits the mark! Why stand around and wait for the action when you can take action and turn every trade show into dollars?" **Danielle Kennedy**
Author, *7 Figure Selling* and *Mathers in the Big League*

"This is great information! Down-to-earth, practical, and sound, your ideas provide a commonsense approach to a much needed area. This is a must for anyone who does or wants to participate in a trade show. All marketers should have this in their library." **Patricia L. Dove**
Senior Marketing Vice President, Educational Institute,
American Hotel & Motel Association

"Marketing is the ultimate leverage in growing rich, happy, and omnisuccessful. *Guerrilla Trade Show Selling* teaches you to become a master marketer. Outperform all the competition with these brilliant insights!" **Mark Victor Hansen**
Coauthor, *New York Times* #1 Bestseller, *Chicken Soup for the Soul*

GUERRILLA TRADE SHOW SELLING

NEW UNCONVENTIONAL WEAPONS AND TACTICS TO MEET MORE PEOPLE, GET MORE LEADS, AND CLOSE MORE SALES

JAY CONRAD LEVINSON

MARK S. A. SMITH

ORVEL RAY WILSON

John Wiley & Sons, Inc.

New York ➤ Chichester ➤ Weinheim ➤ Brisbane ➤ Singapore ➤ Toronto

Library of Congress Cataloging-in-Publication Data:

Levinson, Jay Conrad.
    Guerrilla trade show selling : new unconventional weapons and tactics to meet more people, get more leads, and close more sales / by Jay Conrad Levinson, Mark S. A. Smith, Orvel Ray Wilson.
       p.   cm.
    Includes bibliographical references.
    ISBN 0-471-16568-9 (paper : alk. paper)
    1. Sales promotion. 2. Trade shows. I. Smith, Mark S. A.
II. Wilson, Orvel Ray. III. Title.
HF5438.5.L475 1997
658.8′2—dc20   96-25074
                                          CIP

Preface

Most sales professionals agree: Nobody sells much at a trade show. Visitors flow by like a lazy river, dazed by the halogen lights and overwhelmed by sights and sounds. Most salespeople will tell you that it's just too busy, too noisy, and too crazy to connect with customers. And most of them would be right.

The reason is simple. Most salespeople have never learned how to sell *effectively* in the trade show environment. Only 15 percent—less than one in six—of all trade show exhibitors are effective, intelligent, and focused on serving their customers. And that makes all the difference.

At a sporting-goods show in Las Vegas, two ski manufacturers were exhibiting on opposite sides of the same aisle. The first one didn't sell a thing; not a dime. The second wrote orders for over three million dollars worth of skis in three days.

This smart minority cleans up at shows, leaving with briefcases bulging with orders, while the others go home with empty pockets.

There's no denying, trade shows are big business!

➤ Every year, 1.3 *million* companies exhibit their wares in front of 85 million people at more than 4,300 commercial and association-sponsored trade shows.

➤ Conventions, expositions, and meetings rank 17th among all private-sector industries and generated $49.9

billion of direct spending, producing a total economic impact of $225 billion in 1991.

➤ After magazine advertising, trade shows are the nation's second largest marketing expenditure.

➤ Trade shows account for 18 percent of marketing budgets.

➤ The 200 largest shows have 100,000 participating companies, spending a total of $12 *billion* every year.

➤ The number of shows has grown by 7 percent per year for the past decade and is expected to continue to expand.

➤ Corporate trade show budgets have increased by more than 50 percent in the past two years.

These figures do not include business-to-business expos sponsored by chambers of commerce; local shows such as those held in shopping malls; international shows; or shows held by companies for their vendors, customers, and sales force.

➤ Virtually every one of the 28,000 chambers of commerce sponsored at least one business-to-business expo show this year.

➤ More than 20,000 associations have a trade show during their conventions.

We're going to show you how to take advantage of all this magnificent opportunity.

Guerrilla Trade Show Selling is the first book to apply guerrilla sales and marketing tactics to the unique, high-pressure environment of the trade show floor. We're going to share with you the insider secrets, tips, and techniques that will make you part of that elite 15 percent. This book is for *any* business of *any* size, be it corporate or entrepreneurial or product-based or service-based that wants to use trade shows as an effective marketing weapon.

A sequel to the very successful *Guerrilla Selling, Guerrilla Trade Show Selling* gives salespeople, sales managers, marketing managers, and small business owners an arsenal of *new unconventional weapons and tactics to meet more people, get more leads, and close more sales.*

Guerrilla Trade Show Selling is for people who insist on results. It will show you a step-by-step approach that will multiply your sales results many times over. *Guerrilla Trade Show Selling* is the answer to maximizing your trade show investment.

Guerrilla Trade Show Selling is divided into three parts, organized chronologically. It presents the 12 steps required to maximize sales before, during, and after attending a trade show. You will learn:

➤ How trade show selling differs from a normal sales call, and five reasons why the skills that usually make salespeople effective will *kill* them at a show

➤ How to select the hottest shows for your products and services in order for you to reach the best markets

➤ How to prepare for a successful show mentally, physically, and emotionally

➤ Insider secrets on getting a great booth location without paying top dollar

➤ How to overcome typical success-killing problems and snafus that can pop up at a show

➤ How to make your exhibits more memorable, more exciting, and more approachable without spending a fortune on a custom booth

➤ How to maintain maximum comfort, energy, and enthusiasm during long hours working a trade show floor

➤ How to attract visitors into your booth with dress and clothing, based on image and perception techniques

➤ How to attract the *right* people who want to do business by excluding the tire-kickers, using proven billboard advertising and direct-marketing techniques

➤ How to create powerful presentations based on state-of-the-art adult learning and communication theory

➤ How to meet more people, psychologically connect and establish rapport instantly, and make a positive, lasting impression on every prospect using a new discovery in linguistics

➤ How to deliver a powerful, custom-tailored presentation or demonstration to every visitor

➤ How to get the maximum number of high-quality sales leads from a show

➤ What to say and do to make the prospect *look forward* to the next sales contact

➤ How to move people along gracefully so your salespeople can speak to the next prospect

➤ How to create effective follow-up programs, based on modern computer, direct-mail, tele-sales, and personal selling technology, to make the show really pay off long after it is over.

➤ How to motivate salespeople to follow up trade show leads and close sales immediately

➤ How to measure the results of a trade show, guarantee a bigger budget for next year, and assure the future success of a trade show program

This book offers a solid, "here's what you do to be successful" approach, with a wealth of real-life examples. These concepts will get results, making this one of the most important books in your business library.

Contents

Chapter 4: How to Turn Your Exhibit into a Buyer Magnet   **97**

Chapter 5: The Rewards of Guerrilla Selling on the Trade Show Floor 125

Chapter 6: Setting Up at the Show with No Hassles, in Record Time 149

Chapter 9: Guerrilla Presentations They'll Never Forget

Introduction

■ THE LONG FLIGHT HOME

After stowing your briefcase in the overhead bin, you collapse into your seat and snap the seatbelts together with a click.

It's been a long week; your industry's biggest trade show. These events are usually a drag, but tonight you feel great! This time, everything was different. Instead of long, dull days just standing around, the time just *flew* by. Armed with new guerrilla tactics, your team closed more deals in these three days than in the last three *months* combined, and this business will be much more profitable. Wait until the boss finds out how well you've done.

What a change! After years of boring, expensive shows, *this* time you took command and made some changes. *This* time, everything came off without a hitch. This time the exhibit looked *terrific*, your people were *ready*, and customers just *flocked* to the booth. The only surprise was that *everything* worked, and now you know *exactly* how to get the same results, every time.

You recline the seat and stretch, half-heartedly thumbing the pages of the in-flight magazine as the other passengers board. You recognize a group of your competitor's salespeople as they make their way through the cabin. They look *exhausted*.

"So, what did you think of the show?" you ask, trying to be friendly.

"A total waste," says one.

"Yeah, a real dud!" adds another as he wrestles his carry-on down the aisle.

"I don't even know why we bother," says their manager, "but we have to make an appearance every year to keep up with the competition. We'd be conspicuous by our absence."

Hard to believe they were exhibiting in the *same* show. In fact, their booth was just down the aisle from yours.

"Yeah, I know what you mean!" you offer, trying to look glum to keep them off guard, but inside you're laughing. They don't even *suspect*. You snatched a major account away from them this week, and you did it *right under their noses*. And even though they outspent you ten to one, you've completely outmaneuvered and outsold these guys.

As the plane pushes back from the gate, you recall how you selected this show. For the first time in years, you knew *exactly* why you were there, and you knew *exactly* what to expect. You passed up another show where you've been exhibiting for years; sad to think what a waste of time *that* was. Now you know *exactly* how to select the right show, every time, and you can concentrate your resources where they'll produce *maximum* results.

The plane taxies to the runway, and as the engines spool up for take-off, you feel the vibrations coming through your seat. It's just *amazing* how well this show went. You've been doing trade shows for years, and you *expect* to have problems; these events are *supposed* to be one big headache. Hey, after all, you first learned the trade show business the same way everyone else does, by watching other exhibitors and doing what they do. Sure, your boss coached you a bit in the beginning, but he learned about trade shows the same way—the blind leading the blind. Now that you've learned the guerrilla's secrets of trade show success, you'll never make those mistakes again.

This time the exhibit went together in a snap, and you actually got to bed before 1:00 A.M.! And the labor was so cooperative. It must have been the new way you treated the workers, the way they needed to be treated so they could get the job done. There were a couple of snags, but backup plans worked out, and the issues were quickly resolved. While the competition fumbled around trying to locate samples and literature, you were ready to hit the floor selling from the moment they opened the doors.

It used to be all the big deals passed you by because the companies with the big bucks never stopped at your exhibit. But *this* time, all the heavy hitters came straight to your exhibit and actually *talked* to you. No doubt, a big part of it was the program you designed to make *sure* they *had* to stop by. They sure seemed eager. You're looking forward to getting back to the office to do the full proposal on the deal you shook hands on last night. This could really catapult your company to new heights. This was the first time you've been in a situation where that could happen. From now on, you'll be looking for those deals, and you'll know exactly how and where to find them at every show.

At last year's show, you had to practically stand on your head to get anyone to stop at the booth. Then, when it got busy, you had so many tire-kickers that there wasn't enough time to pitch the real prospects. But this time, your new plan worked perfectly, and almost like magic, because only the *legitimate* prospects stopped in. You were able to spend all your time with people who were *ready* to deal, right there, right then. What a relief not having to deal with all the looky-lous. The new booth design did the trick. You'll never again let an exhibit designer talk you into anything different.

Your plane reaches cruising altitude, and a chime sounds as the captain turns off the seat-belt light. You stand and stretch and remember how you actually closed dozens of sales right there on the trade show floor. You've never taken an order on the show floor before, except for a fluke deal a long time ago. Now you have the keys to closing the sale right on the show floor.

The flight attendant hands you a cold drink. Your advance work really paid off. You got the biggest budget ever for booth space and exhibits, and you were really able to do it *right*. But a guerrilla knows that "right" doesn't necessarily mean big, fancy, and expensive. Your competitors were amazed at how busy your new booth was, even though theirs was much more elaborate; it must have cost them a *fortune*.

And you broke out of the old "exhibit wars." In the past you tried to out-exhibit the competition, and every year your competitors seemed to have even *more* money to spend. But this year, you beat them at their own game. Instead of blowing big bucks on a big new booth, you refurbished a few pieces and rented a few more. Then you put the savings into *staffing*, driving sales activity you *know* is going to make you a hero. And you now know exactly how to do it, every time, every show.

You think about all the VIPs who stopped by to congratulate you, to talk with you, and to express how much they looked forward to doing business with you. You roped them right in by creating different show promotions attracting specific individuals. In the preshow planning, the idea seemed silly. Some of your own salespeople scoffed at the idea. Now they have to eat crow. Your most skeptical VP actually said, "What you did was fabulous! I'm proud of you. Thank you for your contribution to our company."

For the first time, the things that you gave away drew just the prospects you wanted. Your premiums used to be so attractive that people just snatched them up. Some even asked for an extra for their boss or kids. And then they had to stand there and listen to your pitch so they could take the stuff without feeling guilty. What a waste! Not this time. You selected promotional items that only interested the people who *needed* what you sell. In fact, real buyers were dying to get their hands on them. They told you it was the *one* thing from the show they would keep and use, and the rest of the visitors just kept on walking. And just think! Now you know how to do this for *any* product, any service, any show.

You thought about how easy it was to reach out, greet people, and then get them talking about themselves and their needs. It's always been hard to get visitors to move on, but this time you knew how first to qualify their buying power and then to send them gently on their way.

Then there were the competitive snoops. You knew exactly how to handle them this time. What a hoot! You got exactly what you wanted from *them* and seriously short-circuited their plans.

You're glad you kept that grouchy salesman away from the show this year, the one who usually dominates the exhibit. It was easy, and what a pleasure to watch the junior salespeople reaching out, contacting visitors, and making real progress toward a deal. This time, your novice staff outsold the competitor's veterans. This year, you put together a complete team, including salespeople and staff from other parts of the firm as well. And what a great job they did! It seemed a waste to put them *all* through sales training, but it's already paying off in the improvement in their attitude toward prospects and customers, and you can already see the improvement in customer service. This time you brought in a professional trainer. Even after years and years of working shows, you were amazed at how much you learned. There are a lot of unique tricks for selling at a trade show that you'd never use out on the street, things you *never* would have thought of. It really made a lot of sense, and it worked like magic!

You snap open your briefcase and pull out a brown manila folder bulging with new leads. Amazing how much information your salespeople took down in such a short period of time. At past shows, maybe four or five percent of the leads were hot. In this stack, they're *all* hot. One hundred percent! And with complete information like this, your salespeople can pick up the conversation right where they left off and move forward immediately. Your salespeople used to grumble about what a waste of time trade show leads were. "There's no real buyers from that show," you've heard them say. This time, you *know* the leads are solid gold. And now you have a plan for helping them realize the value of the leads. You know they'll willingly follow up and close. They'll know exactly what they have to do next to close the business quickly. With one simple change in the way you collected leads, you got this level of quality.

A few quick extensions on your calculator and you can see that this show is really going to pay off. Projected sales are astronomical. You'll close 25 percent of your year's forecast just on the leads from this one show. If every show were this good, you could double the company with just a few more shows. And you now know how to make every show this good, every time.

Now you consider how little it cost to deliver your sales packages, and with such impact. Your literature is already sitting on the top of your key visitors' in-trays, customized just for them—exactly the way they wanted, and unopened by their administrative assistant. You know that it's one of the first things they'll be expecting when they get back to the office. You never would have done that before. It used to take weeks to get all the leads processed and the literature out, but now you know how to get it done almost instantly. You think about how, for the first time, you wrote the follow-up letter specifically to sell. You even got help from a professional copywriter. Some of the people who reviewed it before the show have already placed orders, and more will be pouring in next week. And you know how to do it for every show. You grin as you think about your competition scrambling to fulfill requests for literature. That stuff won't go out for another two or three weeks. By then, you'll have already made two sales calls on all your new prospects. You're ready to act *now,* and you'll profit from your competitors' tardiness.

You chuckle quietly as you think about the strong competitive data that you were able to collect at the show. What a great way to fly under the radar of your competitors. You even market-tested a new product without them even knowing what was going on.

What a difference this information would have made on your career as a sales manager a few years ago. And you shake your head, wondering why you kept doing things the same way everyone else did for so long. The principles are so simple, and the results are so obvious. You know how to spend less money and have more impact at any trade show just by shifting your emphasis and focus.

There was a lot of resistance, and you had to go to the mat more than once with people who insisted, "We've always done it that way." But the battles were well worth fighting, and now your old adversaries are your staunchest allies. Guerrillas never argue with results.

Given the success of this show, you know that trade shows are going to be a substantial part of your marketing strategy from now on. Now you know how to slash the costs of a sales call and how to quickly generate lots of qualified leads. You know how to make all your other media really pay off, and you'll make them work together, achieving the greatest possible impact.

➤ This Is Not Just a Dream

This story is based on the actual experiences of salespeople who discovered the guerrilla tactics of trade show success.

You're about to launch into the world of guerrilla trade show selling. Some of the things you'll learn are going to challenge the conventional wisdom. And we believe that challenging the conventional wisdom is wise. Guerrillas are contrarians. They look at whatever the competition is doing and do the opposite.

➤ Trade Show Selling Is Different

Whether you usually sell in a showroom, in a retail store, at your customer's office, or over the phone, you'll need a different set of skills to succeed at trade show selling. It requires a unique approach, different from anything else you'll do. The very sales strategies that work so well for you day-to-day will *kill* you on a show floor.

Consider just a few of the differences. At shows, you have an opportunity to talk to people who are usually unreachable. The neutral territory of a show floor offers a unique chance to approach prospects who would otherwise never even talk to you.

On a show floor, you can show off equipment that would be difficult or impossible to take into a customer's location. People can touch, feel, taste, smell, and see your products firsthand.

There's also a peer-pressure effect that you don't usually have during a one-on-one sales call. Crowd enthusiasm can drive sales if you know how to direct it.

And you can reach lots of people in a very short time. Instead of jumping in your car or on an airplane to make those calls, you can put your best presenters right in front of hundreds of your best prospects in just a matter of hours. You can schedule business meetings in environments that would otherwise be very expensive or virtually impossible to arrange.

Buyers go to trade shows because every viable vendor is there. The average visitor spends six hours looking at exhibits and spends time in an average of 17 booths.[1] Buyers can go to the show, get a read on what's available, and make their purchase decisions on the spot. Eighty-six percent of show attendees have buying influence, yet only nine percent of those visitors were called on by salespeople prior to the show.[2] Of executive decision makers at any given show, 95 percent request literature from exhibitors, 95 percent meet with their current suppliers, 77 percent meet at least one new supplier, 76 percent ask for price quotes, 51 percent request a sales rep to visit their company, and 46 percent place orders on the spot.[3]

But changing your approach is critical. We're going to ask you to shift your thinking about what you can accomplish at a show, scrap almost everything you've done in the past, and rebuild. It's really not that difficult, and your sales will soar.

---

[1] "Amazing Numbers." *Personal Selling Power,* Jan.-Feb. 1994, 87.

[2] Exhibit Surveys Inc.

[3] *Cold Facts Hot Tips,* Center for Exhibition Industry Research (CEIR), formerly known as the Trade Show Bureau, 1995.

Chapter 1

What You Can Achieve at a Trade Show (That You Never Thought You Could)

A small handful of exhibitors have it figured out. They only exhibit at shows that are right for them. They use psychology and creativity in place of big-budget exhibit fixtures. They design their graphics and displays to attract just the right prospects. They've learned the insider secrets for a smooth setup, saving money on freight and drayage, and avoiding problems with unions and fire marshals. They work the press and the parties for extra impact. These sales guerrillas hit the floor on opening day full of enthusiasm and maintain their momentum throughout the show. They write piles of orders and go home with heaps of red-hot leads to follow up.

Meanwhile, the majority of their competitors go home empty-handed. Eighty-five percent of trade show exhibitors do things that are inefficient, self-centered, and just plain dumb. It's appalling how much money is simply wasted!

This book will dispel common exhibiting myths and change your point of view on trade shows forever. If you've never exhibited at a show, consider this: Almost *half* of first-time exhibitors experience such poor results that they never exhibit again.

Several factors contribute to this discouraging trend. Maybe these first-time exhibitors picked the wrong show in the first place. Maybe they followed the lead of the other exhibitors, or maybe they just did a miserable job at selling. The exhibitors that return year after year are either doing something right, or they have more cash than common sense. You must avoid being inefficient. This book will show you dozens of guerrilla strategies and hundreds of unconventional weapons and tactics that will make every show a success, no matter what business you're in.

First strategy: stay focused on the real reason you're there—*to get customers.*

➤ Avoid the Kiss of Death

The kiss of death is something that looks attractive but will kill you. Used properly, trade shows are one of the most powerful weapons in a guerrilla marketer's arsenal.[1] Other exhibitors commonly do things that *seem* attractive, but they end up killing sales. Avoid the pitfalls, and you'll sell circles around your competition.

The guerrilla approach is different. You're not there for exposure. You're there to make as much money as you possibly can. *Profits* are the only legitimate measure of your success. The ideas in this book are here for their money-making potential. Some of our criticism of traditional methods may seem harsh, but when you're outnumbered, outgunned, and outspent ten to one, you can't afford to fool around.

The only practical reason for investing the effort and the capital in a show is to find and talk with people who are willing to buy what you sell. That's it. Nothing more. Just sales. If that's not what you want, and we mean *really* want, then you're wasting your time. Return this book for your money back right now. It's not going to do you any good.

---

[1] Levinson, Jay Conrad. *Guerrilla Marketing Weapons—Strategies and Tactics for Winning Big Profits from Your Small Business* (Boston: Houghton Mifflin, 1987).

➤ How to Get Extraordinary Results

If you want average results, do what you see most exhibitors doing. If you want extraordinary results, train yourself, train your staff, and most importantly, *expect* extraordinary results. You don't always get what you want, but you almost always get what you expect. Guerrillas cut through the hype and call the shots as they see them, and these are the success strategies used by companies that consistently produce extraordinary sales at trade shows. This is the stuff that works.

➤ This May Make Some People Mad

Thomas Paine said, "Too often, what should be questionable conduct nonetheless becomes a method of doing business when all know such conduct is intrinsically improper."

Forewarned is forearmed. We're also going to make you aware of many of the dirty tricks commonly used in the trade show industry. There are lots of good, honest, hard-working people in the industry who really want you to succeed, but there are also those who are only after the cash in your wallet. This book will protect you. There are approaches to the business that are in the show producer's best interests, not yours. This book will level the playing field for you.

➤ Don't Just Go for the Awards

If you want your organization to win ribbons and trophies for best exhibit, most innovative exhibit, or best of show, read no farther. While it's nice to have an award-winning booth, your customers couldn't care less if your exhibit gets top honors.

➤ No Holds Barred!

Get ready for an all-out attack on your competition's plans. Expect to turn heads and raise eyebrows. You're going to change the status quo.

Warm up the armored truck. You'll need it to haul all the cash to the bank.

While we've taken every precaution to give you the best possible information, we cannot offer legal advice or guarantee that every idea will work in every situation. In fact, we *encourage* you to pick and choose those weapons and tactics that are *appropriate* for your industry, your culture, and your personal values. We *can* guarantee that, if you adopt a can-do, sales-closing, customer-serving, competition-beating, forward-thinking, nobody-can-tell-me-to-do-it-their-way attitude, you'll be wildly successful.

And then call us[2] and tell us how it went! We'd like to include your success story in our regular newsletter.[3]

We've also listed sources and people you can call for more information about useful products and services. The magic words to remember when you call are, "Please send me your free brochure." While these sources have proven reliable in the past, please treat them as you would any new vendor. Keep in mind that the world changes, and by the time you read this, these offers may no longer be available.

➤ How Is Guerrilla Marketing Different?

1. Guerrillas rely on *time, energy,* and *imagination* instead of the brute force of a massive sales staff or mountains of cash. If you already have mountains of cash, guerrilla marketing will make every dime work that much harder for you.

---

[2] Our number at The Guerrilla Group is 1-800-247-9145.

[3] To subscribe, call us at 1-800-247-9145. The call is free, and so is the newsletter.

2. Guerrilla marketing is based on *psychology* instead of guesswork. Science has learned a great deal about personality, motivation, and behavior, and guerrillas use these discoveries to generate sales.

3. Anyone can generate lots of traffic, anyone can generate stacks of leads, and anyone can write a pile of orders. But for the guerrilla, *profit* is the only reasonable yardstick of success. Profitable marketing is good marketing. All other marketing is bad.

4. Guerrilla marketing is strictly geared to *small* business. Big companies routinely buy our books by the thousands to distribute to their employees because thinking and acting like a small business provides a number of tactical advantages.

5. Guerrilla marketing removes the *mystique* from marketing. Many entrepreneurs and managers are intimidated by marketing because they've never studied it. So they don't *do* it.

6. Guerrilla marketing is based on *cooperation* instead of competition. You see this strategy in action when you're watching a commercial for McDonald's and realize that it's *really* a commercial for Coca-Cola and then realize that it's *really* an ad for the latest Disney movie. Strive to create fusion-marketing partnerships that are mutually beneficial.

7. Guerrillas don't go for the sale—they go for the *relationship*. It costs at least five times as much to create a new customer as it does to sell the same dollar volume to an existing customer. When you consider the economic power of repeat and referral business, the relationship is more important than a single transaction.

8. Guerrillas know that advertising doesn't work; direct mail doesn't work; telemarketing doesn't work. Only marketing *combinations* work. Combine a variety of marketing weapons, and they reinforce each other, making each other work.

9. Consequently, guerrillas use as many marketing weapons as possible[4]—there are at least a hundred from which to choose (and trade shows are only one). While most companies rely on a handful of them to generate business, guerrillas will use 40 or 50 of them. The more weapons in your arsenal, the more profitable your business will be.

■ SHOULD YOU EXHIBIT AT A SHOW?

It's an expensive proposition. It takes a lot of time. It drains your energy. And, if done right, it will generate a lot of work.

But it can also create enormous sales opportunity. Prospects are harder to find and harder to reach. Seventy-three percent of salespeople who have been selling for ten years or more feel that today's buyers are less accessible. This is not surprising. What is more significant is that salespeople themselves estimate that they make *40 percent fewer* face-to-face sales calls than they did ten years ago.[5] Trade shows let you make those critical face-to-face calls because hard-to-reach prospects are often accessible at a show.

➤ The Opportunity and the Costs

You should carefully consider the investment. If you already have more business than you can handle, forget it. If you're running at full capacity and don't want to expand, then don't go. If you're on the verge of going out of business and your reserves are depleted, carefully consider other guerrilla-marketing weapons before committing the sizable resources

---

[4] Levinson, Jay Conrad. *Guerrilla Marketing Weapons* (New York: Plume, 1990).

[5] Center for Exhibition Industry Research, SM34, 1996.

that putting together a successful show requires. You may be better off doing something different to pull back from the brink of disaster.

If what you're doing now gets you all the business you want, don't go to a trade show as an exhibitor.

On the other hand, in markets where technology advances rapidly, like in health care or apparel or telecommunications, the product life cycles are getting shorter and shorter (annually there are currently eight Comdex shows worldwide). So buyers rely on shows to keep abreast of the newest developments. In these fields, shows are becoming more and more segmented and specialized. If your field changes daily, exhibiting may be the only way you can satisfy the unique information needs of leading-edge technology buyers.

Trade shows are rated as *the* leading source for purchasing information, ahead of 12 alternative resources (Table 1.1), according to *The Power of Trade Shows,* a Simmons Market Research Bureau study. Ninety-one percent of 1,009 decision makers surveyed report that trade shows are "extremely useful" when making purchases for their companies.

TABLE 1.1 "EXTREMELY USEFUL" SOURCES OF PURCHASING INFORMATION

Trade shows	91%
Articles in trade publications	86%
Friends or business associates	83%
Directories and catalogs	72%
Manufacturer reps	69%
Ad in trade publications	66%
On-site visits	64%
Conferences and seminars	59%
User groups	41%
In-house purchasing dept.	40%
Outside consultants	39%
Retail sales staff	23%
Newspapers	22%
Other	2%

Trade-show participation can also help a company fine-tune its other marketing efforts. For instance, a typical direct-mail campaign nets about 13 percent readership, and a response rate of two percent is considered good. By contrast, a direct-mail campaign based on contacts made at a trade show generates 45 percent readership and an average response rate of 20 percent.

➤ Are You Ready?

There are lots of good reasons to go to trade shows and lots of good reasons not to go. When you select the right show and apply guerrilla tactics, you'll generate as much business as you can handle. Are you ready for that? Does your team have the capacity to make the sales calls? Does your customer service department have the staff to take care of all your new customers? Can production keep up with demand? Can you deliver top-notch service to everyone who will want it? Can you expand quickly, adding the necessary staff, production, and support services? Do you have financing available for more working capital if you need it?

➤ The Number-One Cause of Failure

Most trade show exhibitors fail because they don't close sales. They won't close sales. They can't close sales. They sabotage their success because they don't know how to attract the right visitors. They get overwhelmed with traffic, yet when the show is over, they haven't closed sales. They work hard. They talk to lots of people. They hand out tons of literature and thousands of trinkets. But they make no attempt to qualify the level of interest of their visitors, or they judge the show by the wrong indicators. They take home a huge stack of leads, but business as usual grabs their attention, and they never follow up to close sales.

Unless you're ready to close sales, don't go to the show. All you'll do is make your competitor's job easier.

➤ Take the Team Approach

Every fast-growing business has several indispensable people that seem to work miracles daily and accomplish the lion's share of the progress. Don't let them take on responsibility for a trade show. They'll accomplish more if left to work on their usual projects.

Instead, create a trade show team, dividing tasks among several people. The creative juices will flow, and a team will be much less likely to overlook something important. And you'll have companywide buy-in to your plans.

➤ How to Lead Your Company to Success

Make selling at trade shows an integral part of your guerrilla marketing plan.[6] That's why we're devoting this entire book to only one of the one hundred guerrilla marketing weapons. Few people have studied the specific principles of successful trade show selling, and even fewer implement the techniques consistently. To ensure your success, assign a designated trade show guerrilla who will lead the team and be held personally accountable for the results from the show as measured by *profit*.

By becoming a guerrilla, you're already on the leading edge. You'll lead the rest of your trade show team to success when you share the ideas in this book with them. Set their expectations high by telling them that you don't want to be like the other exhibitors. You want your company to make *money,* and lots of it. Encourage them to think creatively.

---

[6] Levinson, Jay Conrad. *Guerrilla Marketing Attack* (Boston: Houghton Mifflin, 1987), 56–87.

■ WHAT SHOULD YOU EXPECT?

Of trade show exhibitors surveyed, 54 percent fail to set objectives, and, of those who do, only half follow through. This means that you can gain a tremendous tactical advantage by deciding in advance what results you expect from participating in a show. Objectives can give direction to every aspect of your company's trade show participation. They become the basis of your marketing strategies, budgets, exhibit architecture, graphics, products, literature, and most importantly, staffing decisions. Objectives should stimulate sales performance in the exhibit and be measurable in terms of quantity and quality of results.

You can expect many companies to go to trade shows for the wrong reasons, and you can bet that many others don't take advantage of the incredible business opportunities that a show offers. Make certain that you're doing it for the right reasons.

➤ Top 10 Wrong Reasons for Exhibiting

1. *Because the competition is going.*   Thirty-two percent of companies indicated that they participated in a trade show because their competitors were exhibiting. Only 10 percent said their primary goal was to write orders on the exhibit floor.[7] This can work to your advantage if you're prepared to sell. Guerrillas never let their competition decide how to conduct their marketing campaigns.

2. *Because we've always gone to this show.*   By itself, this reason is not good enough. If the show has been profitable for you in the past, by all means go. But evaluate the opportunity in light of your firm's current goals and objectives.

---

[7] Center for Exhibition Industry Research Report, MS/RR #2050, p. 1.

3. *Because we want exposure.* If exposure is what you want, there are cheaper and more effective ways to get it. At the show, you'll be competing with every other exhibitor for media attention. Guerrillas focus on making impressions on their prospects and customers, not just settling for general, undefined exposure.

4. *Because we're doing an educational session.* A booth may divert resources. The educational session may be all the marketing you need to do. Your best clients, customers, and prospects will attend. Capture their names and follow up. It may be the most profitable show you never attended.

5. *Because we'll get to see all our friends.* If your salespeople use your booth to hold a reunion, they may be driving away customers forever. Visitors complain, time and again, that salespeople are more concerned with holding private conversations with other salespeople they haven't seen for a while than in offering assistance to the unfamiliar face looking for information.

6. *Because we'd be conspicuous by our absence.* You can leave a show that you've been going to for a long time with little or no impact on your business. We'll tell you how in Chapter 2.

7. *Because we have an image to maintain.* Sixty-four percent of companies surveyed by the CEIR cited building image as their primary objective. Guerrillas value identity over image. Spend your time and money getting to know your customers better.

8. *Because we want to support our association.* If you really want to support your association, write them a check.

9. *Because we need to train our new salespeople.* While it's a good place to learn about the competition, a show is a bad place to learn about selling your product. Let them fail in the classroom, not in front of the whole world.

10. *Because the show's in Hawaii.* A successful show is no vacation. Plan your vacation after the show. You'll need the rest.

➤ Top 15 Reasons Why Guerrillas Exhibit at Trade Shows

1. *Sell what you offer to visitors.* Without a doubt, this is the best reason to go to a trade show—not the only reason, but by far the best. An average of only nine percent of the visitors to an exhibit have been called on by a salesperson within the 12 months prior to a show. This means that an average of 91 percent of an exhibitor's visitors will be seeing the exhibitor's personnel for the first time.

2. *Sell what you offer to other exhibitors.* A reverse show, or one where you're targeting the other exhibitors instead of the visitors, works very well if you supply goods and services that the exhibitors use in their daily business or could sell to their customers.

3. *Get leads for your sales force to follow up.* Eighty-six percent of exhibitors go to shows to get leads and leads only. This is a good secondary reason to be at the show, but it should never be your number-one reason.

4. *Network and troubleshoot with other professionals.* You can share your war stories with others who have faced the same challenges and learn from more experienced pros in the business.

5. *Establish industry positioning.* A show is a great place to announce to the world that you're a player.

6. *Meet with existing customers.* You can make weeks' and months' worth of sales calls to your existing customers in a short period of time.

7. *Visit with people who are otherwise hard to meet.* At trade shows, you can get to key buyers who are otherwise unapproachable.

8. *Introduce new products to the market.* This works great if you can coordinate a product launch with a trade show.

9. *Do market research.* In just a few days, you can try new offers out on thousands of buyers and fine-tune your pricing and product focus.

10. *Find new dealers, representatives, and distributors.* If you're looking for help distributing what you sell, put a small sign in your exhibit that says DEALERS WANTED or AGENTS WANTED.

11. *Find new employees.* It's virtually inevitable that job seekers will be walking the show floor.

12. *Conduct business meetings.* You can meet with all your business partners and prospective partners in just a few days. To do the same thing without the show would cost you thousands of dollars and weeks on the road.

13. *Scope out the competition.* You'll get a clear picture of your competition's marketing strategy and a glimpse at their direction at a trade show.

14. *Get smart.* The educational sessions are a good reason to go to an industry or association conference, but be cautious about mixing them with the trade show schedule.

15. *Get media exposure.* The trade press are at industry and association shows. National media are at large consumer shows.

If you want to get the most out of your show, pick one or two of these reasons and concentrate every bit of your effort on hitting the mark.

One of the deadly sins is trying to do too much at the show. You'll spend so much money buying the floor space, preparing the exhibit, and flying the staff to the convention site that you'll want to get every red cent you can out of the show. And you'll end up getting bits and pieces of business instead of concentrating on making the deals that will put your organization exactly where you want it to be.

➤ Why Do Visitors Go to Shows?

The trade show is an excellent forum for decision makers to evaluate new products, make new contacts, enhance supplier relationships, and conduct purchasing activities. Those who attend usually do so regularly, attending an average of three trade shows a year. Of 170 respondents who attended a show in the last 12 months, 26 percent attended one show, 23 percent attended two shows, 15 percent attended three shows, 17 percent attended four, and 19 percent attended five or more.

On average, these attendees spent 7.9 hours viewing the exhibits over an average span of 2.1 days.

Decision Makers Attend Shows in Order to . . .

➤ *Find out what's new.*   Fifty percent of all show attendees want to see what's new in products and services.

➤ *See competitors and compare prices.*   Ninety-three percent compared similar products, 50 percent requested a call from a sales rep, 73 percent asked for a price quote, and 73 percent found at least one new supplier.

➤ *Visit different suppliers, hear their presentations, and compare each vendor's point of view.*   Almost half (49 percent) have made purchases at a trade show. Purchases by trade show attendees average $64,000.

➤ *Collect literature about services offered; take it back to the office and review it with the buying team to evaluate what to put in next year's capital budget.*   The average show visitor stops to talk or acquire literature at 26 exhibits.

➤ *Get a better perspective of what's available in a short period of time.*   It beats hunting for people and spending a lot of time on the phone.[8]

---

[8] Center for Exhibition Industry Research Report PT11, Research Summary, p. 2.

➤ Sell What You Offer to Other Exhibitors

This guerrilla tactic is called a *reverse show,* where you're targeting exhibitors instead of visitors. It works very well if you are supplying goods and services that the other exhibitors use in their daily business.

Just think—in several days, you can make hundreds of calls to current customers and new prospects, and they're all right there on the trade show floor. You can do a year's worth of cold calling in the environment of a trade show and speak to people you would never otherwise reach. Since many companies send their top executives and managers to shows, all you have to do is sniff out who's there and make your approach.

Reverse selling means you need to be out on the floor during setup, before the show opens. Do your scouting during slow periods when other exhibitors are dying to talk to someone so they can complain about their aching feet (a problem you won't have!) Keep your exhibit up for several hours after the show closes, and let other exhibitors know that you'll be there to help them.

Guerrilla Trade Show Selling in Action

A moving-and-storage company decided to do a reverse show at a major computer electronics convention. About two hours before the show closed, they began to hand out cardboard shipping boxes to exhibitors in exchange for a business card to help them pack up their stuff. Most exhibitors accumulate extra stuff at a show, so they were grateful for the extra boxes, and the moving-and-storage company got a number of great leads for computer installation and moving.

➤ Get Leads for Your Sales Force to Follow Up

This is a good secondary reason to be at the show. You can gather more qualified leads from a trade show than virtually any other marketing activity, if you know how.

Once you have made a qualified prospect at a trade show, it typically requires only a phone call or letter to close the sale. Field sales calls cost at least 2.5 times more to close than trade show leads. The average cost of contacting a prospect in the field[9] is $292 versus $185 cost per trade show visitor.[10] Calculate your lead cost from other marketing weapons that you use, such as magazine and newspaper advertisements, bingo cards, telemarketing, radio and TV advertising, postcard decks, direct mail, billboards, and referrals. What is your average cost per lead? You may find that leads generated at a show are far less expensive than those generated from your current sources.

➤ Establish Industry Positioning

Many companies believe they need a monstrous custom exhibit to make a grand impression. Wrong. Floor space is the key. People will equate the size of your company with the *area* of your exhibit. Combine several booth spaces with inexpensive fixtures, rented furniture, plants, and lots of people, and you'll make a big impression on a small budget.

➤ Expand Industry Positioning

If you want to expand your trade show impression, buy multiple, smaller exhibits in the hall so visitors see you several times. Have each exhibit focus on a specific theme or particular part of your product line. This tactic will drive your trade show coordinator absolutely crazy, but it goes with the

---

[9] Cahners Advertising Research Report (CARR) No. 542.1H. Costs include direct costs, compensation, travel, and entertainment expenses.

[10] Exhibit Surveys, Inc. Costs include space rental, booth construction, refurbishing and transportation, show services, plus travel, living, and salary expenses for exhibit personnel.

territory. You're going to the show for maximum sales, not to please your employees.

➤ Maintain Industry Positioning

This is a seriously stupid reason to attend a trade show. If you go to a show because you feel you *have* to be there or it will affect your sales, think again. If a show's effectiveness is declining, it's time to take a long, hard look at whether you should attend that show at all.

The focus, attendance, and impact of a show can change over time, even from year to year. For example, at one time a show for medical professionals granted continuing education units (CEUs) to participants in exhibitor-conducted training programs on the show floor. When the association discontinued the practice, people quit going to the show floor, preferring to spend time in the break-out sessions (where they still qualified for CEUs). This simple change radically affected attendees' behavior and killed the show.

➤ Meet with Current Customers

This is an outstanding reason to do a trade show. You can make weeks' and months' worth of sales calls to existing customers in a very short period of time. This works well for customers you don't often get to see.

To make this work, you must actively invite your existing customers and really give them a reason to come. We'll talk more about preshow promotions that bring in the buyers in Chapter 4.

If you have equipment that's hard to transport, you can demonstrate it to lots of customers for a one-time freight bill. And if you do it right, a new customer will buy it then and there and pay the freight to ship it directly to their facility.

Throw a by-invitation-only customer-appreciation bash one evening during the show. This is a great way for your customers to meet each other, reinforcing each other's success in doing business with you. It's also a great time for the key people in your company to quickly establish a relationship with new customers and strengthen relations with your best customers. And customers will go home and brag about meeting the president of the company.

➤ Visit with People Who Are Otherwise Hard to Meet

At trade shows, you can get to key buyers who are otherwise unapproachable. They are out of their turf, on neutral territory, and fair game for you.

Decide who you really would like to see at the show, and develop a campaign to get them there and into your exhibit. Create a hit list of buyers to whom you want to sell and then do everything in your power to get them dying to meet with you at the show. We'll explore how in Chapter 4.

➤ Introduce New Products to the Market

A trade show can be a very cost-effective platform for testing and launching a new product or service. Many companies introduce new product offerings at trade shows because visitors are there to see what's new and different. They're there to plan for future purchases. They're making a short list of products and vendors to consider when they're ready to buy.

Introducing new products at the show gives you extensive and intense contact with your marketplace. You'll get immediate feedback on features, price, delivery, and other important competitive indicators.

But don't let the trade show schedule drive your product announcements. Companies have been badly burned by preannouncing a new product that wasn't ready to ship, and current sales plummet because customers decide to wait for the new product. And when sales drop, so does the money to fund the product's completion.

Likewise, don't hold off on announcing a product because you're waiting for a trade show. Your sales momentum gets going during the first 90 days of your product announcement. Don't wait and risk having a competitor scoop you.

➤ Do Market Research

The reality of a trade show is that visitors will walk by your exhibit once and only once unless you've given them a very good reason to come back.

You can capitalize on this by using the show for test marketing. Since an individual visitor is likely to see you only once, you can change your exhibit signs to test alternate headlines, prices, even different features and benefits. In just a few days you can try out new offers on thousands of people who buy what you sell and tune your pricing and product focus very quickly.

➤ Find New Dealers, Representatives, and Distributors

If you're looking for help distributing what you sell, put a small sign in your exhibit that says something like DEALERS WANTED. Distributors are often scouring trade shows for new and exciting products or services to add to their line card. Make it easy for them to spot your hot opportunities.

Select one person to be the dealer contact, and have all your exhibit staff refer dealer questions to that person. If you're selecting a limited number of dealers, wait until the close of the show to finalize agreements. Not all the dealers show up on the first day.

➤ Find New Employees

This is a simple and inexpensive way to recruit. When the economy is bad, you'll have job seekers walking the show floor. They're usually easy to spot. They're wearing a suit and tight shoes and carrying a briefcase. You'll probably get a few resumes, so decide who's going to get them and what will happen next.

If you're actively looking, put up a small sign that says, NOW ACCEPTING SELECTED APPLICATIONS. Assign one person to discuss opportunities with candidates, and keep the initial meeting short so that it doesn't interfere with your selling efforts.

➤ Conduct Business Meetings

Conducting business meetings is one of the best reasons to go to a show. You can meet with all your business partners and prospective partners in just a few days. To do the same thing without the show would cost you thousands of dollars and weeks on the road.

Create a small meeting area within your exhibit. Set up a table and several chairs, but don't use this space as a general resting area for your exhibit staff. It's a conference table, exclusively.

If you need more privacy, or if you don't want your competition to see who you're meeting with, a nearby hotel suite is a good alternative.

People involved in meetings should not be assigned exhibit duty. They need to be fresh and alert to do their best at negotiating and moving business forward.

A bonus to business meetings at the show—

➤ The agendas tend to be tightly focused, so these meetings usually don't last as long.

➤ The attitude is usually to get down to business, so the meeting is more productive.

➤ People aren't on their home turf, so they behave better (usually!).

➤ The right people are usually there. Those difficult people who tend to sidetrack your meetings aren't invited.

➤ Go Because Competition Is There

Just because your competition is at a show doesn't mean it's a good show for you, or even for them. If this is the only reason you're going to a show, you're throwing your money away. Keep in mind, your competitor may be attending out of habit, inertia, tradition, or just to support the industry, all of which are poor reasons to go.

The show company's sales rep will often tell you which of your competitors will be exhibiting as a way to entice you into the show. They aren't selling you on the merits of the show or on the match of visitors to your marketing objectives. They're just playing on the fear that your competition will scoop all the business. Accept their invitation only after you're certain the show will pay big for you.

➤ Get Specialized Training

The break-out sessions are a good reason to go to an industry or association conference, but don't confuse these with the trade show goals. We've seen too many people miss their exhibit shift because they were tied up in a heated discussion after an educational session. The lost sales opportunities are costly, and it may be more cost-effective to send your people to a separate conference or seminar instead.

If you've been to the sessions, you know that some of them can really stir up your thoughts and get the creative juices flowing. It's virtually impossible to concentrate on solving your visitor's problems when your mind is racing at warp speed because of a presentation you've just attended. If you attend an educational seminar, allow a period of time after the session and before your exhibit shift to cool down. You may meet important business contacts in the session, or you may want to speak with the discussion panel or speaker about possible business opportunities.

If you don't need the cool-down time (some of the sessions are real yawners), then you can do something else productive, like show up at the exhibit early. But save the report on the session until that evening's show review meeting.

➤ Get Media Exposure

The trade press will be out in force at major industry and association shows. Large consumer shows are covered by national media. Most trade publications have their own exhibits, and many companies hold media conferences during the show. Come prepared to present your story to the media. Bring articles, press-kit photos, and testimonials to make it easy for a staff writer or editor to publish your story. (Better still, bring it all on computer diskettes, so they can upload the text right into their word processors.)

Keep in mind the danger that a competitor may scoop you at the show, sidetracking your carefully laid media plans. We've seen front-page products get pushed to the back page when a competitor launches a counter campaign to kill the new product introduction. Be careful about who knows your advance plans, and develop your media strategy with care.

■ THE KEY TO YOUR TRADE SHOW SUCCESS

A trade show is probably the best place to rapidly get the information, knowledge, and wisdom you need to move your business to the next level of success. When you attend a show targeted to your needs and tastes, many if not all of the people and companies you need to contact will be there. You can get competitive information, find out future plans, and cut sweet deals at trade shows.

➤ How to Be a Guerrilla Show Visitor

Here are 17 little-known insider secrets that let you wring out the best deals and the best information from trade show exhibitors. With this information, you'll make your visit to the trade show pay big.

Plan Your Show Goals

Why are you going to the show? What specific information do you want? What problem are you trying to solve? What's your biggest challenge? What three things, if accomplished, would make the time and energy invested in visiting the show worthwhile?

For example, your show goals may be (1) finding a replacement vendor for the critical assembly, (2) investigating potential OEMs, and (3) looking at new advances in control technologies.

Or you may be having problems with a vendor and not getting satisfaction—you just can't get through to the right levels of the company. At the show, you probably can break through to the top brass and get the problem resolved.

Savvy companies will decide what information they need and then make assignments to the visitors going to the show. Your show goals may be a mixture of personal issues as well as those of your colleagues.

How will you report to the rest of the company on the information you bring back from the show? Will you do a formal or informal presentation? Will you file a report or simply E-mail or voicemail broadcast updates at the end of each day of the show?

Report Back Daily

If possible, check in with the home office daily. If you discover information that impacts your company's strategies, you need to report that immediately.

If you're gathering information for others, make sure you can reach them in case there are surprises. Be prepared to change your show goals based on what you learn.

Plan Your Time Now

Now that you have your show goals, prioritize a list of who you want to visit. Decide which exhibitors are "must see," "nice to see," or "who cares if you see."

For the vendors you have got to see, pick up the phone now and set an appointment to visit them. The top officers of most companies are busy with meetings, press conferences, and negotiations. Make sure you're part of that schedule. You'll also want to be invited to their hospitality suite or party.

For the "nice to see" vendors, plan a prioritized route with the show guide, so you'll have time to see those who are most important.

Update Plans at the Show

Pick up a copy of the show guide and look for new ideas and changes to the show line-up. Last minute exhibitors may cause you to reevaluate your priorities and schedule. The first day, take a quick walk down the aisles, previewing the show. Don't stop yet, but notice booths that catch your attention and decide how they fit into your show strategy.

Take Time to Explore

Sometimes, your best discoveries are new vendors with interesting ideas or technology that hasn't received a lot of press. Plan for a little free time to wander the aisles with the curiosity of a child. Ignore the vendors you know, and search out the ones that are new to you.

Some companies have found whole new worlds of business by finding—and partnering with—small, undercapitalized vendors discovered at a trade show.

Who's Not Exhibiting?

It's equally important to know who's decided not to exhibit this time around. Call the companies up and ask them why. Not exhibiting may indicate business difficulties about which you need to know. Or it may be that the trade show is no longer effective for that company—it happens. If the company is going to a different show, you need to know.

Ask, "What's Hot?"

Ask everyone you meet, "What's the most exciting thing you've seen?" or "What's the hottest thing here?" Getting another perspective gives you a good idea on what other visitors and exhibitors think is exciting. This is a good way to detect future trends. Plus, it's a great conversation starter in the bar!

Exhibitor's Psychology Gives You Secrets

Trade shows are exciting! Exhibitors lavish plenty of attention and resources on the booth. The competition is making a similar showing. Exhibit staffers are out of their normal environment and comfort zone. Some feel like they're out on the town and tend to behave recklessly.

Many companies staff their exhibits with people from a wide range of departments—from R&D to sales, from marketing to customer service, from corporate officers to field salespeople. These people often have different agendas, different instructions, and different attitudes towards visitors and the reasons for being at the show.

For these reasons, exhibit staff tend to be more willing to discuss future plans, insider secrets, and information that's normally hard to get. Ask everyone you meet in the exhibit, "What's new? What's coming next? What are your future plans? Tell me about your competition. What's your show special?" It's amazing what you can learn by asking lots of questions and being interested, especially from people who don't normally sell.

Decide what you need to know for your future plans. Know who's providing the information. Companies' plans change, and you don't want to make a decision based on information that isn't sanctioned by the top brass.

Ask to Meet the Boss

Ask the staffer to introduce you to the founder, sales manager, CEO, or other people who will ultimately be making decisions. If you have a specific problem to solve, these are the people who will do it. At a trade show, they're under pressure to keep things moving smoothly. It's amazing what problems you can get resolved by talking with a decision maker on a busy show floor.

Making the contact at the show face to face sets up the business relationship rapidly. It also lets you call your contacts after the show with, "We met in your booth, and I had a follow-up question. . . ."

Get It Done Your Way

You're the prospect or customer. Tell the exhibitors what you want to have happen. Don't just sit through their canned presentations if that's not what you need. Don't carry home their literature if you would rather have them send it. Tell them what you need to do, see, or hear to consider doing business with them.

Be Choosy

Choose carefully what you take from exhibitors. It's easy to become loaded down with literature, catalogs, toys, trinkets, and trash. You don't want to be a pack mule. You certainly don't want to expend your precious energy dragging around pounds of unwanted stuff.

And besides, how much of what you take actually gets home? And how much of that actually gets used? Do yourself, and the garbage dumps, a favor: Think carefully before accepting anything from an exhibitor.

Many exhibitors feel that serious buyers are not literature collectors. A bag full of literature may pigeonhole you. You may wish to save the literature collecting until toward the end of the show. You may be much better off asking the exhibitor to send you an information and literature package. It's one less thing for you to carry, and by their response, you'll get an indication of how the company treats its customers.

Ask about Show Specials

You may be able to pay for your visit with the discounts you get at the show. Most companies offer sales, discounts, and allowances as show specials. You can often buy merchandise right off the show floor. You may be able to buy the demonstration machines or floor samples at the end of the show for a healthy discount. It's one less thing the exhibitor must ship back for refurbishing or return to inventory.

Ask a sales decision maker, "What could you do for me if I said yes right now?" Exhibit staffers want to be heroes by closing sales on the spot. You can take advantage of this psychology to get better deals for you.

Ask for a Media Kit

If you want detailed information on a company and what it sells, ask for a media kit. Most savvy companies have these stashed away, ready to hand to the press and radio and TV reporters. Companies will usually be glad to give you a copy. If not, ask them to send you a copy after the show.

You'll get background information on the company, including information on the founders, business history, and some future plans. You'll get all the media releases, which can indicate the company's abilities to meet their stated deadlines. And you'll get detailed information on what they sell, often including articles written about the company.

Hit the Parties

You can get great intelligence information by going to the show parties. If you're not specifically invited, go to the exhibit of the company and ask, "Where's the party?" Most will tell you.

Ask people you meet, "What parties are you going to tonight?" Join them if the party represents a group with which you need to do business.

A key party strategy is to stay sharp and not drink alcohol. Instead, drink look-alikes such as water with a lime or alcohol-free beer. Work the room, asking for introductions to key people. When you've exhausted the opportunities at that party, move on to the next.

Take Notes

It's hard to remember everything that goes on at a show. You see something, intend to return to the exhibit later, and then can't find it. Or you have lots of discussions, and you forget who promised what.

One way to solve this problem is write notes on 3 × 5 index cards—one or two cards for each vendor you meet. Then it's easy to organize your notes and thoughts when reporting back after the show. Another way is to use a microcassette recorder. Speak notes into the recorder, either on the spot or in a quiet place during a break. Have the tape transcribed when you return home for complete notes.

Consider taking photos of key exhibits and vendors. If you're planning a formal report to a group, shoot slides of the show to make the meeting exciting and memorable.

Get a Press Pass

Do you publish? If you write articles for any publication, or your company publishes, consider getting a press pass. And then watch the doors open. You'll be invited almost anywhere and told almost anything, and you'll get lots of free stuff, too.

Plan, Observe, and Question for Success

The first secret of success when visiting a trade show is to plan what you want to accomplish and how to accomplish it comfortably.

The second secret is to be very observant. Watch who's talking to whom. Watch for increases and decreases in exhibit space from last year. Watch for clues to hidden behavior—what are they not telling you?

And the third secret is to ask lots and lots of questions, just like Peter Falk's character, Colombo. You'll get the best information when you act as if you don't already know the answer.

Do these things, and you'll make your visit to the show pay big.

➤ Set Your Goals and Create Tools to Measure Results

You will get out of a show what you put into a show. One exhibitor will say, "Best show ever for us!" while another at the same show will say, "Terrible show. A waste of money."

What are you expecting from this show? Target a specific number of contacts, a specific number of leads collected, a specific number of demonstrations done. Decide how many sales you will close from contacts at the show. Then, using the ideas in this book, decide how you will meet those numbers and set up systems to measure results. Decide which of these items are important to you and write down exactly what you need to make the show a success for you.

If you're new to trade shows and aren't sure what would be realistic, write down numbers you feel you need to make the show successful, and then analyze them to understand if they are achievable and realistic. You'll learn some rules of thumb for estimating returns at the shows you attend.

Decide what you need—

- ➤ How many leads?
- ➤ How many new contacts?
- ➤ How many current customers?
- ➤ What percentage of the visitors?
- ➤ What payback? What time period?
- ➤ What market information?
- ➤ What competitive information?
- ➤ What product information?

Now that you know why you're going and what you want to achieve, let's figure out what shows will pay off big for you.

➤ Making Your Show Budget Pay Handsomely

Many senior managers were middle managers back in the days when a trade show was an excuse for getting rip-roaring drunk and thrown in the pool. Unfortunately, they may still believe this perception to be true for modern trade shows.

When exhibits coordinator Charlotte Reczek arrived at electrical component manufacturer Danial Woodhead, the prevailing budgeting strategy was, "Whatever you spend, you spend." Today Reczek counts every dollar, follows every lead, and directs every expenditure according to marketing goals. "Our shows support our mainstream marketing efforts," Reczek says. "We're generally in those shows for the markets that we've targeted." Result: In the six years she's been on board, the trade show budget has tripled. And upper management has approved funding for two new custom-built exhibits, and four mobile exhibit trailers.[11]

Gaining upper-management support is less a matter of your persuasive skills and more a matter of how well you do your homework. Be certain to have answers to these questions:

1. How much is this going to cost?
2. What are we going to get out of it?
3. What have we gotten out of it before?
4. Is the plan on target with our overall corporate and marketing goals? How do we know that?
5. Does it fit with our other marketing objectives and strategies in advertising, public relations, and direct marketing?

From our experience, you can make a ballpark estimate of your exhibit-related expenses by multiplying your exhibit space cost by five. This won't include follow-up or travel expenses, but it will give you a good starting point for deciding whether to attend.

The big secret: View the initial planning budget as a strategic starting point for the year's trade show schedule. If you want your management to approve a generous budget for your next show, fill out the *Marketing Return on Investment* form (p. 41) and present it to the person responsible for allocating funds. This tool lets you decide where you need to invest for the greatest number of sales. You'll also find the *Trade Show Budget Planner* worksheet (p. 42) an invaluable addition to your guerrilla arsenal.

---

[11] *Exhibitor* magazine, May 1993. To subscribe, call toll-free 1-888-235-6155.

Under the Media column of the ROI form, list the marketing media you are using now, including magazine and newspaper advertisements, bingo cards, telemarketing, radio and TV advertising, card decks, direct mail, billboard, and referrals.

List the cost for each time you execute a run, insertion, or campaign in the Cost per time run column.

Determine how many leads you get from each campaign and put this in the Average number of leads column. (If you can't do this, your marketing department is out of control and costing you a ton of money. Tracking lead origin and quality is critical to success. If you've been successful without this, it means you're making enough money to pay for your mistakes. But watch out—when you stop being so successful, your mistakes will kill your organization.)

Calculate the cost per lead by dividing the cost per time run by the average number of leads. This is a good starting number to indicate what it costs for you to contact someone who could potentially do business with you. What you do with them is up to you and leads us to the next question: How much did you sell to them?

Place the number of sales closed in each of the one-, three-, and six-month time periods. You may need to select shorter or longer time periods depending on what you sell. This gives you an idea of how quickly the leads are converted to sales. It gives you a way to predict your sales into the future, all other things being equal.

Enter the average sales per lead closed. This is sometimes difficult to calculate, but do your best, estimating if necessary.

Calculate your return on investment (ROI) for the medium by multiplying the total number of leads closed by the average sale per lead closed and dividing the result by the cost per time run.

With these numbers charted, you can calculate your return on investment for each of your marketing weapons. Most companies find that well-executed trade show activities give them the highest number of leads per dollar spent and the best ROI of any of their marketing activities.

MARKETING RETURN ON INVESTMENT (ROI) FORM

Media	Cost per time run	Average number of leads generated	Cost per lead	Number closed in 1 month	Number closed in 3 months	Number closed in 6 months	Average sale per lead closed	ROI for media
1.								
2.								
3.								
4.								
5.								
6.								
7.								
8.								
9.								
10.								
11.								
12.								
13.								
14.								
15.								

YOUR TRADE SHOW BUDGET PLANNER

	Budget	Actual
Exhibit Space		
Space Rental		
Location premium		
Member discount		
Prepay discount		
Exhibit		
Design		
Rental		
Construction		
Graphics design and creation		
Refurbish or touch-up		
Lighting		
Storage/warehousing		
Amortization over other shows		
Split with other partners		
Freight from exhibit builder		
Furnishings for Exhibit		
Carpeting (rent or own)		
Garbage cans (rent or own)		
Tables		
Chairs/stools		
Plants and flowers		
Computers (rent or borrow)		
A/V equipment (rent or borrow) Supplies (bulbs, etc.)		
Your samples, equipment, etc. Supplies (batteries, consumable, etc.)		
Music/video permissions/licensing		
Back-up audio/videotapes		
Survival kit		
Transportation		
Freight from exhibit builder		
Exhibit freight round-trip		

YOUR TRADE SHOW BUDGET PLANNER (CONT.)

	Budget	Actual
Transportation (Cont.)		
Materials shipments		
Carry materials as airline baggage?		
Express shipments		
Drayage		
Hundredweight minimum		
Surcharge for blanket wrap		
Overtime		
Late shipments (minimum per piece charge)		
Airfare		
Charter discounts		
Advance purchase discount		
Show airline discount		
Ground transportation		
Van		
Car rental		
Mileage reimbursement		
Taxi		
Hotel shuttle		
Show Services		
Install and dismantle		
Straight time		
Overtime		
Double time		
Supervision		
Electrical		
Shared with another exhibitor		
Pre-order discount		
Electrician labor		
Extension cords/covers		
Water, gas, air		
Preorder discount		
Plumber labor		
Materials charge		

YOUR TRADE SHOW BUDGET PLANNER (CONT.)

	Budget	Actual
Show Services (Cont.)		
Telephone, FAX	_____	_____
Preorder discount	_____	_____
Installation labor	_____	_____
Long-distance charges	_____	_____
Equipment (rent or own)	_____	_____
Cellular phone rental or roam charges	_____	_____
Cleaning service	_____	_____
Photography	_____	_____
Security	_____	_____
Projectionist for performances	_____	_____
Electrician for performances	_____	_____
Temporary help	_____	_____
Promotion		
Preshow	_____	_____
Advertisement updates	_____	_____
Design and creative fees	_____	_____
Production and printing	_____	_____
Assembly	_____	_____
List rental	_____	_____
Postage	_____	_____
Telemarketing	_____	_____
At-show	_____	_____
Design and creative fees	_____	_____
Production and printing	_____	_____
Assembly	_____	_____
Postshow	_____	_____
Design and creative fees	_____	_____
Production and printing	_____	_____
Assembly	_____	_____
Postage	_____	_____
Telemarketing	_____	_____

YOUR TRADE SHOW BUDGET PLANNER (CONT.)

	Budget	Actual
Promotion (Cont.)		
Premiums		
Design		
Production		
Shipping		
Seminars		
Speaker expense		
Audience handouts		
A/V support		
Media kit		
Creation		
Production		
Postage		
Follow-up calls		
Media/press conference		
Location rental		
Invitations		
Hospitality		
Lead Management		
Lead form		
Creation		
Printing		
Lead form imprinter (rent or own)		
Data entry		
Express charges		
Show Staff		
Time value/opportunity cost		
Hotel		
AAA or member discount		
Week-end package discount		
Early check-out surcharge		
Meals		
Entertainment		

YOUR TRADE SHOW BUDGET PLANNER (CONT.)		
	Budget	Actual
Show Staff (Cont.)		
Show registration	_____	_____
Preshow discount	_____	_____
Special clothing	_____	_____
Cellular phone/pager	_____	_____
Training	_____	_____
Education sessions tuition	_____	_____
Preshow discount	_____	_____
Special Events		
Hotel Suite	_____	_____
AAA or other member discount	_____	_____
Corporate rate discount	_____	_____
Hospitality suite/reception	_____	_____
Food	_____	_____
Drink	_____	_____
Entertainment	_____	_____
A/V equipment	_____	_____
Decorations	_____	_____
Sales meetings	_____	_____
Total Budget	_____	_____

➤ Seventeen Hidden Budget Busters

Now that you have your Budget and ROI projected, take out some success insurance by watching for these common pitfalls that can bust your budget.

    1. *Carpet and trash-can rental.* You can rent carpet at the show, but you can usually buy a higher grade for the same price and be money ahead. At the show, you'll pay twice the hardware-store purchase price to rent a trash can. Check out the Trade Show Success Checklist in the Appendix.

2. *Installation/dismantle dates.* Pull out next year's calendar and check the days of the week that installation/dismantling will occur. Weekends mean overtime labor, but also watch for floating Monday holidays. Some cities have idiosyncrasies that affect installation/dismantling. For example, deer season opening in Michigan and St. Patrick's Day in New York or Chicago will severely limit labor availability.

3. *Fire codes.* An exhibit with a large, two-story area or ceiling is hit hard by fire codes in some cities. In Los Angeles, it might mean installing a sprinkler system; in Chicago, it could require fire watchers. Check with show management to see which rules apply.

4. *Union jurisdictions.* Which union does what? It varies from show site to show site. The carpenters' union may lay carpet in one city, while the carpet layers' union does it in another. When planning setup, you don't want carpenters when you really need carpet layers. Ask show management about union jurisdictions for each show.

5. *Exhibit house drayage.* Drayage is the charge to move materials from the show loading dock to your exhibit space. Trade-show teams often overlook the drayage from the storage warehouse to the truck and back again. It can be as much as $500 each way if you use a custom exhibit. Ask your exhibit house about these charges.

6. *Exhibit inspections.* It can cost big bucks to have your exhibit vendor inspect or do a preview setup of your custom exhibit. Inspection charges can be calculated per crate or per hour. Full setup previews may also be billed per hour, adding up to 80 percent of your at-show setup bill. Or you may pay for footage for previews, $2 to $4 per foot. Decide well in advance how often the exhibit should be inspected.

7. *Check-cutting surcharges.* If your exhibit house cuts checks for drayage, labor, and so on, you could be paying anywhere from 15 to 40 percent above the bill

for that service. Instead, provide a credit-card number to pay show expenses.

8. *Music licensing.* If you dub copyrighted music into a video for show use or even play music in the background, you're responsible for paying a license fee. Try using "needle drop" or "buy out" music, which comes complete with the license fee prepaid.[12]

9. *Independent contractor fees.* Some shows charge you a fee if you use an independent contractor instead of the general contractor. Though this charge is usually minimal, these hidden costs can add up.

10. *Last-minute new product introductions.* The cost of adding shows, space, product pedestals or demonstrations can be deadly to the budget. This is where good communication with your marketing and product managers is essential.

11. *Cleaning fees.* Suppose you have a 600-square-foot exhibit, 200 feet of which is a storage room that does not need to be cleaned. If you use cleaning services, your first inclination would be to budget for cleaning 400 square feet. Wrong. You will be charged for cleaning the entire exhibit; all 600 feet.

12. *In-booth electrical adjustments.* If your exhibit requires a lot of electrical power, it's essential that you plan for it. Find out whether the power comes from the ceiling or floor. Work out where to place outlets. Last-minute changes are very expensive.

13. *Travel changes.* If you're subjected to numerous last-minute flight changes that double the airfares, ask upper management to issue a memo explaining that once arrangements are made, any costs incurred by last-minute changes will be paid out of the individual's department budget, not the trade show budget.

---

[12] For a free sample CD of license-paid music, contact The Music Bakery, 1-800-229-0313.

14. *Last-minute shipments.* Drayage costs skyrocket when packages are shipped and handled separately. Each separately arriving package will be charged the minimum hundredweight drayage fee.

15. *Overly complex exhibit assembly.* The extra time needed to set up the booth translates into labor overages.

16. *Personnel costs.* Travel, entertainment, and related expenses can be the biggest exhibiting costs, but they're not always accounted for up front. Set spending limits for your staff.

17. *Ordering services from the show floor.* Expect to pay a premium of double what you would have paid for services ordered in advance.

Even the most successful managers are often asked to make cuts during the early rounds of budgeting. Guerrillas only cut expenditures that don't relate to sales. For example, you could reduce the number of new graphics or ask exhibit staffers to share hotel rooms. Some managers start by cutting the extras like preshow mailers or exhibit training. We strongly advise against cutting preshow promotion, since guerrillas know it's one of the most effective ways to attract visitors.

Chapter 2

How to Pick
the Right Show

Selecting the right show means lots of sales, leads, business deals, and success. The right show is one that attracts a large number of people who are already buyers or prospects for your product or service. The right show is the right *size,* attracting a cross section of vendors in related fields, but not so big that you're going head-to-head with everyone in the industry. The right show is in the right *place,* situated geographically to attract buyers in your market area, be it local, regional, national, or international. The right show is scheduled at the right *time,* when you have the capacity to service the surge of new business you'll generate. And finally, the right show is organized by the right *management* with a track record of success.

There are only two kinds of shows: expensive and inexpensive. Picking the wrong show is expensive in time, money, energy, and emotions. The right show is inexpensive because, whatever the costs, they are offset by sales results.

While there isn't always a clear equation for selecting a show, if you think about a few critical issues, you can pick winners every time.

➤ How to Find Shows That Work

What, specifically, do you want to accomplish at the show? If you wish to expand your market, look for a show that targets your new market segment. If you want to do market research, look for a show that attracts the market you're interested in. Don't be blinded by dazzling numbers. Big crowds don't always translate into big sales; in fact, the opposite is often the case.

The best way to find the best shows to attend is to ask. Ask your best customers what shows they attend when they need to make critical buying decisions. If you want to expand into other markets, ask people that you'd like to have as customers what shows they attend when they make crucial buying decisions. Another good source is your friendly competition— that is, the other players in your industry that don't compete with you head-to-head.

➤ Finding *New* Shows That Work for You

It may seem that you get calls about prospective shows every day. One way to evaluate these new shows is to take a look at who's there: how many visitors and exhibitors are expected? Also ask about the track record for the show's management. If they've done a lot of successful shows in the past, they probably know what it takes to launch a new show.

➤ Send a Spy

Never jump into a new show right away. If the show sounds interesting, go as an attendee, or send one of your managers to review the show from the attendee's point of view. Your spy should ask attendees, "Are you finding everything you need? Has this show been useful for you? If not, why not? Was the mix of exhibits what you expected?" Information is one of your secret weapons, and direct reconnaissance is the best, most reliable source. If it meets your needs, consider exhibiting there next year.

➤ Take a Hard Look at Traditional Shows

Scrutinize every show you attend every year. Is the show's target audience still your market? A show's focus and target market can drift away from the intended market in a year or two when floor space is sold to eager, but inappropriate, exhibitors.

Don't allow tradition to drive your selection. You change, your company changes, and the shows change.

■ SHOWS TO CHOOSE

There are three basic types of show events: public shows, industry trade shows, and association shows.

➤ Public Shows

Public shows are those to which all are invited, like lawn-and-garden shows, home decorating shows, and sporting-goods shows. These shows are usually created by a show promoter, who may run from a few to a few dozen shows a year.

Public shows target specific regions and lifestyles. They're held Friday, Saturday, and Sunday. They attract a wide variety of visitors, from the casual and curious to the checkbook-in-hand, we're-ready-to-buy-today people.

Most major cities will host several public shows each month, if not several in a weekend. The visitors to public shows usually arrive by car and usually travel not more than an hour to get to the show.

Find these shows by calling the convention and visitors bureau (CVB) in your target city. They are glad to give you a list of local shows, their dates, and information so you can contact the show promoter.

➤ Industry Shows

Industry trade shows are produced by show promoters and are usually sponsored by major trade associations, industry trade magazines, and journals. These shows are rarely open to the public, so well-qualified visitors walk the aisles. These shows are almost always held on weekdays.

Find out about industry shows by going to your public library and asking the reference librarian for one of the trade show directories.[1] There are several available, and they all cost a ton of money. For pocket change you can copy the pages you want and get all the information you need.

Most of these directories have extensive cross-references so you can find shows by geographic location, markets served, industry affiliation, and key words. Select the shows that you think will best reach your market and copy the information about these shows from the directory.

Another approach is to call the magazines that serve the industry you want to reach. Ask for information about the shows that they sponsor and other shows that serve the industry. Selecting publications that target the markets you want can automatically help you select the best show for you.

➤ Association Shows

Association shows are usually held in conjunction with national and regional meetings of a professional or trade association. There are currently over 27,000 associations in the United States and 85,000 associations worldwide, and a thousand new ones being formed every year. Virtually all of them are listed in the *Gale Encyclopedia of Associations* (available at your library). Many of them feature a trade show during their conventions. There are plenty of opportunities to reach very targeted markets through association shows. Some are very

---

[1] See the Appendix for a listing of available trade-show directories.

small, with just a dozen or so exhibitors. Others are massive, filling the convention halls of major cities.

Associations tend to attract people with similar ideals and goals (fraternal organizations), professions (professional associations), and interests (fan clubs and affinity groups).

In many cases, associations are the best way to target a very select group of buyers. For example, if you want to reach cardiologists who practice in the United States, you should go to the American Heart Association's conference and show. If you want to reach people who speak for a living, go to the National Speakers Association convention and show.

➤ Business-to-Business Expos

Along these same lines are chamber of commerce business-to-business expos, fraternal organization shows, local gun-club shows, craft fairs, and other local events. Take a very close look at these shows before deciding to participate. Some are very well done, attracting visitors with money burning holes in their pockets. Others don't work well at all, bringing in a mix of window shoppers out for a Sunday drive. You may feel compelled to participate since you're a member of the organization. Beware! This attitude will severely limit your selling ability. If you go, make sure you *really* want to go and be sure you can write heaps of orders.

➤ Regional Shows Offer Unique Advantages

Too often, companies plan their trade show schedules by rote and wind up exhibiting at the same national events year after year. If your company has fallen into this scheduling rut, it may be time for an approach more conducive to guerrilla marketing. Fast-growing regional shows offer new opportunities at a fraction of the cost. According to the Center for Exhibition Industry Research, at least half of the new trade shows in the next decade will be regional in scope.

Company reps don't have to commit the time, travel, or resources required for a national event, so more decision makers and influencers are likely to attend. Trial introductions and new product tests are less expensive and easier to set up. Regionals are not as crowded or as busy, giving you more quality time with prospects. Input from a diverse group of attendees may spark new marketing and product-application ideas.

➤ International Shows

Guerrillas know that one of the fastest growing opportunities for small business is in the international arena. The U.S. Department of Commerce offers the Certified Trade Events Program. Certified trade events offer the best opportunities for companies new to international commerce. Companies exhibiting in certified events benefit from extensive exposure in local markets as well as U.S. Embassy assistance before, during, and after the show.

The Department of Commerce also sponsors the *Foreign Buyer Program,* which heavily promotes selected large U.S. trade shows overseas to attract attendance from abroad. Multilingual promotional materials help to draw a global audience. Participating in such shows is an inexpensive way to explore the international market in your products without going overseas.

Every country has unique customs and requirements for trade show success. Although this book was written with North American trade shows in mind, our experience internationally suggests that most of these techniques apply worldwide.[2] Ask your distributors or Department of Commerce about local customs and procedures. A list of resources for international shows is listed in the Appendix.

---

[2] For specific assistance with international trade-show planning, contact Joseph Ciprut at Tradex Associates. You can call him at 1-617-969-3326, or E-mail tradeshows@aol.com.

VAT *Refunds*

When you exhibit internationally, you'll be charged value-added tax (VAT) ranging from 12 to 33 percent on goods and services. VAT can be refunded when purchases leave the country. You can also receive VAT refunds on travel bills. Ask your show management about VAT refunds. There are VAT rebate agencies that work on commission.[3]

➤ Nonprofits

Nonprofit shows can be extremely profitable. You can also target buyers with specific income ranges by selecting affinity organizations and participating in their shows. Many influential buyers participate in nonprofit activities as their way of giving something back to a world that's been good to them.

➤ Professional Associations

One of the best ways to educate yourself about effective exhibiting is to get involved in any of the several professional associations serving the exhibition industry. See the Appendix for a listing.

A number of universities and community colleges offer courses on trade show marketing. If you have the time and resources, this may be a great way to develop skills and avoid expensive mistakes.

Many associations depend on the fees collected from trade show exhibitors to fund their operations. The membership dues cover a small portion of the budget, and the lion's share comes from the trade show at the national convention.

---

[3] One such agency is Meridian Vat Reclaim Services USA, 575 Eighth Ave., New York, NY 10018, call 1-212-554-6650.

But the associations sometimes don't do a good job at filling the exhibit hall with buyers.

Make sure you understand what promotional activities have been used in the past and what promotion is planned for this show to guarantee you'll have a steady stream of buyers.

■ HOW TO EVALUATE THE SHOWS YOU'VE SELECTED

Many savvy trade show producers offer exceptional shows. Expo producers like to think they have the exhibitors' best interests at heart. They want to help, but business is *so* good that they have no motivation to behave differently.

➤ Expo Landlords

Expo producers act like landlords, and you know how difficult it can be to have a good relationship with your landlord. Their primary goal is to sell space. They set up minimum standards for exhibit architecture and sales behavior. The best show producers do a *lot* more, like getting people in the door, but usually the rest is up to you. When it comes to packing your exhibit with buyers, don't expect much from your show producer. You're responsible for selecting the right show, attracting qualified buyers, and then doing whatever is necessary to achieve your sales goals.

The expo salesperson's job is to sell exhibit space. Unless you're vigilant, you could be talked into a show that really isn't right for you. It happens innocently enough; you've always done the show in the past, or you're told that your competition is exhibiting. Just because your competitors are at a show doesn't mean it's a good show for you or for them. An unscrupulous few will even resort to scare tactics, implying that you're making a huge mistake by passing up their show. When you have clear marketing objectives, you'll avoid these traps and select the right show every time.

Scrutinize every show you attend every year. Is the show's target audience still your market?

Savvy show producers bring together the right visitors and the right exhibitors. They won't let their sales force sell to everyone they call on. They know that it's better to have the right people at the show than to have a tutti-frutti mix of exhibitors. Visitors don't want to waste time at exhibits that they don't care about.

➤ Key Information You Need to Make a Decision

Who's There?

Who are the show attendees? What are their buying needs and interests? What is their buying authority? Where do your target buyers go when they want to go shopping? Some visitors can insist on a purchase. Others influence the decision or make recommendations as part of a purchasing team. What is the economic health of their industry? Do they have money they *can* spend or *must* spend? While preshow visitor rosters are usually available, don't rely too heavily on them; they aren't always accurate.

Why Are These Attendees There?

Are they there to review the market for new vendors and business relationships? Are they looking to make purchase decisions? Do association attendees just want education?

Where Is the Show?

Some destinations attract visitors, while other cities are avoided. Just think about the crimes you've heard reported on the evening news and the cities associated with them. No doubt about it—show location does influence attendance (see Table 2.1). Having said that, though, some people will attend a show no matter where it's held, if it's the right topic and the show matches their interests.

> ### TABLE 2.1   TOP 10 SHOW SITES*
>
> 1. Atlanta
> 2. Chicago
> 3. Orlando (tie)
> 4. Toronto (tie)
> 5. New York City
> 6. Dallas
> 7. Las Vegas
> 8. Washington DC
> 9. San Francisco
> 10. New Orleans
>
> *These are the 10 cities that hosted the most expositions in 1996.

Since more and more organizations are carefully scrutinizing expenses, conferences at costly locations are getting the ax. For example, consider a show in Hawaii. The vendors think it's great; the company pays the bill for a Hawaiian vacation. But the visitors are faced with larger airfare and hotel bills plus the extra travel time. Many companies won't go that distance.

Where Will Your Exhibit Be?

What will promote a steady stream of visitors into the exhibit area? What will be your location on the floor relative to the educational sessions and other proceedings? Where do people have to go to eat and drink in respect to the exhibit hall?

What Are the Exhibit Hours?

This is particularly important with association trade shows. What other activities and programs conflict with your show time? It's really frustrating not to have set show hours. A steady stream of people will keep you in a good mood. If conference attendees don't have a time to come and see your products, you'll stand for long hours on the empty floor and waste your time.

What Are the Costs?

What's the cost of exhibit-space rental, utilities, freight and handling, and so on? What other attendance fees are required? Is union labor required? What are the typical travel, hotel, and entertainment costs? List everything!

How Can You Get Attendees into Your Exhibit?

Are there preshow mailings being done by the producer? Are the exhibits actively promoted during association sessions and with program materials? Can you place signs outside the hall directing visitors to your exhibit? Can your staff sell outside the exhibit, in the lobbies, or outside the hall?

How Responsive Is the Show Management?

Will show management make sure all the support systems are in place? Can they solve problems quickly and professionally? For references, ask for a copy of last year's exhibitors' list and call a sampling of those who would be selling to your customers.

You need show management to be professional and have all the support mechanisms in place. There'll be times when the installation crew has put up your exhibit incorrectly (a problem we'll show you how to avoid in Chapter 10), and you'll have to work with them to untangle the problems.

Does the Producer Offer Exhibitor Support?

Better show producers will include consultation, training materials, manuals, and even advanced preshow training for your employees. We are routinely contracted to provide these services for a number of show organizers. These services are seldom publicized but are often included in the price of the exhibit space.

➤ Other Critical Information You Should Know

How Many Other Exhibitors?

Who else is going to be exhibiting? How does your company fit in with the rest of the mix? What direct competition will be there, and where will they be located with respect to your exhibit? By all means, ask to keep away from your direct competition!

How Many Attendees Are Expected?

Don't just settle for big numbers. What are their buying habits and qualifications? You want good, qualified leads, not just a sea of traffic. You're better off going to a smaller show where there's little traffic but great leads over a larger show where there's lots of traffic and few buyers.

When you compare expected attendance with last year's numbers, you can get a trend within that target market. One long-term trend we're seeing is that companies are sending fewer people with a broader decision-making responsibility.

What Are the Show Restrictions?

Are giveaways allowed? Are there height restrictions? Can you take along your own exhibit? Some shows try to level the playing field by requiring everyone to use the same pipe-and-drape background.

The generic exhibit approach is gaining popularity. For example, both the Federation for American Health Systems show and the Austin Chamber of Commerce business-to-business expo provide standard exhibits that are used one day by the vendors while the buyers circulate—then the next day by the buyers while the vendors circulate. This approach removes the hype from the exhibits and turns the attention to networking, getting business, and closing sales.

Smart associations and show producers go a long way to facilitate your trade show success. Ultimately, it's up to you to set your goals and select the right show to meet those objectives.

➤ How to Quit a Show

You can quit going to a show in which you've participated forever with no impact at all. Reallocate the funds you would have spent for that show and put them into an advertising campaign, direct-mail program, or public-relations strategy like a blitz to your industry press. Tell your customers and prospects that you've decided the show isn't as effective as it once was and that you would rather give your customers added value instead of spending it at the show. Make your *not* being there a benefit to your customers.

➤ The Best Possible Locations

Location can dramatically increase the traffic at your exhibit. Best locations are where the visitors *have* to pass to get into the show, such as at the show entrance, on the way to the bathrooms, and near concession stands.

When it comes to repeated exposure to visitors walking the aisles, an island works best. This is where you have a space that is surrounded on all four sides by aisles. You get a chance to get the visitors coming and going. At a building-supply show, a manufacturer of hardwood flooring set up a twenty-by-twenty-foot island covered with the company's beautiful flooring product. The island became a popular shortcut to the bathrooms. Most exhibitors would have complained, but these guerrillas loved the traffic.

The next best location is at the end of a row where three sides of your exhibit are on aisles. This works well if you can set up a production line. For example, at the Retailers Bakery Association show, an equipment company set up a complete working bagel line, featuring a mixer at one end, followed by a dough roller and former, proofer, and cooker. Attendees could pick the hot, fresh bagels right off the end of the line. A real show-stopper!

Another way to increase exposure is to rent space on opposite sides of the same aisle so the visitor sees you on both sides. This works well when your company offers different product lines that attract different visitors at the same show, or when you're joining forces with fellow franchisees. A tool company used this strategy effectively at a hardware show, featuring automotive tools in one exhibit and construction tools in another just across the aisle.

The easiest way to establish yourself as a player in an industry is to attend the industry trade show, buy a lot of floor space, and create a "village." This is effective if you have lots of money and really want to launch yourself into a market quickly. Set around a few pop-up exhibit towers, add plants and lots of salespeople, and you've made a big impression. It's better to buy floor space and rent exhibits than to buy a very expensive exhibit at the expense of floor space. We guarantee that you will be the talk of the show, and virtually every visitor will want to know who you are and what you do.

Many companies believe location is *everything* at a show. A Fortune 500 executive once told us, "The key to trade show success is location, location, location," and he's wrong, wrong, wrong. The location myth is perpetuated by many trade show organizers who charge a premium for prime locations. Companies who pay extra for their location will also pay big bucks for fancy, complex exhibits to capitalize on that location. This is great if you have lots of cash to waste. The bad news is that these same companies don't usually invest in training their exhibit staff to close sales, and then they do a weak job on after-show follow-up, so the investment in preferred locations is usually wasted.

Location is not nearly as critical to getting leads and closing sales as some promoters would like you to believe. It's far better to have a cheaper location and a less elaborate exhibit and invest the savings in a strong preshow promotion, sales training for your exhibit staff, and a great after-show follow-up campaign.

A well-known and respected computer firm that attends hundreds of trade shows per year invests an average of a *million dollars* per show. Yet, in four out of the past five years, this firm did *nothing* to follow up the leads collected at these shows. Nothing! Those in charge are spending too much on the wrong things and getting no return on the investment. One executive told us the show was for exposure. Try paying dividends to your stockholders with that.

➤ How to Get the Best Possible Location

When it comes to selecting your location on a show floor, you're usually stuck. Most trade show producers apply a formula that includes how long your organization has been exhibiting and how much floor space you've bought in the past. Sometimes they use a weighting factor that awards people who have been with the show since the beginning. This all conspires to put the small, first-time exhibitor at a disadvantage when it comes to location selection.

The best way to improve your location is to ask show management to let you know when a better location opens up. Make friends with the show manager. When another exhibitor drops out or downsizes space, the show manager will call you. Be sure to review the offer to make sure it really is a better location for you.

You can often improve your exhibit location when you arrive at the show. Before you set up, ask the show manager if there have been any last-minute cancellations. A few exhibitors usually drop out at the last minute for a variety of reasons, including bankruptcy. The show manager doesn't care—they've already been paid, so they just fill the unoccupied space with potted plants and chairs. Look at those locations, and if they're better than your current location, take the best one. That's why guerrillas never use phrases like "See us in booth #257" in their preshow promotion.

Picking the right show takes time, energy, and imagination, and this may seem like a lot of work. Most companies do more research evaluating a $3,000 copier than they do when planning to spend $30,000 to exhibit at a show. The wrong show can burn up a lot of resources and leave you tired and bitter. But once you've found the right one, the battle is half won.

➤ Create a Show Timeline

Create a timeline with a schedule of checkpoints for the tasks, events, and bills that must be paid before, during, and after the show. A successful exhibit is a combination of event planning, execution, and follow-up activities that peak at the show. You'll save money by taking advantage of preshow specials, you'll get the best rates on printing, you'll not have to pay overnight shipping charges, and you'll avoid rush charges.

Careful planning and follow-up are critical for a successful and profitable show. Many companies have regular meetings beginning as early as six months before the show date to ensure an effective and trouble-free show.

➤ Trade Show Success Calendar

Here's a list of tasks and the best time to do them to guarantee your show's success. Some of the events may seem to be scheduled way ahead of time. We have found that this scheduling will give you the jump on your competition, so you get prime hotel space, pay the lowest possible price, and avoid budget-killing rush charges, overtime labor, and express freight bills.

52 Weeks Before

- ☐ Send a spy to make sure the people you want to sell to attend in numbers that make the investment worthwhile.
- ☐ Contact show management for the exhibitor kit.
- ☐ Review show suitability.
- ☐ Work up a preliminary budget, padded by 10–20 percent.
- ☐ Reserve exhibit space.
- ☐ Sign and return contracts.
- ☐ Reserve hotel suite space.
- ☐ Find out how your company can lead some of next year's educational sessions.

25 Weeks Before

- ☐ Check to see if you can get a better location because someone's dropped out of the show. Do this monthly until the show date.
- ☐ Confirm your company's participation in the educational seminars.

16 Weeks Before

- ☐ Budget and planning meeting. Bring together the departments involved to set show goals, assign responsibilities and accountability, and finalize budget.
- ☐ Develop message and theme, integrated with other marketing plans.
- ☐ Create preshow promotion plan.
- ☐ Select sales, technical, and support staff.
- ☐ Review the exhibitor kit to understand show deadlines.
- ☐ Book hotel rooms for the staff. Confirm hotel suite.

14 Weeks Before

- ☐ Plan exhibit layout and design.
- ☐ Develop graphics design requirements.
- ☐ Develop a media kit and promotion strategy.
- ☐ Plan staff training session.

12 Weeks Before

☐ Get company details to show management for show directory.
☐ If an outside contractor is used, schedule labor for exhibit installation and dismantling labor. Alert show management.
☐ Send preshow media releases.
☐ Update advertising and newsletters to include show details.

10 Weeks Before

☐ Order premiums now to avoid rush charges and express freight charges.

8 Weeks Before

☐ Confirm staff participation and scheduling. If hiring temporary help, confirm arrangements.
☐ Confirm graphics design is on schedule.
☐ Confirm exhibit construction is on schedule.
☐ Check travel, liability, theft, and catastrophe insurance coverage.

6 Weeks Before

☐ Plan travel itineraries and book airline tickets for the staff with the most predictable travel schedule. You'll get the best deals now, since most companies will book 3 to 4 weeks out, and the cheap seats will be gone.
☐ Make ground transportation arrangements.
☐ Order on-site show services.
☐ Create back-up show services vendor list.
☐ Request visitor information package from convention and visitors bureau for inclusion in your "survival manual."

4 Weeks Before

- ☐ Develop demonstrations.
- ☐ Create lead form and database template.
- ☐ Create follow-up package.
- ☐ Write and test follow-up letters.
- ☐ Write follow-up telemarketing script.
- ☐ Complete exhibit construction.
- ☐ Complete educational seminar handout materials and graphics.
- ☐ Check demo inventory, samples, and literature; are quantities adequate for follow-up?

3 Weeks Before

- ☐ Mail preshow promotions to arrive 10 to 14 days before the show.
- ☐ Schedule inbound and outbound freight.

2 Weeks Before

- ☐ Confirm on-site show services.
- ☐ Confirm travel arrangements for all staff.
- ☐ Create "survival manual."
- ☐ Assemble survival kit.
- ☐ Package and ship materials to show by traceable carrier.

1 Week Before

- ☐ Final all-hands staff meeting and training.
- ☐ Get enough rest. You'll need your energy for the show.
- ☐ Staff and stock hotel suite.
- ☐ Pick up badges.
- ☐ Train temporary help.
- ☐ Conduct daily staff meetings.
- ☐ Process leads daily.

1 Week After

- ☐ Conduct aftershow review—discuss what went well and what gets changed for the next show.
- ☐ Deliver staff recognition and awards.
- ☐ Follow up with leads.
- ☐ Send thank-you notes.
- ☐ Close sales.

2 Weeks After

- ☐ Reconcile expenses and review against planned budget.
- ☐ Survey publications for media coverage. Calculate value.
- ☐ Decide whether to do the show next year.

4 Weeks After

- ☐ Measure your sales results from show activities.

8 Weeks After

- ☐ Do a post-show survey to measure sales effectiveness.

16 Weeks After

- ☐ Do a second post-show survey to measure sales effectiveness.

Chapter 3

Why a Potent Exhibit Strategy Sets the Stage for Maximum Sales

In this chapter, you'll learn how to bring all the components of your exhibit together in a cohesive and effective strategy. You'll see how to combine fixtures, people, signs, giveaways, costumes, and literature into a cohesive theme that will achieve maximum sales results.

➤ Floor Plans for Success

Busy exhibits are open, inviting, uncluttered, colorful, and attractive. They do not present barriers, like tables or desks, between the visitors and the exhibit staff. There are people who love clutter but will put up with clean, and there are people who hate clutter and won't put up with it. You're much safer to have a clean, uncluttered exhibit. You don't have to display everything you offer—a representative assortment will do.

Make sure your exhibit isn't a challenge to enter or exit. We've seen exhibits that looked like a carnival fun-house maze. Make your exhibit tough to get into, and you'll be as lonely as the Maytag repairman.

You may have noticed that we haven't used the word "booth" (as it's known in the United States) or "stand" (as it's known to the rest of the world). There's a good reason. You are exhibiting what you sell, so think of it as your exhibit. This simple change in vernacular helps you focus on the real reason you're at a show—to get business!

➤ Get Out from behind the Table

We have no idea why, but show decorators always set up the standard eight-foot-draped-and-skirted table right across the front of the exhibit space. This is *not* where it belongs. Novice exhibitors compound this mistake by leaving it there, creating a barrier between the sales staff and the show traffic. They further aggravate the error by sitting in one of the two chairs (also provided) *behind* the table and blanketing the tabletop with literature. With this exhibit strategy, there are only two types of visitors who will stop and talk—those who want what you're giving away, and those who know you already.

The key is to open up the space. If you have a small exhibit, push your table to the back and place your samples there. Or push the table to the side and use it to support a demonstration aid like a TV and videotape.

Using the chairs can also cause a problem. Visitors like exhibitors who are like them. If you're sitting down and your visitor is standing, you're now *un*like them, just as placing the barrier of a table between you and your visitors limits your ability to reach out and greet them.

If you *must* stand behind your table to demonstrate what you sell, place the table at an angle so people can come into your exhibit space. Then you can move around to the front when traffic is slow.

A cosmetic company brought us in to work with their salespeople at a local show. Because of a scheduling conflict, only half the staff was able to attend, but those who used these ideas had substantially improved results. In a two-hour period, the salespeople who stood behind a table got an average of just one lead and complained about the show. Those who stood in front of the table averaged six hot leads per hour and thought the show was great! One salesperson closed a substantial amount of business at the show, something she had never done before!

➤ **Select a Theme**

CONSIDER PATRIOTIC THEME
> FLAGS
> FLAG POLE?

Should you use a theme? Depending on what you are offering, a theme exhibit can be very powerful. The theme must reinforce your message in a creative and memorable way.

You can make a strong impression and draw big crowds with devices like era themes (the 50s), occupation themes like medical and police, or fantasy or futuristic themes.

Be careful about themed exhibits. Don't make the theme so intriguing that everyone wants to stop and visit—unless everyone is your prospective customer. Make the theme so that it's attractive to only the visitors with whom you want to do business.

When you do build themed exhibits, be wary of copyright and trademark infringement. If you want to use the latest movie theme, you'll draw a letter from the movie production company's lawyers unless you're using licensed products to decorate your exhibit. If your artist uses a logo or other graphics that have been protected with copyright or trademark status, you're infringing and will risk a $10,000 fine (in the United States) for *each* infringement.

With themed exhibits, uniforms or costumes are often employed. While this can be a lot of fun, salespeople in costume get silly and forget why they're at the show. We've observed visitors shying away from costumed actors. Do the advantages of the theme outweigh this barrier to business? Weigh this downside to costumes against your sales goal.

■ YOUR LITERATURE STRATEGY

A key element to your trade show sales success is your literature strategy—how you use brochures, fliers, and sales collateral at your show. What do you hand out to show visitors?

How do you make it most effective? How do you make sure that you're not wasting your money?

At most shows, you see two different literature-strategy camps—the "load 'em up" exhibitors and the "give 'em nothing" exhibitors. What is effective for you depends on what you're selling.

➤ Simple Ways to Save Money on Literature

Use it sparingly. People are going to see so many companies that the majority of what is picked up gets tossed out.

If a visitor is burdened with literature, the literature doesn't make it home. It will end up in the garbage at the show or in the hotel-room trash can. What good does a huge shopping bag of literature do for you?

➤ Why Handing Out Literature Can Lose Sales

For a complex product, literature can actually *hinder* the purchasing process. If your prospects review the literature and don't find exactly what they're looking for, they may think you don't offer it, and you're out of the running. You're much better off talking to your visitors and finding out their needs than having them interpret your literature later.

And another thing—you'd rather have the literature collectors keep walking.

➤ Give Them Just a Bit

If written materials are what you need to close the sale at the show floor, then have that material available for your visitors. If most buyers require more detailed information, or need to go to a committee to purchase, then you only need limited information at the show. Follow up after the show with the right material to support a buying decision in your favor.

If you have a large catalog of products, you may wish to use sales literature as a key part of your trade show selling process. For example, bring the best and most appropriate literature for the show, and display sample copies. Let your exhibit staff detail products from the literature, and use the customer's interest in the literature to get leads. It doesn't make sense for you to pass out a telephone-book-sized catalog at the show, but offering to mail them a catalog in exchange for a business card will get your visitor to respond.

If what you offer can be sold quickly from a simple brochure and your brochure is a brief overview, reference, and reminder of your product, take a supply to the show. If a visitor shows interest, give that person a brochure on the spot. Ask the visitor to hand it off to the person in charge of purchasing. For this strategy to work, you must still get the visitor's contact information, and follow up after the show to make sure the brochure got into the decision maker's hands.

Or you may take the middle ground. You want to keep your exhibit clean and professional-looking, and literature tends to clutter it up. Make appropriate material available to your visitors, but don't weigh them down. Offer to let them order the literature they want and fulfill the request quickly. Get their literature to their offices by the time they return from the show, or at least within the next three or four days.

For some consumer shows, all you want to do is give enough information to let prospective buyers know if the product is for them, and then invite them to call your toll-free number for more information.

No matter what your strategy, if a client or prospect at the show really wants detailed information and wants it now, make sure the person gets it. You never want to turn your back on hot prospects—give them what they need. Some people are leaving the country with the information. Others need to make a decision in the next day or two. Talk with them now!

For many organizations, you'll be better off if you set up a time after the show to discuss what you sell than to hand out literature.

➤ Create Special Literature Just for the Show

Given the cost of attending most shows, creating a targeted promotional piece for that particular audience is a good investment. Write a one-sheet flyer describing your key selling points. Make sure the benefits are critical to the visitors at the show. Make the piece current and topical, and distribute it exclusively at the show. This will save you money in the long run, because you won't give away your more expensive sales pieces, you'll reduce the amount of literature your visitor has to carry, and you'll deliver a focused message to your target buyer.

➤ How to Use Fusion Marketing

If you have any fusion-marketing partners exhibiting at the show, create a one-sheet flyer with a map on one side identifying the locations of your business partners on the show floor. On the other side, print short summaries of the specific benefits your business partners bring to your buyers, and have your associates hand out copies of this flyer at their exhibits. This approach boosts your image by tying you to other companies in a cooperative way. People like to buy from team players.

Giving away anything without first getting contact information from your customer is like throwing your literature into the trash can. Walk down the aisle from companies that hand out materials left and right, and you'll find a trash can full of their literature. Even if you want to buy what they sell, the psychological impact of thousands of other people discarding their offer leaves a negative impression. Most companies that do this are at the show for "exposure," not sales. It's far easier to give something to a visitor than to actively sell something.

➤ Developing Literature That Works

Many companies still write their sales literature in a customer vacuum, with no input from the sales force or buyers. Savvy companies take a more aggressive approach.

Your approach to literature development must keep the decision makers in mind. What are they looking for, and how will they decide? Is the decision made by a team or an individual? What criteria are being used to evaluate your product? How can your literature help to close the sale?

You may have a product that is sold to three different markets. Create a sales piece for each market's special needs. If what you sell requires a team to make the decision, make sure you have literature that covers the physical details, the financial details, and the people details. Testimonials are one of your most important sales tools. Include them, too.

Design your literature to show the benefits and advantages that meet the needs of the customer. The best pieces avoid long-winded paragraphs and are easy for your sales force to use. Buyers need assistance, so use your piece to assist in the discussion of your buyer's needs, and generate questions your salesperson can answer.

Use your knowledge of your sales force when creating your literature. Challenge your people to get as much information as possible about what the customer really wants from promotional material.

■ HOW TO SAVE BIG MONEY ON YOUR EXHIBIT

Your exhibit doesn't have to be complex, elaborate, or fancy. But it does have to communicate your sales message to visitors and be in harmony with your corporate identity.

You may want to forgo using an exhibit altogether. Instead of the normal blue-curtain backdrop of a trade show booth, one guerrilla stacked up piles of the company's shipping crates as high as the show officials would allow. The exhibit drew attention and reinforced the theme that they were now shipping the newest update of its product.

We would have a very difficult time recommending custom exhibits to anyone these days. The return on the investment just isn't there. We know this will make the custom-exhibit houses mad, but the buggy-whip makers got mad at Henry Ford.

Custom-exhibit houses have turned out some real showstoppers. And they require a budget to match. Most of the large exhibit houses will provide design services free of charge. And most companies solicit designs from several exhibit houses. Obviously, most of the designs are not chosen, but someone has to pay for the designers' time. For this reason, some custom exhibit houses mark up the retail price of what they sell by 10 percent or more. This is just to cover the costs of business they lost!

When you buy from these custom exhibit houses, you're paying the design costs of some other company's decision not to buy their design. And you lose.

➤ Use a Portable Exhibit

We cannot recommend custom exhibits to a guerrilla because they're big, heavy, and expensive. You need a truck to move them and an army to assemble them. Guerrilla marketers will use several sections of lightweight portable exhibit.

The wave of the future is to move away from complex, heavy, expensive, labor-intensive, and ineffective custom-built exhibits. Companies are spending fortunes on these exhibits and realizing little increase in sales for the tremendous costs involved. Any time you need to change your corporate look, you either eat the expensive reengineering fees or dump the exhibit (there's a booming second-hand custom exhibit market) and start over.

Portables are either panel systems or pop-ups. Panel systems use a skeleton of channeled frames and grooved panels that slide into the channels. Pop-ups have a collapsible latticework frame of aluminum spars from which you hang a flexible skin of fabric or plastic sheeting, usually attached with magnetic or Velcro® strips. The sheets roll up and the latticework scissors fold down into a compact package. You can take it to small shows, add sections for larger shows, and rent more sections for your largest shows. This lets you keep your transportation costs low, and you can change the configuration of your exhibit rapidly. You can update the signs and upgrade your image for much less than custom designs.

Using portables, you'll save lots of money at least four ways:

1. *Initial costs are much less.* Since you are configuring standard modules into your own design, costs are substantially lower. You'll save from 30 to 80 percent over a custom-designed exhibit. And you'll get every bit as much business at the show.

2. *Shipping is much cheaper.* A portable exhibit weighs between 35 and 130 pounds and can be hand-carried or wheeled by one person. It can be transported in a car trunk or shipped via common carrier such as UPS. It can even be checked as airline baggage. Even after paying excess baggage and overweight surcharges, it's cheaper (and faster) than Federal Express. Never use the post office to ship your exhibit. The post office only offers tracking on overnight shipments, and delivery reliability isn't as high. Since you don't have to hire a moving and storage company to ship your exhibit around, you save a lot of money on transportation.

3. *Drayage is much less expensive.* Drayage is the outrageous fee that exhibit producers charge you to move your exhibit and materials—usually with union labor—

from the loading dock to your exhibit floor space. In some cases, that several-hundred-foot delivery will cost you more than shipping your materials thousands of miles. The charges are usually figured by the hundredweight (CWT), plus overtime after normal business hours and on weekends. Portable exhibits are much lighter, so you pay less drayage. And if you have a smaller exhibit, you can wheel the exhibit in yourself (if union rules allow), avoiding drayage charges altogether.

4. *Storage is much cheaper or free.* If you have a custom exhibit, you'll probably have to store it in a warehouse, complete with storage and insurance fees. Most portable exhibits will store neatly in a corner of your office, or ask your exhibit vendor to store your exhibit for you. Some will do this at no cost as a service to you. Ask about it or negotiate for it.

➤ Rent an Exhibit

Unless you do more than two or three shows a year, you should simply choose to rent for each show. There are at least five advantages:

1. *You don't have to store your exhibit.* It gets shipped from your exhibit vendor before the show, and you ship it back to them after the show. Storage charges for a custom exhibit can cost thousands of dollars a year— money you could have working for you to make sales.

2. *You don't have to refurbish the exhibit between shows.* The exhibit comes fresh from your exhibit vendor, in perfect condition, ready to go.

3. *You pay much less.* Most rentals cost 10 to 20 percent of the purchase price. It's much better to spend your money on a powerful preshow promotion and a strong aftershow sales campaign. You'll get a substantially higher return on your investment, and that will let

you buy more floor space at the next show, so you can get more sales next time.

4. *You're not stuck with an exhibit that doesn't meet your needs.* You can rent a larger exhibit or a smaller exhibit each time. You pay only for what you need.

5. *Renting will keep your exhibit fresh-looking and save you lots of money.* Most companies buy a new exhibit or refurbish their exhibit every two years.

➤ Lease Your Exhibit

If you do more than three exhibits per year, you may wish to lease your exhibit. Lease during your busiest trade show season, cutting out your lease expenses during the summer and holiday periods when you don't have shows.

Leasing gives you all the advantages of renting, except you store the exhibit and you have to make sure it's in top condition for the next show.

Leasing will save you money when you see your organization growing rapidly.

➤ Buy a Used Exhibit

If you do many shows a year, you'll want to buy your exhibit. Get your ego out of the way, and think about buying a second-hand exhibit.

There is a strong second-hand exhibit market. Companies expand and sell their smaller exhibits. Companies go broke and sell their ineffective exhibits. Companies get tired of looking at their exhibits and sell them.

Just like when you drive a new car off the dealer's lot, your exhibit loses a lot of value after you take ownership. So, you can save from 50 to 70 percent from the list price on a used exhibit. You'll spend up to 20 percent on refurbishing, but you'll still save money overall.

Your exhibit vendor, who stands to make more money on a new exhibit, might not be happy with your decision, but point out how you'll be needing the vendor's services in the future as you grow your business. And right now you need to spend the money on sales-generating activities, not new equipment.

If you're comfortable shopping for your own exhibit, put an ad in your local business paper. "Pop-up exhibit wanted for our next trade show . . ." Offer 20 to 30 percent of the original purchase price.

Shame on Them

One of our clients got a quotation from a large, well-known custom-exhibit house for a small pop-up display. Included in the price was several hundred dollars for "assembly and client viewing." When the client objected, the salesperson agreed to rewrite the quote. The new quote didn't have the assembly charge, but it did have a new "assembly drawings and shipping" charge for the same amount. The client went with another vendor that didn't try to rip his company off.

➤ How to Negotiate the Lowest Exhibit Price

Standard margins for most trade show exhibits are 37.5 to 40 percent. The manufacturer will often pay freight from the factory to your location. Question every additional charge. If it doesn't seem reasonable, ask for an explanation. We believe everyone is entitled to fair profit, but no one should take unfair advantage of you.

If you have questions and doubts about your quotation, call another exhibit vendor and ask if the quotation is fair. Most vendors are tooth-and-nail competitors and are glad to reveal the inside scoop just to get a shot at their competition and a crack at your business.

Shopping around and getting competitive bids on pop-up exhibits seems like a good thing to do, but you can waste lots of time going for the deal that really isn't there. There is so much competition in the pop-up exhibit market that products have little differentiation, and you pretty much get what you pay for. Lower-cost exhibits tend to require frequent refurbishing, and more expensive exhibits need fewer repairs between events.

Waiting until the last moment will cost you a lot of money for sign creation rush charges and overnight express shipping. You can lose every bit of your price advantage— and pay much more than you were expecting—with rush charges. An exhibit vendor's very reasonable quotation can get very expensive if you add rush charges for graphics, photographs, and overnight shipping charges. You can easily blow your budget because you held off choosing a vendor until the last minute.

Choose the vendor you believe will give you the highest level of service, and give this company your business. Try to give your vendor as much time as possible. Establish a partnership.

One question to ask a vendor is, "What do you sell?" If the answer is "exhibits and signs," the vendor has missed the point. If the answer is "a successful and profitable trade show," the vendor understands what you need!

➤ Avoid Dollar-Wasting Exhibit Traps

Avoid custom add-ons to portable exhibits. We've seen quotations on custom add-ons like counters, tall sign headers, and TV towers that double the cost of the exhibit and won't get a single additional lead or make another sale.

One of the biggest money-wasters has already been mentioned—rush charges for sign making and graphics and overnight shipping charges for your exhibit. Planning and ordering in advance will save you these ridiculous and unnecessary charges.

Never rent your exhibit from the show management company. You won't have the control over the signs and graphics you need to excel. The exhibits tend to be tired and worn-out older models that haven't been refurbished, and the show management company will charge you a substantial percentage of full purchase price to rent them to you. If you feel coerced into renting from show management, think twice about doing the show. It means you're too rushed to do the show right, and you'll not get the return you deserve on your investment.

Likewise, don't buy your signs and graphics from the show management company, either. They are expensive and, in general, of mediocre quality. What a waste of time, money, and energy. Guerrillas know that people don't buy because of who you are; they buy because you satisfy a need that they have. Besides, most shows provide a basic sign with your company's name for your exhibit.

Scrutinize every aspect of your exhibit. Make every feature work overtime to communicate your sales message, build credibility, and get you business. If it doesn't contribute to the sales process, it's not an investment, it's a cash drain. Ask, "Does this increase our sales message?" If the answer is no, rethink and redo until everything about your exhibit works hard to get you business.

Display Manufacturers

Call the Exhibit Designers & Producers Association, Milwaukee, Wisconsin, 1-414-276-3372, for a list of members and information on how to select an exhibit designer and producer. Then call each of the vendors listed in the Appendix and ask for a free brochure.

Thirty-Two Questions to Ask When Shopping for Your Exhibit

1. How many shows do you think you'll do in the next three years?

2. Will you be using the exhibit for an occasional event, or will the exhibit see heavy use throughout the year?

3. How will your size requirements change over that time?

4. Will you be sharing the exhibit with other partners? What are their graphics needs?

5. What kind of graphics will you use: computer graphics, photos, silk-screened signs, transparencies?

6. Will you use back-lit photographic art?

7. How often will you update your graphics?

8. What identity do you want your exhibit to portray?

9. What kind of covering do you want? Fabric, laminate, graphic panels? Is it important to match your corporate colors?

10. Do the panels need to appear seamless?

11. How will you be transporting the exhibit to the show? Will it be hand-carried, checked as airline baggage, or sent by freight?

12. Will the cases meet the UPS and airline size and weight maximums (usually 70 pounds and 130-inch-height-plus-width-plus-length dimension)?

13. Do the cases load horizontally or vertically? Vertical cases mean lifting; horizontal cases mean hands-and-knees work.

14. Do the cases have sturdy wheels or removable casters that will withstand rough handling? (Nothing is more frustrating than a case with a missing wheel.)

15. Do the cases have strong lifting handles that won't get snagged in transit?

16. What happens to the exhibit when it is placed on an uneven floor (the norm in exhibit halls)?

17. Who will be setting up the exhibit? Will it be you, your staff, or show labor? Will it be set up by a six-foot, two-hundred-pound man or a five-foot, one-hundred-pound woman?

18. How easy must it be to set up? Does it require any special tools?

19. How fast does it need to be set up? Will you be working under a 30- or 60-minute union-imposed deadline?

20. What happens if a part breaks during setup? How quickly can you get the part?

21. Is there a toll-free number you can call for answers to questions, help with setup problems, or replacement parts? Is it available 24 hours a day?

22. Will you need to change the exhibit configuration in the future to 360°, V-shaped, L-shaped, zigzag, or free-standing island?

23. Will the display have to support your products? What weight will it have to support?

24. Will you need shelves for placement of items? What weight will they need to support?

25. Will you need to add more shelves and fixtures later?

26. What type of lighting is available?

27. Are the replacement bulbs readily available? Are they available in other voltages for foreign shows?

28. Are the lights easily adjusted without a ladder?

29. What are the warrantee terms? What's covered and what's not?

30. Where do you get the exhibit repaired? Is it the responsibility of the dealer or the manufacturer, or both?

31. How long does it take to get repairs done?

32. How will you be storing your exhibit? Under what temperature conditions?

Before you buy any exhibit, assemble it yourself under the vendor's direction. Look for potential assembly problems, such as needing three hands to put a piece together or having parts that can be easily bent or broken. Take pictures of the assembly procedure so that your staff can put the exhibit together later. Ask for a spare parts kit.

■ GET THE EDGE

You'll gain a substantial edge over your competition when you plan for every aspect and potential problem that could arise at the show. Use the experience of your team to look for potential problems.

CHECK WITH SILVERGRAPH RE: EXHIBITING PRINTING

➤ Assemble Your Show Team

Bring together your marketing and sales team as you begin your trade show plans. Remember to include your manufacturing people in the planning of your show. If you hire consultants, invite them to your initial meeting so that you can tap into their trade show expertise and experience. They'll help you foresee potential pitfalls you may not have even considered.

➤ Beat Murphy's Law

If something can go wrong at a trade show, it will. Murphy's law—whatever can go wrong, will—rules at shows. And when something goes wrong, you'll pay the highest price possible for repair or replacement. The costs are more than just budget-blowing expensive. They also take a toll on your sanity, energy, and peace of mind. You can minimize your costs and beat Murphy at his own game.

➤ Create a Backup Plan

People get sick (or hung over). Demonstrations go awry. You don't know what happened to your exhibit shipper. Computer equipment doesn't work. Vendors forget. Someone steps on a sign. A critical piece of the exhibit breaks. The list goes on and on.

Create a Plan B for everything. Brainstorm the worst-case scenario, listing all the things that could go wrong and develop a plan to attack each problem. Have alternate vendors available for virtually *every* aspect of your exhibit. Have contacts in the computer-rental business if you use computers. Find out where you can get replacement parts for your exhibit. Carry spares. Organize backup transportation for your salespeople. Line up alternate vendors for shipping and other services. Ask your travel agent what other airlines can serve you in the event that problems—like labor strikes—crop up. Research alternate hotel accommodations. We've seen shows where the original hotel booked was a flophouse and a very scary place to stay. Or what happens if there is a disaster like a fire or flood the night before you arrive?

Make backup plans to deal with bad weather or other natural disasters. What will you do if there's heavy snow? What will happen if there is an earthquake? What if there is civil disturbance? Will you cancel your participation? Canceling will certainly salvage a show that is doomed from the start, and you may get concessions from the show management.

How will you respond if disaster strikes? Keep a record of contact information for decision makers in your company. Carry contact information for your insurance carrier. List home phone numbers for all your people attending the show. More than once we've had to call a staffer's home to get medical information on someone who got sick or lost en route.

➤ Prepare for the Worst

You can blow your entire show if you lose a critical piece of equipment and you don't have backups or a repair team on standby. If something does break, get it out of your exhibit so it won't embarrass you and you don't have to apologize to visitors all day.

At a recent show we saw the exhibit of a major copy-machine company where the flagship machine was scattered in pieces across the floor. What an embarrassment for the rest of the salespeople! They literally did not want to speak to visitors. Few people were actually interested in the big machine, and they missed opportunities to sell the rest of their products to visitors who were oblivious to the problem.

Our advice would be to get that machine off the show floor and take it to a back room where it could be repaired beyond the prying eyes of visitors. This approach would limit the impact on the salespeople who could then at least sell the rest of the line.

■ GUERRILLA TACTICS FOR SAVING BIG MONEY ON LITTLE THINGS

With so many ways to spend money to make a show successful, you have to watch every expenditure. Here's a list of ways you can save money.

➤ Save on Hotel Accommodations

Hotels with lower rates than the sponsoring hotel are usually found within a short walk from the show. You can save thousands by shopping around. Ask the local convention and visitors bureau for hotels near the convention center that are priced for tourists.

For example, in Anaheim, California, the hotel attached to the convention center charges about five times more per night than the tourist hotels next door. Yes, the convention hotel is more upscale, but the tourist hotels are clean and quiet, and you save over a hundred dollars a room/night that can be spent on more productive things.

The exception to this rule is that the chief officers should stay in the sponsoring hotel. They will have meetings with management, customers, and vendors before, during, and after the show, and having an on-site hotel room is important for these VIP meetings. Put your officers on the concierge level, if possible, where meeting important contacts will make the best impression. Let the rest of the staff know why the brass gets the more expensive hotel room.

Before the airlines started offering upgrades to first class, you could pay for first-class seats with the business you got from the contacts there. The private lounge at the concierge level of hotels is now the place to meet movers and shakers.

Many companies ask exhibit staff to share rooms. This can cut expenses, but can also cause a staff revolt. By offering them single rooms at a lower-cost hotel, you'll save money, and the staff will be happy. Just point out, "You can stay two to a room at the expensive hotel, or you can have your own room at the lower-priced hotel."

➤ Airfare Savings Tips

Shop carefully for airfare savings. Often the show management will arrange with a sponsoring airline for a discount. This can be a good deal, but you can often get a better rate by shopping for yourself.

If your conference is scheduled over a weekend, you can get the super-saver tickets intended for tourists who can stay over a Saturday night. If your trade show is in Las Vegas, you can get the super-saver fare if you stay just three days—a Saturday night stayover isn't required in Vegas.

Find your best deal on your airline tickets, and then call the official show airline to get an additional five to ten percent discount.

Think twice about requiring your staff to stay over a Saturday to get the better airline fare if the show isn't over the weekend. We've seen clients save money at the front end only to be hit with heavy rescheduling penalties when the staff needed to leave early to get back for a business deal that was put together at the trade show. Certainly your chief officers should travel on unrestricted tickets in case business plans change at the beginning or end of the trip.

Better still, link the show to another required business trip. If you can combine several stops into one ticket, it will save a ton of money, particularly if the trip covers a weekend.

➤ Transportation Shortcuts

Ask the hotel manager if shuttle service is available to and from the airport. Find out when it runs or if the hotel will pick you up on demand. You'll save cab fares or rental-car and parking charges.

If you ship your literature, samples, and other last-minute packages directly to the show, the show management will charge each individual shipment the minimum drayage, usually 100 pounds. Save by shipping your last-minute boxes directly to your hotel, marking them "Hold for guest (*Your name*) arriving on (*date*)." Do not ship boxes to arrive at the hotel more than 72 hours in advance of your arrival. Because of storage limitations, many hotels will reject shipments to be held for guests more than a day or two in advance. Use your UPS or FedEx tracking service to get the name of the hotel employee who signed for the boxes, then call ahead to verify that they have arrived, and find out where the boxes have been stored. This one step can save you hours of frantic searching when you arrive.

If you're taking a truckload to the show, load the truck in reverse order of need, so that the materials you'll need first are the ones first out of the van. This will expedite your setup, and you'll reduce wait-around time and labor costs.

Ask for early move-in times to avoid paying overtime charges.

Instead of shipping back boxes of product, take them with you to the airport and check them with the skycap. You can avoid forty-dollar-a-box excess baggage charges by tipping generously. While standing in line, we've observed that perhaps one in three passengers checking luggage will even bother to tip their skycap, and even then the standard gratuity is a dollar a bag. Slip your skycap a $20 bill up front and watch him light up like a Christmas tree as he quietly checks everything right through. But be aware that if the gate agent catches you with a half-dozen claim checks stapled in the ticket folder, you may be questioned.

➤ Getting Utilities at the Show

Common utilities you may need at the show include electrical power, water, sewer, compressed air, and telephone lines. Carefully calculate what utility services you'll need at the show and which you can do without. Order utilities well before the preshow deadline. Ordering utilities at the show gets very expensive.

Electrical power is typically sold (in the United States) as four outlets with certain amperage capacity—15 amps, 20 amps, 30 amps, and so forth. The higher-amperage outlets tend to be a better deal. Group together electrical equipment so that the group gets the higher amperage deal. Use power strips to distribute the power to the various clusters.

Flat power cables—not round cords—are required if you need to run them under carpeting. Bring your own and save lots of money.

If your electrical equipment is sensitive to voltage variations or can cause you grief if power is lost, invest in an uninterruptable power supply (UPS). This device contains a battery that continues to supply power to your equipment if power is lost, and it provides substantial power conditioning as well. This is very important when there are lots of motors and switching machinery operating at the trade show.

If your electrical needs are limited, find out from show management who your neighbors are going to be. Call and ask them if you can use one of their electrical outlets. In exchange, you might offer a sample of what you sell, a $20 bill, or a beer. All you need to do is bring extension cords. Some show management may prohibit this.

When exhibiting overseas, check to see if the electrical equipment, including lights, are compatible voltages. Do you need converters or special adapter plugs? Just because your computer has a 110/220 switch on it doesn't mean that the cord will fit into the outlet.

➤ See the Light on A/V

Reserve A/V equipment early to save late charges for rush shipments. Because of freight and drayage charges on the equipment you bring, you may save money by renting. Besides, when you rent, someone else is responsible for making sure it works!

Call A/V companies in outlying towns. They'll often drive for an hour or two to deliver, and their rates may be much cheaper. Understand that they'll have a slower response time if you have to call for service problems.

Tell the A/V supplier what you want to accomplish, and ask for options. They may offer cheaper alternatives that you haven't considered, such as a playback-only videocassette player instead of a high-quality (and more expensive) VCR. Also, when showing a video at international shows, check to make sure you have the right videotape format; is the equipment being provided NTSC, PAL or SECAM standard?

Negotiate all quotes. Get an agreement in writing, and look for a better deal.

Look for sponsors who will underwrite part of your exhibiting expense. Explore co-op programs with your suppliers and fusion-marketing partners.

You can also barter your goods and services for printing, equipment rental, travel services, and other necessities. Trade out with the A/V company to save cash.

➤ Phones in Your Exhibit

Think twice about having a phone in your exhibit unless you really need it to make outbound calls, schedule on-site appointments, process credit-card transactions, or fax orders to the home office. Phone lines at shows are rented at premium rates, and the long distance is charged at the maximum rate possible. Some shows even levy a surcharge for local calls.

It will almost always be cheaper to use a cellular phone in your exhibit than to get a phone line installed. Not all convention halls have good cellular coverage. The high-power transportables seem to work better, in general, than the hand-held portables. You can also use a fax machine with a handset and dial pad to do double duty.

Set up a communication clearing center either at the show or at your home office. Getting to the pay phones at trade shows is virtually impossible. This way, when you *do* get through, you can set up meeting times, catch important calls, and still do your best at the exhibit.

Try to avoid doing phone-based business while at the show. Sometimes you just have to, but for your own sanity, keep it to a minimum. Too many salespeople are on the phone to current customers instead of meeting new customers and making new sales at the trade show. A staffer talking on the phone in the exhibit is a major turn-off for visitors. A phone in the exhibit invites abuse. So remove temptation, unless you'll use the phone to close sales at the show.

ESTABLISH ABILITY TO ACCEPT
CREDIT CARD ORDERS

➤ Furniture and Accessories

Renting furniture and accessories from show management is always an expensive proposition. You probably can get it cheaper and in better condition from a local rental company. Make sure the company can deliver and set it up without excessive drayage charges from show management.

If objections are raised to your using an outside vendor because show management isn't getting a cut of the action, just say that the official vendor doesn't supply the selection and quality you need.

Never rent things like trash cans and lights. It's almost always cheaper to buy them locally and just throw them away than to rent them from show management.

➤ Flowers and Plants

Plants and flowers add warmth and decor to an exhibit. You can order them from the recommended supplier, but you can usually get cheaper plants and flowers from a local florist. Ask if they will rent.

➤ Carpet and Pad

If you rent carpet from the show management, it is usually low-quality and very thin. It's almost always better to bring your own, even though you'll probably have to pay drayage and a union carpet layer to install it. Quality carpet will make your exhibit stand out from the others. Always get carpet pad. Order the midline pad; that's all you'll need. You want the carpet to be comfortable, and you won't be on it enough to wear it out.

We've seen companies use double layers of carpet pad to increase the cushion of the carpet, but distracted visitors paid more attention to the strange feel of the carpet than the sales message. In addition, the exhibit staff was fatigued from standing on "marshmallows" all day. So don't use excessively thick pad. Consider Stander's Choice Health Mat[1] in your exhibit. It greatly reduces fatigue simply by providing a varied surface.

---

[1] Stander's Choice Health Mats, A Division of Certified Carpet Services, Lancaster, PA, 1-800-537-3731.

How to Turn Your Exhibit into a Buyer Magnet

A little advance planning and promotion can go a long way toward achieving your trade show goals. These factors are far more critical to your success than any other aspect of trade show marketing, because if the right visitors don't come, or if they don't come to *you,* you can't sell to them.

You can't always count on the show organizers to deliver an audience, let alone the *right* audience. We've attended shows where exhibitors outnumbered visitors, and it's a depressing sight. But worse, we've seen exhibitors swamped with inquiries from visitors who had no need, no budget, and no buying authority, while the real prospects walked right by.

Guerrillas turn their exhibit into a magnet for qualified prospects with immediate buying power before the show opens.

In this chapter, you'll learn what to expect from the show producer, how to prepromote your exhibit, and how to get your most important prospects and customers to come to the show and seek you out.

➤ **What to Expect from the Show Producer**

Savvy expo producers market to bring buyers to the show. When you investigate a show for the first time as well as when you return for the next, find out what promotional activity the expo producer is planning. How will the right visitors know to come? What markets are targeted? What budget is planned? What promotional activity will occur for the next show compared with the last show? What special events will draw visitors? Between your preshow promotion to customers and prospects and the expo producer's preshow promotion, you should have plenty of buyers at the show.

➤ Your Preshow Promotion

Your preshow promotion will do more to get you business at the show than any other activity. The idea is to target the people to whom you want to sell, make them aware of your exhibit, and make them look forward to seeing you.

Target those people who you really want to actively walk into your exhibit, find out more about you, and do business with you. The very best preshow promotions are multiple, distinct promotion programs aimed at various target visitors.

One part of the promotion aims at hot prospects with whom you really want to do business. Pull out all the stops to make sure these VIP prospects visit your exhibit. The investment will be considerable on a per-contact basis, but the pay-off will be large.

The second part of the promotion targets existing customers. You're inviting them to stop in, see what's new, and meet the company president and other key employees. This campaign is less costly. You're reminding customers that you're alive and active and would love to see them. Perhaps you'll hold a customer-appreciation party one evening at the show. The preshow promotion piece is their ticket to get into the party.

The third part of the promotion targets prospects in general. They could be people who have inquired about you in the past. They could be people on a rented list. They could be the attendee list from last year's show. The focus of this third promotion must fit in with the theme and message of your exhibit. It should compel them to visit you with a problem that you can solve. If they can't attend, encourage them to pass the invitation on to someone who can use it. Always go for a referral!

Make sure you remove the names of your customers and hot prospects from your general promotion list. This will save you mailing expenses and keep you from sending mixed messages to your best prospects and customers.

➤ Targeting Your Hottest Prospects

Create a top-gun hit list. Who are you drooling to do business with? Which accounts would you kill for? If you could have any one new client, who would that be? If you could have your pick of any ten new customers, who would they be? These names make up your hottest prospect hit list. Now, devise a program that will compel them to stop in and see you.

➤ How to Reach Difficult Prospects

No doubt, you have prospects that you just can't seem to reach. They're always busy. Their secretaries keep you at bay. You just can't seem to get an appointment with them.

Find out from their secretaries what associations they belong to and what conventions and trade shows they attend. At least one of those conventions should match your trade show list. (If it doesn't, you're targeting the wrong shows!)

Now all you need is a plan.

➤ How to Absolutely Guarantee Your Hottest Prospect Will Visit You

A Bribe

The polite term for them is *advertising specialties,* but guer- rillas call them for what they are: bribes. Do a little snooping around. Find out what your prospect likes and wants. Ask peers, secretaries, and others who know your prospects about their favorite leisure activities and interests. Do the research you need to show them you're serious about doing business.

Once you know where to start, create an offer that is so irresistible, so compelling, and so desirable, that your prospect would be motivated to do something to get it (see Table 4.1). But make your prospect earn the incentive. He'll have to come to your exhibit to collect it and visit with the person or organization that contacted him.

There are many things that are worthwhile bribes, but the rule of thumb is that it can't appear too much like a bribe. Many companies won't allow executives to accept gifts beyond a token value of about $50. So your job is to figure out how to make a token gift have great value!

Autographed merchandise makes a great incentive because of its high perceived value. Have a baseball, basketball, or football signed by a major star from your prospect's hometown team. Or get an autographed piece of artwork or sculpture, or an autographed book by a favorite author. Autographed works have a high perceived value and are actually fairly easy to get. For sports figures and authors, contact an entertainment agent in your town and tell him what you want. For a fee he will get it for you. For autographed books,

TABLE 4.1   EIGHT FACTORS THAT INFLUENCE PROSPECTS TO VISIT YOUR EXHIBIT*

1. Obligation
2. Habit
3. Personal invitation
4. Trade-journal publicity
5. Other advertising
6. Mail invitations
7. Recommendation
8. Random selection

*Siskind, Barry. *The Successful Exhibitors Handbook* (Toronto: International Training & Management Company, 1989).

contact the publisher for the author's address, and send the author a letter explaining what you want. In return, offer to send an honorarium to the author or a favorite charity.[1]

A Media Conference

A media event will draw the experts and interested parties out of the woodwork.

If you're releasing a new product, hold a media event to announce it. Instead of just having your officers and people at the event, invite important and well-known industry experts and observers. Have them make statements on your behalf explaining why the market should sit up and take notice and how important this is to the industry.

Now, invite your hot prospects to be a part of the event, either as members of the audience, to meet others in the audience, or to make a statement of their own.

We've been able to get great supporting statements out of companies that hadn't yet used a product because of the magic of the media. But unless you have something new, don't hold a media conference. You'll annoy the press and waste your money.

Introduce Them to Someone Special

Most people will show up to meet someone they really want to get to know. Capitalize on that and create a special inner circle that gets to meet someone important on an exclusive basis. Imagine bringing in your prospect's favorite sports figure or entertainer to meet with them. What an impact, and no repercussions on taking a bribe!

For a fee, most celebrities can be hired for the day. Contact a speakers bureau (usually the best deal; look in the yellow pages) or call a local entertainment agent. Ask about fees and travel expenses. Some celebrities are inexpensive,

---

[1] We will gladly autograph all the books you want. Call us at 1-800-247-9145.

but others are outrageous. You may do better if you look for celebrities that live in the same town as the show. Many performers have a local rate that is significantly less. And you don't have to pay for travel.

Go Online

Publicize your trade show participation in your home page on the Internet. You can also refer media representatives to your site to download prewritten press releases, articles, product announcements, and other pertinent information about your firm. By offering these materials in machine-readable form, editors are more inclined to use them, and write about you.

➤ Hot Preshow Promotions for Other Prospects

The hottest preshow promotions compel your target visitors to actively search out and come to your exhibit. They'll have you on their list and won't leave the show until they've stopped by to visit.

The most compelling reason to visit you is a promise of something of value. That value could be a bribe: T-shirt, cap, jacket, or other item. It could be the promise of a sneak preview, to see the news before it's news, an opportunity to see something others haven't seen and won't for a little while. It could be a chance to meet someone important, or it could be a chance to solve a problem they've identified, which would make them a hero back at the office.

For sneak previews, have them call a toll-free number ". . . now, to reserve your place in the briefing. Seating is limited."

For bribes, print and mail a coupon that the target visitor redeems for the gift at your exhibit. This lets you track and measure the effectiveness of your preshow promotion.

A very effective preshow tactic is to send your target visitor the first half of a two-part bribe. For example, send them a baseball stand, and they get to pick up an autographed baseball. Send the headphones, and they pick up a Walkman. Send a key, and they pick up a briefcase. Send a roll of film, and they pick up a camera.

The two-part approach works well when the bribe is substantial—more than a throwaway pen or trinket—and works best when you target a selected number of people who you really want to see. A distributor of welding equipment and supplies sent its best customers a single welding glove (mailing equal numbers of lefts and rights, so as not to wind up with a box full of unmated gloves) along with a map directing them to the company's exhibit, inviting them to stop by and pick out the mate to make a pair.

➤ Effective Media Relationships

Many shows have a pressroom or an area for you to schedule media conferences and leave copies of your media kit.

If you have important news, make sure you schedule time with the most important media in your industry. Contact the media directly, send press releases, and work with your public-relations company.

Most media kits are pretty lousy. They don't contain any real news, so journalists just pitch them. Most are simply packaged in off-the-shelf theme folders with pockets jammed with material. Some are obviously very expensively prepared.

The best media kits include a table of contents and a media release on top that discusses the newest product introduced at the trade show. They include, in a pocket, black and white photographs and perhaps a color transparency (usually a 35-mm slide). All the company information is in a backgrounder (a separate document in the release detailing the organization), and at-show contact information is included, such as the hotel and number where interested media contacts can reach the PR person for more immediate details. Put your company name and contact info on each document, just in case a page gets separated on the editor's desk.

Most media releases brag about the company and have little focus on what the company's new offering will do for users and for the industry. Editors want to know the impact of what you sell on the market, in real terms, so give it to them.

As you read each line of the release, ask yourself, "Will this line make a jaded editor say, 'So what!' or 'Is that so?' " You had better be sure that every line makes an editor who has seen it all say, "Is that so!"

Good media releases grab the editor's attention in the headline and keeps the interest going until the end of the release.

➤ Cooperative Relationships with Partners

Trade Show Maps

If you have a number of fusion-marketing partners in attendance that work with you, create a map of the show floor, identifying where they are. On the back of the map, write a paragraph on each partner and how the business relationships are beneficial to your customers. This gives visitors tangible proof that you are a major player in the industry.

Joint Exhibits

Invite business partners to share floor space with you in your exhibit, and in exchange, you take space in their exhibit. This is a great way to build credibility in your industry, ride the coattails of a better-known partner, and add real value to your relationship.

Some exhibit managers prohibit subleasing of exhibit space, so make sure they know you're displaying joint ventures, not subleasing. If your partner contributes to your expenses, why should the exhibit manager know that?

For example, one guerrilla company invited two of their well-known business partners into their exhibit, demonstrating how well their technology worked together. The benefit is that people stopped to see the well-known business partners and were introduced to our client by a gilt-edge company, giving the client instant credibility. The partners loved it. They were able to have an extended presence at the show, which meant talking to more people and making more sales.

➤ How to Get Your Name Spread across the Trade Show

Ask your business partners or associates at the show to display a sign in their exhibit touting your partnership.

If you have a product or service that can be used by other exhibitors at the show (printing, lighting, fixtures, graphics), offer it to them at no charge in exchange for a professionally made sign in their exhibit that alerts visitors that they are using your product.

For example, if you sell carpeting, offer free carpet and pad for exhibitors who agree to post a sign in the exhibit stating that you're the supplier. Create an at-show special to resell the carpet at a substantial discount over your normal price. You'll probably sell more carpet of the same color to the buyer and probably pick up jobs from the people to whom you loaned the carpet, and of course, your name is plastered all over the show.

■ GET BUYERS TO STOP

Your exhibit signs are the first step to selling what you have to the visitors. This is the attention getter that brings visitors into the exhibit to see you, talk with you, and get a feeling for what you offer.

But before you can design your signs, you have to have a *unique selling proposition,* or USP.

➤ Your Show USP

What is it that you are proposing that is so compelling, so hot, so different, that visitors will flood your exhibit dying to do business with you?

That is your USP. The best USP puts the spotlight on something of real value to your buyer and keeps the spotlight off you. What do you do *better* than your competition? What do you *exclusively* offer that's of real value to your buyer? Do you have a better *guarantee?* Faster *delivery?* Lowest *price?* Longest *life?* Largest *selection?*

USPs that don't work include bragging rights such as "longest in the business," "same location for 30 years," or "most employees." Hey, nobody cares!

The USP must be clear, concise, and obvious to the visitor who will buy from you. When buyers understand your USP and experience your exhibit, they must come see what you offer.

➤ Why What You Do Is More Important than Who You Are

Your prospect, in general, doesn't care what company you work for. There have been so many mergers and buy-outs over the years that it's hard to know who owns what. While the brand name is still a big draw for many buyers, it is not as important as it used to be.

Most things are now a commodity. You can get similar goods or services from other vendors. Think about it. In most parts of the United States, the only monopoly left is the water company. You can get almost every other service from another provider—you can get telephone service from a cellular provider; soon you'll get phone service from your cable TV company. You can even put up solar cells or a windmill and sell electricity back to the power company. There are very few products left that truly hold an advantage in the marketplace. Even if yours does, it probably won't in a year or less.

The point is that who you are is less important than ever, so you must focus on making your exhibit clearly communicate what you can do for the visitor.

➤ Creating Your Message

Once you have a USP, the next step is to create your message for the show. The message must communicate one strong idea that is a benefit to your buyer.

Think billboard advertising. What can you say in five to seven words that your prospect will read in seconds that is clear and memorable, and will—

- ➤ Capture your visitor's attention
- ➤ Create an interest in what you offer
- ➤ Cultivate a desire to have what you sell
- ➤ Call your visitor to take a specific action

One very effective message seen hanging in an exhibit was a large sign that simply said

VIDEO HEADS.

Would you walk into that exhibit?

If no, then *good,* because these people don't want to talk to you. Not unless you're a buyer of video heads. If you said yes, then they *absolutely* want to talk to you, because they are eager to discuss your video-head needs. The message on the sign only speaks to those who are interested in buying and only captures the attention of the visitors who are qualified.

Clever, catchy, and cute messages will attract everyone. That's great if everybody is a prospect for your product. That's rarely true at a show. Coy messages will either fly over the head of your buyer or attract a crowd of curiosity seekers who will waste your time while you explain what you mean. All the while, real buyers will be strolling past your exhibit, moving on to organizations that communicate in their language.

➤ The Headline Test

If the copy on your sign was the headline of a newspaper, would it make your target visitor pick up the paper and read about it?

Use the headline test for all of your signs. Each sign you have must compel your target audience to walk in and find out more. If any sign fails the headline test, get rid of it and replace it with one that works.

A great way to learn about headlines is to study the tabloid newspapers. If you read the headline and get a bit embarrassed, that means you're getting close. Look at the headlines for formulas that you can use for your exhibit. Make up several signs, and then test them by alternating them every hour and analyzing the resulting traffic.

➤ How Visitors Read Your Signs

There are differences in the way visitors read signs. There are those who will scan your signs, make an instant decision, and either move along or stop to talk with you. If they move along, they're gone, either because you didn't communicate to them—your loss—or because they don't need what you sell—your gain.

A second type of visitor will walk in and talk to you about what you do and virtually ignore the signs.

The third type of visitor will look at your graphics and decide based on your pictures whether to find out more. Keep this in mind, especially if your customer and prospect base has a high level of functional illiteracy.

All this means that your graphics have to be just as strong as your signs. Do your graphics pass the photo caption test? Do they clearly communicate what you do so that your target visitor feels he must walk into your exhibit to find out more? If this graphic were a picture in a newspaper, would your target visitor pick up the paper and read the caption underneath?

Identifying *new* products helps stop prospects. The word *new* stops the viewer's eye and forces a double take. The prospect is challenged by the word *new* and is compelled to learn more. Always make up a separate sign with just the word *NEW!* on it. Don't make this word part of an existing sign. It should stand out as its own message. This is sure to cause a second glance and bring attention to your exhibit and product.

Focus on one single, strong graphic if you have a smaller exhibit. Think billboard, not bulletin board. Billboards don't use lots of small pictures—small pictures will be seen only by the person who puts them up and takes them down.

➤ Learn from Museums

If you want a great education in creating signs and graphics for a trade show, visit your nearest major museum. A well-done museum exhibit is a perpetual trade show that's selling knowledge. Each exhibit is competing for your attention—and the dinosaur exhibit usually wins at least some of your attention. How can you make your trade show exhibit the "dinosaur attraction" of your next trade show?

Look at the museum's exhibits and displays. Look at the graphics. Notice how large they are and how they entice you down the corridor to learn more.

Look at the signs. Look at the brief, engaging message that makes you curious for more information. Notice how each of the artifacts in the display is labeled, and how the graphics and text work together to tell a story. And notice, too, that each display focuses on a single important point—the point the museum wants you to remember.

➤ Why Professional Exhibit Designers Can Kill You

If you take a look at the sales literature from most exhibit vendors and design houses, 80 percent of it doesn't tell you anything about what the pictured company does and gives no compelling reason for you to walk in and find out more. These brochures are designed to showcase the exhibit *fixtures,* not the exhibiting firm's products and services. Consider this: You're going to the show to sell *your* products, not *theirs.*

The reason why exhibit designers do what they do is because they often come from advertising agencies. Advertising is all about stunning pictures, flashy graphics, song and dance, clever headlines, anorexic models, pretty boys, name recognition, and other kinds of foolishness that big corporations with more money than sales sense came to believe as necessary and required. This stuff doesn't close sales. All it does is make the designer feel good.

As a guerrilla, you don't use any of these flashy devices when you sell to your prospects. You meet them, gain rapport, and show them you're just like they are. You find out what problems they have and then demonstrate how you can solve those problems. The only flashy stuff you might have there is your sales literature, and how often have you closed a sale on your literature alone?

Advertising agencies and most exhibit designers don't know a thing about closing sales. All they know about is creating an image, and they charge a ton of money to do it. The infomercial and home-shopping-network world has proven beyond a shadow of a doubt that you don't need awareness or image to close sales. All you need is a compelling message that fills a need. Now you know how to test for what works.

■ GIVEAWAYS THAT WORK

Premiums and incentives have been a staple of the trade show business since the beginning of civilized sales. The polite term is advertising specialties. Guerrillas call them what they really are: bribes. Show visitors' offices are littered with pens, coffee mugs, note pads, and other trash and trinkets (two other terms often heard in the trade show world).

You've been to shows, swiped goodies from the candy jars, collected your bag of trash and treasures, and then taken them home, either to throw away or give to the kids. Now ask yourself what impact these giveaways had on your buying decision.

If you choose to use a giveaway, make sure that you're trading the prize for your visitor's name, address, and phone number.

Any advertising specialty item should reflect the quality of your product and the good reputation of your firm. You don't want your logo on a cheap pen that doesn't write. There is a subconscious discounting of who you are when a prospect has to throw away something you've given them.

The giveaway should be something genuinely useful, and it should be kept in a place where the prospect will refer to it when the need for your product arises.[2] A good example is the Domino's Pizza refrigerator magnet. You come home, find nothing in the fridge, and call Domino's delivery. If you can't position your giveaway effectively, don't use it.

The best premiums are those that help your visitors get their jobs done faster or better. They have a high perceived value and cost you very little to reproduce. Information premiums have the highest perceived value and the lowest relative reproduction cost. Examples are <u>reprints of articles</u>, special reports, audio and videotapes, computer software, and books related to your field. Such premiums self-select your prime prospects, because they are of little use to the general public.

An effective guerrilla premium is a laminated wallet card covered with valuable reference information that your customers use regularly. For example, a Century 21 office in Denver gives out a threefold city street guide that doubles as a business card. Spectranetics, a company that builds lasers for clearing arterial blockages, created a plastic wallet card summarizing the recommended treatment options for various patient conditions. The cardiologist can discreetly

---

[2] For a free database search of over 400,000 ad specialty items that may work for your business, call Dave Kilmer at Design House International, 1-888-333-2291.

review the technical details of the procedure before scrubbing up. A welding-equipment distributor gives out wallet cards with recommended amperage settings for welding a variety of alloys.

One of the most effective promotions we've ever used is a laminated wallet card that includes the Trade Show Success Checklist.[3] It includes valuable information that any trade show exhibitor will need, it's a reminder of what we do, and the contact information is discreetly included so that clients can easily contact us with their questions.

The next best premium is—

➤ Something that the visitors want

➤ Something that helps them do a better job

➤ Something they wouldn't necessarily buy for themselves

➤ Something their organization wouldn't necessarily buy for them

➤ Something that is specialized enough to self-qualify whoever wants it as a potential buyer

Specialized tools make excellent premiums. For example, hand out a dive table card for scuba enthusiasts or a plastic slide rule for landscapers who need to calculate application rates for fertilizer. Another example is a wine selection book for a meeting planner, or a keyboard-mounted calculator for a computer programmer.

If you decide to use premiums, select something meaningful and useful to your customer or prospect and then use it as a parting gift. Say, "Thank you for stopping by. Here's something for you to take with you as a thank you for your time. We'll talk after the show." Insist on making your giveaway work hard to get you sales. Some organizations only use incentives if they have a new product release or a new application, and then it's closely tied to the product.

---

[3] Call 1-800-247-9145 for your free copy.

You can also use controlled giveaways to attract visitors and qualify them. Some of the most desirable giveaways are apparel items like T-shirts, hats, and sunglasses. Ask the visitor to complete a survey or a questionnaire, or have the visitor listen to a presentation to qualify for the prize.

Professional-association shows often prohibit certain giveaway items like food, candy, newspapers, posters, T-shirts, bags, and novelties. Ask show management what you're permitted to do before ordering 10,000 imprinted Frisbees.®

Don't get caught in the Bag Wars, where others give away better-quality bags than you do. So you move up to more expensive bags, and they counter with even *more* expensive bags. What's the point? Bags seem attractive for two reasons: Everybody wants one, and they become walking billboards. The problem is that they fail the guerrilla's dual criteria for self-selection and utility after the show. We suggest avoiding bags and containers altogether! The only really effective bag promotion we've ever seen was when United Parcel Service distributed specially designed bags, offering to ship them back to the visitor's office at the end of the show—for a fee!

➤ Why Your Candy Bowl Turns Visitors into Thieves

When you set up a candy bowl or offer other trivial giveaways to all visitors, you actually turn visitors into thieves. You've seen them: They sneak up, snitch a piece of candy, and slink away, avoiding eye contact. If you do make eye contact, they say hi-how-are-you and move away at full speed.

A candy bowl really doesn't add any value in getting the right visitors into your exhibit, and it takes up valuable exhibit space. (An exception, of course, is if you *sell* candy and you're giving away samples.) How many times have you been asked, "Can I have another for my kids?" You have to say yes or you look like a jerk. Then the person asks you what you do, and you end up doing your pitch to someone who is really only interested in a snack.

Everything in your exhibit has to work to get you business. If your giveaway doesn't buy you customers, don't give it away. Otherwise you're throwing away your money that could be put to better use closing sales.

➤ Drawings and Prizes

Avoid gimmicky promotions like pop-the-balloon or miniature golf because they waste time and money with people who will never do business with you. Perhaps you've seen these acrylic grab-the-bucks boxes with cash blowing around inside. This type of promotion will attract everyone. That may be appropriate for your business, but more likely you're just blowing your cash.

If collecting names for your mailing list is one of your marketing goals, hold a drawing to give something away. Consider giving away smaller prizes more often throughout the day versus a bigger, single prize at the end of the show. More visitors will drop their name and address in your fishbowl when they think there is a reasonable chance to win a prize.

These contests, like advertising specialties, should self-select for qualified prospects. At a consumer electronics show, two competitors were both selling refurbished toner cartridges. The first vendor put out a fishbowl with a sign, DROP YOUR BUSINESS CARD TO WIN A COLOR TV! The competitor put out a fishbowl with a sign, DROP YOUR BUSINESS CARD TO WIN A FREE TONER CARTRIDGE! If you were selling toner cartridges, which stack of leads would *you* rather take home?

If your goal is to collect the names of all the visitors at the show, consider not going at all and, if the show offers it, buy the registration list instead. If it's an association show, you either rent the membership list or get it when you join. You may be even better off skipping the registration list and buying a good, proven mailing list to target your customers.

Unqualified giveaways mean you collect unqualified leads your sales force won't follow up. Unqualified leads come from giveaway items that attract every visitor, whether they can buy from you or not.

An insurance company held a fishbowl drawing for a set of steak knives. This is one of the dumbest giveaways we can imagine for a professional organization. Let's not mention your liability for having meat-cutting razor-sharp knives laying around your exhibit. Besides, few people need or even want a set of steak knives.

We looked at the fishbowl full of business cards and asked the salesman how many of those cards were prospects for his business.

He said, "None of them. The hot ones are here, in my pocket."

"So what will you do with the names in the fishbowl?" we asked.

"Pitch them," he replied.

"How many of your hot leads want a set of steak knives?"

"I'll give them *all* a set if they want."

So, he would have been much better off offering a free set of steak knives (ugh!) with every consultation appointment. That way, he would have only talked to people who wanted to do business with him.

Draw for something that is only interesting to visitors with whom you can do business. Never give away things that are of general interest, like stereo equipment, travel, cameras, or TVs.

As a professional, lawyer, physician, accountant, consultant, or trainer, you could give away an hour of your services. Yes, you'll get some unqualified leads, but the number will be much lower than if you were giving away a Hawaiian vacation.

As a sporting equipment company, give away nine holes of golf with your owner or president.

If you're in the automotive industry, give away something that has to be installed by you, so the winner has to come to your shop, or your dealer's shop, to get it. Then you have a chance to sell them more.

At smaller, specialty conferences, you may want to consider having a drawing for various levels of prizes, including airfare, room and board, and registration fee for the next conference. That way, the incentive brings the winner back to next year's show.

➤ Pick Your Winners

Since this is *your* contest, *you* get to make the rules, and while a fishbowl may imply that the drawing is random, guerrillas reserve the right to strategically *choose* the winners to help achieve their marketing goals. You might choose to have your top ten customers win, or your top 50 prospects. To be perfectly ethical, you may even choose to have *everyone* win. Use the winning notification as an opportunity to contact a buyer.

■ HOW TO LURE PROSPECTS TO YOUR EXHIBIT

Now that you're all set up, your next challenge is attracting visitors. And not just any visitors. The guerrilla wants to connect with only two very special types of visitors: *prospects with buying authority,* and *current customers with current needs.* And they want everyone else to *keep walking!*

If somebody cannot or will not buy from you, that person is wasting your time and energy.

➤ Multiply Your Exhibit Success

Use all five senses—sight, touch, sound, smell, and, where appropriate, taste—to multiply your exhibit success. Guerrillas know that the more senses they appeal to in their marketing, the more effective the marketing strategy will be.

Sight

Four seconds. That's how much time it takes a visitor to walk the ten-foot length of your exhibit space. Just four seconds. You're in stiff competition with all the other distractions in the hall. You only have four seconds to tell your basic story and grab the visitor's attention, so your signs must tell your story graphically.

Your graphics must show what you do. They must be clear and compelling. They must be colorful and attractive, and they must sell! Your graphics and signs are, without a doubt, the most important part of your exhibit.

Don't let the creative people drag you into expensive graphics that look cool but don't deliver your sales message. Many organizations waste exhibiting space by making their company logo the most prominent item in the display. This is a carryover from the old advertising-agency adage, "If the client doesn't like the ad, put in a picture of the factory. If he still doesn't like the ad, put in a picture of the company president." Even if your firm's name is a household word, why would that compel a visitor to stop and see you? And how would that qualify them anyway? Your signs must deliver a compelling sales message targeted *specifically* to your ideal visitor.

Use your graphics and signs to tell your visitor how you can help them and why they should stop in your exhibit. Then, let your company name and logo be the second thing they find out about you.

Sound

What sounds can you use to increase the effectiveness of your exhibit to deliver your sales message? Will it be music? Sound effects? A live presentation describing what you can do for your visitors?

Speakers for music are commonly placed in the rear of the exhibit, aimed toward the aisle in an effort to attract visitors. This positioning will enrage your neighbors and reduce your sales, and unless the music is unique, it gets lost in the din of a noisy show.

Because the visitor usually faces the exhibit and therefore also the speakers, the music will compete with the salesperson for the visitor's attention.

The solution is to install the speakers in the *top* of your exhibit, aiming them down towards the floor. This will create a sonic blanket of soft music that screens out other noise. Set the volume at levels that won't interfere with your conversations.

Do You Need a Performance License?

Playing unlicensed music in public is a violation of applicable copyrights, so if you decide to use music in your exhibit, it must be licensed or you risk penalties and fines. All popular music requires licensing, and many classical recordings require licensing as well. Licenses are obtained by completing an application and paying a royalty. The main U.S. licensing organizations are Broadcast Music Inc. (BMI), the American Society of Composers, Authors and Publishers (ASCAP), and the Society of European Stage Authors and Composers (SESAC).

The show management is usually responsible for securing a blanket license for the show, so check to see if your show producer has made such arrangements. In that case, you can use whatever music you wish, and it will be covered. If no such license is obtained, there could be trouble. According to an ASCAP representative, the performance-rights organizations won't come after *you* for the infraction but *will* enjoin the trade show producer if there is a violation.

You will also need a performance license if you plan to use a live band or recorded music at a hospitality suite, party, or function. It's *your* responsibility to get the performance license, not the band's or the DJ's. The music license for the hotel or meeting facility only covers the common areas and doesn't cover the meeting rooms that you're renting.

Damages for not having a license can range from $500 to $20,000 for *each* infringement, and both BMI and ASCAP have been beefing up enforcement.[4]

If you use popular music in the introduction or background of an audio or videotape brochure to hand out at the show, you can obtain a mechanical license, which charges a per-copy royalty. This royalty is literally pennies per title per copy, but can take eight to twelve weeks to obtain.[5]

Creating Long-Playing Tapes That Don't Repeat

You can use a hi-fi VCR to record music onto a videotape. Use the super-long-play (SLP) mode. This gives you six uninterrupted, non-repeating hours of near-CD-quality music with a two-minute break for the tape to rewind. You don't have to hook up a TV to play it back; just use the stereo audio outputs of the VCR.

You can also hire a disc jockey to create a seamless mix of music that creates the mood and energy level you want in your exhibit. Make sure the DJ uses music you approve of and that fits in with your theme and your corporate image.

Smell

Bakeries and movie theaters are the masters of olfactory marketing. Look for ways you can use aromas to enhance your exhibit's buying climate. Can you use flowers, perfumes, incense, food smells, or leather smells? What smell will evoke the memories or moods that will make your visitor want to buy?

You may wish to consult an aromatherapist to discuss ways to use aromas to enhance your buying environment.

---

[4] Contact ASCAP (1-800-755-1019), BMI (1-800-669-4264), or SESAC (1-800-826-9996) for an update on licensing requirements.

[5] For more information about mechanical licenses, contact The Harry Fox Agency, Inc., 711 Third Avenue, New York, NY 10017 (1-212-370-5330).

Aromas can help set the appropriate mood and emotional mindset for your buyer. Occasionally put a few drops of aromatic oil on a light bulb. Vanilla makes people feel sexy, rosemary is energizing, and peppermint is refreshing.

You can also use aromatic sprays. But aerosols aren't very effective for trade shows because you'll have to use them frequently, and you don't want to do that while visitors are in your exhibit.

There are aroma products available that you just sprinkle on your carpets in the morning after your exhibit is cleaned and vacuumed. The products blend right into the pile, releasing a scent as the granules are crushed by the weight of foot traffic. As your visitors walk through your exhibit, the breezy scent reaches their noses, and they unconsciously respond.

Fragrances can create an energized environment, a relaxed environment, or a balanced-feeling environment. These are economical, considering they put your visitor into a buying frame of mind.

Consider the negative smells that may affect your visitors, too. Many times you'll be setting up in an area where the janitorial staff has used an industrial cleaner on the floor. Or, if your literature has just come from the printer, the solvent from the ink will permeate your area.

Taste

If your product is edible, you obviously want people to sample your wares. But keep in mind that classic trade show sales story:

> Simple Simon met a pieman going to the fair.
> Said Simple Simon to the pieman, "Let me taste your wares."
> Said the pieman to Simple Simon, "Let me see your penny."
> Said Simple Simon to the pieman, "I fear I haven't any."

Before offering a sample, the pieman *qualified* his prospect, checking for economic buying power. Applying this idea to your samples, always ask for something in *exchange* for giving your sample. Get information.

A pizza restaurant was handing out slivers of their product at a restaurant show, but the staff would ask each visitor a simple and very powerful question: "How do you like it?" Further investigation revealed that the restaurant was experimenting with new sauces, right there at the show. Not only did the staff get immediate feedback about the new recipe, but when a visitor with a mouth full would mumble, "I fink iss great!" he would receive a coupon and an invitation to the restaurant.

Find out if they're buyers, get their cards, get a referral, ask for a commitment, and make a sale.

Touch

Some people just have to touch things to get the idea into their brain. You can accommodate these visitors by giving them the opportunity to touch what you sell! Understand the guerrilla adage, "Never let your prospect handle your product unless you want them to buy it." Insist that visitors touch and play with your samples, knowing that once you pet a puppy, it's likely to follow you home.

What can you let your visitors touch, feel, and play with? Getting your visitor physically involved in what you do intensifies their desire to have what you offer. We'll discuss the secrets of doing powerful demonstrations later on in Chapter 9.

Touch is a factor even when what you sell is you. That process begins with a handshake, and you'll learn more about that in Chapter 8.

Shoot a Commercial at the Show

If you sell a product that customers can sample and purchase on the spot, try this super sales success secret. Shoot TV commercials in your exhibit with live on-camera testimonials from visitors who have just tried your product. This gives them a shot at their 15 minutes of fame, while you sell a ton of your product.

This guerrilla tactic accomplishes several things:

➤ You'll attract a lot of attention for very little money.

➤ You'll have the public selling the public on trying what you have to offer.

➤ You'll have excellent testimonial footage to use in future commercials, infomercials, and print and sales materials.

➤ You'll have the people on camera make their own sales close.

You'll need at least a 10-by-20-foot exhibit. In the middle, place a TV camera, complete with bright lights and photographic background. Put up signs that state you're filming TV commercials and are looking for testimonials from real people. On either side of the exhibit, run TV monitors with commercials taped the day before, or that day, or the hour before, so that people can see what you're doing. People *love* to see themselves on camera.

On one side of the exhibit, have people try what you sell. If they like it, have them get in line for a ten- to fifteen-second testimonial. As each person stands in front of the camera, have the interviewer ask this vital question: "Will you allow us to use your voice and picture to promote our product without payment to you for as long as we need to?" When the person says yes, you have an on-camera talent release.

Then videotape the person's response to your product. Say thank you, and pass the person on to the sales rep. It's a simple matter to hand the visitor an order form to complete the transaction. If the person balks, just say, "Oh, from what you said on camera, I thought you were dying to get this. You really did mean what you said, didn't you?"

➤ Heavy Traffic Doesn't Mean Success

Many companies use traffic and activity as their measure of success and do everything they can to make sure they have lots of traffic in their exhibits without regard to whether the exhibits are filled with the right people. These companies use magicians, jugglers, or entertainers. Some hire attractive models to pass out materials and literature. Unfortunately, these strategies only attract people who find the *entertainment* interesting. Use entertainers at your parties and receptions, not your sales exhibit.

Lots of exhibit traffic doesn't mean the show is a success, and light traffic doesn't mean it's a failure. Which would you rather have? Ten people who walk into the exhibit and place orders or a hundred who only want literature? The answer's obvious, but it's easy to forget.

➤ Get Help!

Professional exhibit designers, decorators, movers, and lead follow-up services are in business to help you get the most out of your show. And, yes, they are expensive. Minimize your expense and maximize your profits through careful planning and deployment of your own resources in advance.

Everything that the *public* sees should be done professionally. Any hint of amateurism in your marketing materials erodes your credibility. Consider *prototyping* all of the components before handing them over to a designer for professional execution. By using your own time, energy, and imagination, you can leverage your investment a hundredfold.

Chapter 5

The Rewards of Guerrilla Selling on the Trade Show Floor

When you take a guerrilla approach to selling at your exhibit, your salespeople will actually look forward to the opportunity. The show provides an opportunity to build camaraderie and teamwork, and it can be a real morale boost for the whole company. Different people in different departments get to meet customers face to face, and everyone gets a bird's-eye view of the competition. The show provides a fantastic opportunity to fast-track everyone's training.

When you're getting ready for an important trade show, one of your assignments is deciding who will staff your exhibit and preparing them with the information and skills that they will need to be effective.

At your next trade show, you'll meet a lot of new business prospects. An overwhelming majority of visitors haven't yet done business with you. If your experience is like ours, you'll find that nine out of ten visitors will be people you haven't met before. Seven of ten attendees will be decision makers who want detailed information about the company and the product. They'll make snap judgments on whether your firm is a viable vendor based on their interaction with one salesperson.

You're going to make a big impression on your industry, and you want it to be a good one. It takes *eleven* positive impressions to overcome a *single* negative impression. Once you lose a customer to a negative impression, you may never recover the lost business.

Your sales staff's mission is to complete the job that your exhibit begins. If your people are professional, efficient, and well-mannered, it will pay big dividends for the company in new sales and new opportunity.

A Fortune 500 computer manufacturer with whom we consult was recently at a major business trade show. A large man, about six foot three, walked into the exhibit dressed in overalls and a plaid flannel shirt. The sales staff didn't quite know what to do. This guy didn't fit the profile of the typical computer customer. With the long beard, he looked more like a biker than a buyer. One salesman took the initiative, introduced himself, and started a conversation. He quickly found out that this man was a *key* buyer for a large federal agency with responsibility for millions of dollars of computer equipment purchases.

The salesman quickly introduced him to the rest of the exhibit staff and saved the day. The visitor eventually placed a very large order with the company. If this savvy salesman hadn't taken the initiative and used his common sense to treat this visitor with respect, millions of dollars in sales would have been lost.

What would your sales staff have done?

Who to Take?

Since your travel budget is limited, you can't take everybody you want, so you usually tap into your sales staff to fill out the exhibit staffing schedule. While this certainly fills the schedule, are you making the best staffing choice for the best return on your trade show investment?

Sensitize your staff. Train them. Make them aware of trade show selling issues and how to be successful. This investment will have a major impact on your trade show success.

➤ Why the Best Salespeople Don't Always Make the Best Exhibit Staff

Talk to outside salespeople who are working at trade shows, and you'll find that they would rather be out making regular calls. Many actually dread "doing" a trade show. No wonder they're frustrated with the long hours standing on a hard floor, the flood of questions, and the boredom of absolutely nothing going on. They're accustomed to controlling their own time and activity and may feel uncomfortable leaving their destiny to the whims of show traffic.

➤ Trade Show Selling Is Different

It's important for your staff to understand the difference between trade show selling and a normal sales call. Behavior that is appropriate and effective in a traditional sales call will kill sales at a trade show. When the salesperson uses the tried and true methods and they don't work, frustration and resentment will follow. Certainly you've heard them complain, "This was a *lousy* show! Nothing but a bunch of tire-kickers." We contend that it is the *salesperson's* interaction with the visitors that makes the show lousy.

Your salespeople are probably experts at on-site sales calls. This is how your people work best. In a half-hour appointment, they can qualify, present, and close for the order. Paperwork in hand, they return to the office feeling triumphant. Unfortunately, at a trade show, you don't have a half hour to make the sale. You have only a few seconds, perhaps minutes. Because your salespeople don't see the immediate success of being able to close, they feel they're spinning their wheels.

Many salespeople are excellent at demonstrations. Their technique is based on demonstrating the product, letting the features sell the benefits. At trade shows, you may not even have room for a demo unit, and you certainly won't have time to demo every visitor. Unless your product demos quickly, this strategy limits your success.

Some old sales pros are burned out on trade shows. They've worked too many that weren't done right and failed. They put up with trade shows as a necessary evil of the job, and their negative attitude shows. Visitors can tell, and the sales process fails.

With experienced salespeople, a trade show more often becomes "old home week." They see people for the first time in years, and they really want to catch up on the news. While they swap stories and slap each other on the back, your prospects continue to stream past, each a potential sale walking away.

Choose Staffers Who Are . . .

Experienced—They demonstrate a combination of skills that produce success.

Committed—They are there to meet new prospects and sell, not just to enjoy a day away from the office.

Knowledgeable—They know what you sell and how to explain it in ways that your buyers can understand.

Prepared—They have the skills necessary to sell at trade shows and are ready to use them.

Confident—They believe in what they sell and know it's the best for their customers.

Bold—They must be able to reach out and talk to people who are initially reluctant to visit.

Friendly—They can meet strangers and turn them quickly into friends. While many people don't know how to do this, it can be taught.

Enthusiastic—They are the people who are most excited about your company and your products, and, most important, they are looking forward to working the show.

Persistent—Visitors often say no. But some visitors say yes! Ideal exhibit staffers stay with it, looking for the yes that makes the whole show worthwhile.

➤ How Many People Should Staff Your Exhibit?

Here's how to calculate how many people should staff your exhibit:

$$\frac{\% \text{ Visitors interested}}{100} \times \text{Total attendance} = \text{Number of prospects}$$

For a show to be successful, the number of interested visitors should be greater than 15 percent of the traffic. You can estimate this by reviewing the show demographics. For example, if your buyers are executives, look at the percentage of visitors whose titles indicate an executive position.

$$\frac{\text{Number of prospects}}{\text{Total productive show hours}} = \text{Average visitors per hour}$$

Subtract show hours when visitors are unlikely to come to the show floor, such as during keynote sessions and major presentations.

Assuming each visitor spends five minutes in the exhibit, permitting 12 visitor interactions per hour:

$$\frac{\text{Average visitors per hour}}{12 \text{ Visitors per salesperson per hour}} = \text{Number of staff needed}$$

The number of visitors per hour your staff can effectively serve depends on the level of detail needed to qualify and close prospects. Five minutes each, or twelve per hour is an average across industries, but guerrillas will optimize their staffing by role-playing likely sales scenarios with a stopwatch to determine the time required for an average visitor. Remember to factor in break times.

You should also consider how much space your exhibit will occupy. You'll need about 50 square feet per salesperson on duty. Never put more than two people in a 10-by-10; you won't have room for visitors.

$$\text{Number of prospects} \times \text{Closing ratio} = \text{New customers}$$

Determine the likely closing ratio from sales history, and then check your predicted outcome against your sales goal.

$$\frac{\$ \text{ Sales goal}}{\$ \text{ Average sale}} = \text{New customers needed}$$

Guerrillas choose their battles. After running the numbers, do they all add up? Will this show deliver the profits you need to make it worthwhile? If not, abandon your plan now. Does the forecast suggest that you need more people, more space, or more prospects? If so, make the necessary adjustments to be sure that you have enough people to handle the traffic and enough traffic to challenge your people.

■ AVOID THE SIX DEADLY TRADE SHOW SINS

The biggest problem with people selling at trade shows is that they don't follow the trade show sales process.

1. *They tell instead of sell.* *Telling* is speaking to the visitor about your own favorite parts of the offer. This may satisfy you, but doesn't do a thing for your visitor. *Selling* is speaking to the visitors about *their* favorite parts of the offer. This satisfies them and lets you do business.

2. *They try to do too much.* The sharper the focus of your exhibit and your offer, the more you'll sell. Since trade shows are confusing, noisy, distracting, and psychologically overloading, when you try to do too much, visitors give up and move along.

3. *They ignore visitors' wants.* We see this one repeated again and again. The company focuses on what *it* needs and ignores what the *customers* want. Focus on what your customers want, and you'll never worry about having enough business.

4. *They don't respond to the wants with benefits.* People don't buy things for what they are but for what they do. At the risk of using a cliché, people don't buy a drill, they buy a hole. What, exactly, do your customers buy from you?

5. *Spending too much time with visitors.* A trade show is perishable. Every minute spent with a visitor beyond doing business is a minute that is wasted. Visitors usually walk by an exhibit only once. If you're not available to meet them, they are gone, and you won't get them back. This is an easy trap to fall into, especially when you're speaking to someone with whom you have a rapport. It's easier to continue talking with them than to meet a stranger and face possible rejection.

6. *They don't try to close business.* Most exhibit staffers are serious wimps when it comes to closing business. You can and should try to close business on the show floor. If a sale on the spot seems unlikely, guerrillas go for an *advance,* or a commitment to the next step in the process—a sales call, a request for literature, a follow-up phone call. People are dying to be led. That way they don't have to take full responsibility for their actions. Take the initiative and suggest what your visitor should do next. Advance the sale!

➤ How Trade Show Selling Differs from a Normal Sales Call

At a trade show, the buyer and seller are outside their normal environments.

Shows are disorienting and distracting. There are lots of lights, sounds, and activities. Exhibits communicate on a number of levels, from subtle and subconscious to blatant and animalistic to shocking and stunning. Most visitors respond to this mental barrage by wandering from exhibit to exhibit in a daze. Focused visitors—those there with a specific agenda—move from exhibit to exhibit with deliberate purpose. When you see these people, know that they will buy what you sell if you meet their needs.

Five Reasons You Can't Sell the Same Way at a Trade Show

1. Visitors get a large dose of information in a short time and remember only the information that is most important. In a normal sales call, you make a strong impression because you physically occupy their attention for a period of time. At trade shows, you'll get seconds to minutes, and your impact diminishes substantially.

2. Visitors are talking to your competition at the show. They can get conflicting information—you say one thing, your competition says another. You must have your facts completely straight about your competitor's products, because you won't get a second chance if your competition proves you wrong.

3. Visitors are tired. After walking on the hard cement floors covered with flimsy carpeting, their feet are sore, their legs are tired, and their back is aching. Their arms hurt from carrying the bag full of literature. They may be suffering from jet lag or other travel ailments. Fatigue dulls their mental faculties, and they don't always respond normally.

4. During a routine sales call, prospects will give you their attention for 30 minutes to a few hours. You won't have that time during the show. Visitors feel compelled to see more of the show; they don't want to miss anything.

5. The new trend in commercial businesses is team buying, where individuals bring their expertise together in making decisions, usually for major capital equipment. Companies send fewer people to the show but

require them to gather more information than ever before. These teams will ask questions, schedule in-house presentations, order literature or catalogs, and possibly even inspect your product at the show. But they seldom place an order. Learn how to work with teams in Chapter 7.

■ WHY CUSTOMERS BEHAVE DIFFERENTLY AT A SHOW

The stream of traffic moving past your exhibit will be composed of a mix of people with differing needs and conflicting agendas. Understand their needs and you can serve them better.

Buyers—These people are there to select vendors for their company. They want you to solve their problems. Your first priority is to identify these people and spend time with them.

Competitors—Your competitors will be at the show, whether they have an exhibit or not. They want to find out everything they can about you. Are they wearing a badge? If not, beware. They may be your competitors. Do they have a business card? Sneaky competitors will always say, "I'm out of cards." Honorable rivals will introduce themselves up front and arrange to meet later.

The curious—These people have come to check it out. They're interested in finding out about your offer, often in detail, but they won't buy.

Customers—People who have bought from you before will be there. They want to know what's new and how to upgrade or trade in what they've bought, and they want to complain about problems they've had. Have ready answers for them, but don't spend too much time with them.

Educators—Professors and teachers will be on the floor. Some will be doing research. Others want to keep up with the industry trends. Some educators will ask you to donate goods or services. This can be a great way to promote your products to future customers and decision makers. Establish a policy for dealing with educators and stick to it.

Industry partners—People in the industry are there to meet with their business partners. They may be looking for new partners and new opportunities.

Influencers—Part of the buying team, these people influence and direct the opinions of the group that makes the decision. They are looking for information and facts to support their recommendations.

Job-hunters—People will come to a show to look for work. They're the ones with suits and briefcases. They want to know if you're hiring and if you'll take a resume.

Market researchers—Companies looking to enter a market will often visit a show to get a good look at what they're getting into. These people ask lots of good questions, some of them very probing and detailed. Watch out for companies that will enter the market to take business away from you.

The media—The press, radio, and TV will be at the show, depending on its size and importance to local trade news. These people are almost always up front about what they want—they want to know what's new. This is a leveraged marketing opportunity that the guerrilla is well prepared to take. Have your press kit handy.

Meeting attendees—Certain people, like health-care professionals and teachers, come primarily for the educational sessions to fulfill mandatory continuing-education requirements. It's sometimes difficult to get these people into the show floor, but they are usually well qualified buyers.

Other exhibitors—They walk the floor, seeing what's available, scoping out the competition, and getting ideas for the future.

Speakers—When there are educational sessions, the speakers will often take a quick stroll through the exhibits.

They may or may not be prospects. You can usually recognize these people by the ribbons on their badge. Ask them what their session was about, and how many attended, and how it went.

Spouses—These people may have come along for the ride, but beware. Even if they're wearing a staff badge, they may have little knowledge of the industry, and they often don't care. On the other hand, they may play a very influential role in their partners' business decisions. A kiss of death is assuming that female companions of male visitors are "just wives." Guerrillas always strive to include them in the discussion until their disinterest becomes obvious.

Students—Some shows have a student day, when local educational facilities are invited at little or no charge. Students are fascinated by what you're doing and will ask lots of questions. Dealing with students is a tricky situation. They may not buy from you now, but they certainly will avoid buying from you in the future if you blow them off. We still hold grudges against companies that mistreated us decades ago when we were students.

Vendors—These people want to sell you something. Some of these people aren't registered with the show, and usually their solicitation is against show rules. Some of them are exhibitors at the show who are targeting other exhibitors. They want your business. Give them a few seconds, and then ask them to contact you later if what they offer is of interest to you.

➤ What a Salesperson Needs to Know about Working a Show

There are four essential trade show selling skills:

1. Product knowledge
2. Competitive knowledge

3. Guerrilla selling skills

4. Moving people on gently and quickly

Product Knowledge

Visitors attend the show to learn about what's new and to get detailed information. Product knowledge is what they're after. Visitors are impressed when they can speak with someone who knows the product well enough to answer their questions. They don't necessarily expect all their questions to be answered, but they do want the important ones addressed. Product training is important, especially for new releases. What is the impression that leaves with your visitor if you can't answer a question on your newest and hottest offering?

Competitive Knowledge

It's very important that you study and know what your competition does. Your visitors will ask how you stand in comparison to your competition. And it's even more important that you keep the information up to date. We've seen a case where a company introduced the new version of a product at a show—this product solved a major problem with the previous release. Unfortunately, a poorly informed competitor kept talking about the now-fixed problem as if it were still a problem, getting egg all over their face. It's tough on your reputation when you say one thing and your competition proves you wrong on the spot!

Guerrilla Selling®

The guerrilla's secret weapon is asking questions and seeking to *dis*qualify visitors. This means looking for a reason *not* to do business with them. That way, you'll naturally spend the right amount of time with the right people. When you run into a sale-stopper, whether it's a conflict with product need, budget, timing, or buyer profile, move the person on immediately. We'll show you how to do that effectively in Chapter 8.

➤ Bring Non-Salespeople as Well

Balance your sales team with product development, engineering, and customer service staff. These people can be available to answer the hard questions that serious prospects often ask. They are also great fielders for curious tech-heads, keeping your crack salespeople free to work more visitors. Your telemarketing people may be your best choice for staffing a trade show. They're more comfortable initiating conversations with strangers, and customers are delighted when they can put a face with the name and voice with which they've been dealing.

■ WHAT TO TRAIN

Advance training for your sales team can make a tremendous difference in effectiveness. Training can take many forms: books, audiotapes, videotapes, competitive reconnaissance, classroom instruction, one-on-one coaching, peer review, even tag-team selling with a veteran. A thorough treatment of advanced sales skills is covered in our previous book, *Guerrilla Selling—Unconventional Weapons and Tactics for Increasing Your Sales.*[1]

➤ Build a Trade Show Training Resource Center

Magazines

Guerrillas regularly subscribe to the magazines, journals, and newsletters that serve professional selling. These include

---

[1] By Levinson, Gallagher, Wilson (New York: Houghton Mifflin, 1992).

Sell!ng magazine, *Personal Selling Power, Sales & Marketing Management, Potentials in Marketing,*[2] *Entrepreneur, Success,* and the *Guerrilla Marketing Newsletter.*[3] Check with your reference librarian for examples. Many of the associations listed in the Appendix publish articles and newsletters on sales skills.

Books

Assign required reading before the show. This book would be a good start, particularly Chapters 7, 8, and 9. Use the bibliography as a shopping list for books. With paperback books you can practice *razor reading,* or cutting the book apart at the spine and distributing chapters or sections to your team members. Instruct them to review the material and do a verbal book report at your next sales meeting.

Audiotapes

The average commute in America is 22 minutes. Provide skill-sharpening audiotapes for your sales team to review while driving to and from work.[4]

Videotapes

Nine out of ten homes in America have a VCR, and if you make training videos available to borrow, your salespeople are more likely to take them home and study them on their own time.[5]

---

[2] To subscribe, call 1-800-328-4329.

[3] To subscribe, call Guerrilla Marketing International at 1-800-748-6444.

[4] For a free copy of the 28-minute audiocassette, *The Seven Steps to Trade Show Success* by Mark S. A. Smith and Orvel Ray Wilson, call 1-800-247-9145.

[5] See the Appendix for titles, or call for a free catalog, 1-800-247-9145.

Competitive Reconnaissance

What you don't know *can* hurt you. Consider this: What if you spend weeks with your R&D, marketing, and sales staff, creating your next product introduction, and one month later, you read in the trade press about a similar announcement from your competition? How would you feel? What would your boss say? What would your customers think? Why didn't you know about the competition?

There are good reasons why otherwise savvy companies don't know enough about their competitors. That is, most people assigned the task of gathering competitive intelligence don't look forward to the job. They feel it's a painful, long, drawn-out, pointless process. They don't know how to start, where to go, who to call, or what to ask.

Gathering competitive intelligence is actually fun and easy to do, and it can make you a hero in your own company. You'll avoid "stepping in it," and you won't be doomed to repeating the failures of your predecessors. Your well-thought-out marketing plan won't be shot down, since you can demonstrate you know what the competition is up to. With a successful plan, you'll get more marketing dollars.

When you know more about your competition than they know about you, they're dead! It's actually fun to become a "Corporate Columbo" and sleuth your competition.

➤ Thirteen Ways to Sleuth Your Competition

1. *Adjust your viewpoint.* Most sales and marketing people look at their competition with disdain and contempt, even hatred. These emotions create barriers to clear thinking and effective planning. Fear and loathing lead to competitive myopia. View your competition as your prospects and customers do. They're curious, open minded, and probably excited. They're trying to solve a problem. We tend to be more critical than most customers and usually focus on things

they don't really care about, such as, "I hate that color," or "That's a bad place for the on/off switch."

When you analyze your competition, do so as if you were a prospect or someone with positive expectations; take the "I've-got-money-to-spend" viewpoint. Or better yet, watch real prospective customers review your competition's products to get an idea of what they think is important.

Then, look at what your competitors sell as if you were seeing it for the first time. Or ask someone who's unfamiliar with your competition to review its products. You'll be surprised at what you've missed in the past. In the passion of looking for dirt, more than one company has been baited by false information, or worse, has redirected marketing plans down dead-end paths. Savvy sales and marketing professionals don't let the competition blindly set their marketing strategy. Objective intelligence gathering leads to a pragmatic and successful market attack.

2. *Create your competitive intelligence network.* Enlist all of your colleagues, associates, and vendors in your quest for competitive intelligence. Let them know you're always interested in competitive information and reward those in your organization who become "industry experts."

Make competitive intelligence gathering part of your everyday awareness, and you'll never be blindsided by your competition.

3. *Watch for the competition's publicity.* Have your entire staff looking for news items about your competition.

Watch the employment ad postings. Often they'll reveal information about upcoming projects. You can determine a lot from staffing requirements, especially when you've been watching them for a while.

4. *Get all the literature you can.* Call your competition and ask them to send you their catalog, samples, brochures, and literature. Tell your competitor who

you are, what you do, and that you'd like the literature so you have a clear understanding of what the company tells your customers.

If they balk, call back, this time giving your home address, or ask one of your customers to request the information for you.

Study their literature, just as if you were an excited customer getting ready to buy. Punch these materials for a three-ring binder and add them to your training library.

5. *Ask!* You'd be surprised what information you can get just by asking your competition. For example, Mike, who's the sales manager at a major hotel in New Orleans, had an association executive previewing the property for an upcoming conference. Mike asked, "Where was the best conference you've had?" The exec mentioned last year's conference at a high-profile hotel in Las Vegas.

After the meeting, Mike called the sales manager of that hotel. "Hello, I just had one of your customers in here raving about you. Would you do me a favor? Would you fax me last year's contract?" Mike patterned his proposal after the Las Vegas contract and won the business.

Just because you wouldn't give your competition the information doesn't mean that they won't give it to you!

6. *Go where the competition hangs out.* Where do the workers go after work for a drink? Where do they go to lunch? You can pick up lots of interesting information just by sitting back and listening. Or encourage the competition's people with a round of drinks and then listen to them complain.

We've heard about more than one industry secret revealed in an overheard conversation in a restaurant, bar, or airplane.

7. *Interview disgruntled former employees.* Check the grapevine for someone who has just left your com-

petitor. Invite this person out for dinner and drinks and do some brain-picking with questions such as: What do you think they do really well, better than us? Where are we falling down? What three things should we be doing that we're not?

Steer clear of asking the person to violate any nondisclosure agreement that may have been signed. You may be liable for misuse of obviously confidential information.

8. *Take your competitor's customers to lunch.* If you want to understand your competitor's marketing strategy, ask your sales force about a deal that was recently lost to the competitor, and offer to take the buyer to lunch. Explain that you're only interested in finding out how to improve what you sell so that next time around, you'll have a shot at earning their business.

Sure, this feels like eating humble pie, and so you might be tempted to reject this idea. But you've already lost the sale, so swallow your pride and don't lose the intelligence the sale generated.

Objectively, without arguing with what you hear, ask questions such as: How did you find out about our competitor? What steps did you go through as you made your decision? What were the factors you used to decide? Comparing how we did with the competition, what did we do well? What could have we done better?

Focus on what the competitor does to win customers, not on how to save the deal. When customers are pushed to reconsider a decision, their natural reaction is to defend and exaggerate the deciding factors. Your job is to ask questions and bite your tongue. You want the unvarnished truth from them.

So consider the lost deal an investment, perhaps an expensive investment, in planning the next battle.

9. *Take stock.* Call a discount stock broker and order one share of your competitor's stock. You are now, in the truest sense of the word, a shareholder. You are entitled to all the information and privileges of a shareholder, and the company information will be automatically sent to you. You are also entitled to attend the shareholder meetings. If you really want to have fun, buy a share of stock for everyone possible in the company. Take a road trip to the annual shareholder's meeting, and sit in the front row.

Don't disrupt! But can you imagine the impact on your competitor's CEO when he explains how the company will increase sales next year and the competition is literally hearing it first. Enjoy the look on their face when you ask for a plant tour.

10. *Become the competitor's customer.* Experience your competitors firsthand. Buy from them. When most companies buy from the competition, they rip apart their purchase and look for the bad things to point out to their salespeople. This works in creating a traditional competitive analysis. But you still don't have an insight as to why others buy from them.

What works better is to use your competitors' products just as their customers do. Most buyers gleefully bring their new acquisition into their lives. To truly understand the mind set of your competitor's customer, you must (begrudgingly or otherwise) do the same.

When the competition turns around and orders from you, we suggest treating your competitor's orders as you would your most important customer. Scare them with your exceptional customer service. They'll assume that if you give this level of attention to your competition, you must really be going out of your way for customers.

11. *Use trade show reconnaissance.* A great source of competitive intelligence is a trade show. The exhibits are often staffed by those in the know who haven't been briefed on what topics are safe and which are out of bounds. Because of the unfamiliar show envi-

ronment, these people are just insecure enough to feel that, by talking about "insider information," they'll command respect. It only takes a little prodding to get them started.

At trade shows, the unwritten rule is "seller beware." Walk up without your badge and start asking questions. Entire marketing plans have been unwittingly revealed to competitors at trade shows.

12. *Get online.* Compile competitive profiles that include online research from Dow Jones, Lexis, Nexis, DiaLog and the World Wide Web. Go to newsgroups that customers are likely to frequent and post questions about competitors' products as well as your own. You'll find the responses pointed and pragmatic.

An advertising agency was competing for the business of a very large, Fortune 100 account. One of the salespeople got on the computer and looked up the prospect's corporate home page on the World Wide Web. Posted there, for anyone to read, was the target account's marketing plan. By adapting their presentation to the plan point-by-point, the agency was able to persuade the corporate marketing department that the best way to achieve its goals was to switch agencies, and in doing so, they won the account.

13. *Take mug shots at the show.* On the opening day of the show, have one of your people take pictures of the competitors' exhibits, particularly close-ups of their staff (a telephoto lens is handy). Have a one-hour photo finisher develop the film (or better still, use one of the new digital still cameras that download the pictures right into a computer[6]). Make up a *Wanted* poster so that your staff will recognize competitors when they come snooping.

---

[6] For a free brochure, contact Kodak at 1-800-23KODAK.

➤ Video Feedback

This is perhaps the most powerful way to prepare your people. When you do your preview setup, take a camcorder and have your people role-play various visitor scenarios. Play the tape back so they can see how they came across. Some rules to follow: Concentrate on the positive (they can clearly see how badly they've done) and emphasize the skills you want them to use. Use the freeze-frame feature to stop the tape and discuss key points, like pointing out when a visitor is asking a buying-signal question. (For example, "Can I write a check?" *This* is a buying signal.)

➤ Objection Hit List

The best time to answer an objection is *before* it arises. Brainstorm with your team to develop a list of your top ten most frequent objections, and then collaborate with your sales veterans to develop scripted answers that everyone can use. The same technique can be applied to common complaints that visitors are likely to bring up at the show.

This tactic instantly cures call reluctance. New hires and non-salespeople staffing the exhibit are afraid to talk to visitors because they don't have the answers to the hard questions. Give them the list and fear evaporates.

➤ Questioning Skills

Asking good questions is, in itself, an art form. Here is a list of questions that will take a prospect all the way through the buying process. Your team members should memorize them until they can recall on demand, "What's question number 10?"

The 37 Magic Selling Questions:

1. What is your main objective?
2. How do you plan to achieve that goal?
3. What is the biggest problem you currently face?
4. What other problems do you experience?
5. What are you doing currently to deal with this?
6. What is your strategy for the future?
7. What other ideas do you have?
8. What role do others play in achieving your goals?
9. Who else is affected?
10. What are you using now?
11. What do you like *most* about it?
12. What do you like *least* about it?
13. If you could have things any way you wanted, what would you change?
14. What effect would this change have on the present situation?
15. What would motivate you to change?
16. Do you have a preference?
17. What has been your experience?
18. How do you know?
19. Is there anything else you'd like to see?
20. How much would it be worth to you to solve this problem?
21. What would it cost, ultimately, if things remained as they are?
22. Are you working within a budget?
23. How do you plan to finance it?
24. What alternatives have you considered?
25. What benefit would you personally realize as a result?
26. How would others benefit?

27. How can I help?
28. Is there anything I've overlooked?
29. Are there any questions you'd like to ask?
30. What do you see as the next step?
31. Who else *besides yourself* will be involved in making the decision?
32. On a scale of one to ten, how confident do you feel about doing business with us? What would it take to get that up to a ten?
33. Are you working against a particular deadline?
34. How soon would you like to start?
35. When would you like to take delivery?
36. When should we get together to discuss this again?
37. Is there anything else you'd like for me to take care of?

➤ Outside Consultants

If you are inexperienced in managing a trade show sales team, consider using an outside expert to facilitate your preparations. Such support is often available through your expo producer and may already be included in the price of your exhibit space. Many shows offer special preshow workshops for exhibitors and their employees. By arriving at the show early, you can take advantage of this special training.

➤ Preshow Sales Meeting

Set aside two hours the night before the show opens to review your trade show goals and objectives with your team. Let them know exactly what is expected of them, when their shifts will be, and what you consider acceptable dress, conduct, and sales performance. Take time to refresh and review critical trade show selling skills and procedures for lead management. Use a quiz-show format or other device to make it fun and interesting. Award prizes for the right answers, and, by all means, get them to bed early so they can be fresh and alert, ready to sell from the moment the doors open.

➤ Create a Master Show Guide

Bring together all the information that your sales staff needs to know in a single booklet, including exhibit staffing schedule, responses to the top ten objections (see previous section), show floorplan, area maps, VIP visit schedules, emergency contact information, hotel information, transportation schedules, and other relevant details. You need not type it up; simply photocopy all the various pages and staple them together. Mark it CONFIDENTIAL with a red rubber stamp.

➤ Daily Debriefs

Each day, immediately after the close of the show floor, call a team meeting to discuss and review the day's progress. Review performance by tallying the number of leads, contracts, and dollars closed that day. Review new information gleaned about competitors. Announce any changes in your strategy. Review the staffing and show schedule for the next day, including any last-minute changes. Finally, select a salesperson of the day. Hewlett-Packard awards its daily top producer a $50 gift certificate from Victoria's Secret.

Chapter 6

Setting Up at the Show with No Hassles, in Record Time

Imagine arriving at the show and having everything you need, all stacked and ready to go. The labor foreman is friendly, the union people are helpful, and everything goes up without a hitch. Imagine being finished with your move-in, hours ahead of schedule, and looking on as your competitors get frustrated trying to locate lost shipping crates and missing cartons of literature. While they struggle late into the night getting ready, you and your crack guerrilla selling team head off to one of the vendor receptions where you can relax, network, and meet new and useful contacts.

■ INFORMATION IS YOUR SECRET WEAPON

➤ The Show Manual

You can create an instant advantage by reading the show manual well in advance. This is the number-one complaint of show management—exhibitors don't read the manual.

This document will usually tell you everything you need to know about how the show is organized, how the floor will be laid out, and where and when things will happen. You can gain an immediate advantage by reading the manual, because most of your competitors won't.

➤ A Master Exhibit Guide

Along with the guide created for the sales force, create a master exhibit guide, including contacts, vendor contacts, alternate vendors, show rules, and staff travel schedules.

➤ Shipping Your Stuff to the Show

Check the exhibitor's manual for target and cut-off freight receiving dates and work with your freight carrier to hit the target dates. Missing dates will cost you time and aggravation.

At the same time, arrange for return shipment. You'll save time during teardown if you prepare the return bill of lading and shipping labels now.

Ship all freight prepaid or billed to your account. For small exhibitors, the discount freight rates negotiated by the show management are often very good. They may not compare with a national contract, but they can be good for the little guy.

Before you leave for the show, trace the shipment to make sure it's arrived. Provide show management with a list of your freight so they can confirm arrival of all the pieces. The best show managers will call *you* to confirm when the shipment arrives. Don't wait until you arrive at the show to locate your cartons. We've experienced difficulties tracing a shipment after arriving on the show floor because many other people are trying to trace their shipments at the same time.

Bring a copy of the bill of lading with you to the show, and forward a copy to your installation and dismantling contractor as well.

➤ What to Do with All These Boxes

To speed teardown, put small boxes inside big boxes. Mark your boxes with 8½-by-11 EMPTY signs printed on the computer. Include a box number (such as *1 of 7*), your company name, and your space number in large printed letters and numbers.

Don't send anything to storage other than empty boxes. Once they're in storage, you won't have access to them until after the show. Set the boxes on the threshold of your exhibit where the contractor will pick them up. If it's important for you to have the boxes returned early, make arrangements with the general contractor in advance.

Although you may be tempted to keep your boxes in or behind your exhibit, the fire marshal often won't allow it.

➤ At Teardown

Your empty boxes will magically appear after the show closes. There usually isn't much you can do to accelerate this process, so wait patiently. Check the box count, and start packing.

When you're done packing, tear off the EMPTY labels and apply the return address labels. Leave the boxes in your exhibit, and the contractor will deliver them to the freight carrier. Don't leave the bill of lading with the boxes; give it directly to the show contractor. Take a copy with you.

When you return home, run a trace to ensure everything has come back.

■ WHEN TO ARRIVE

If you're traveling out of town to your show, make sure you arrive at least one day before the show opens to set up your exhibit. If you have a complex exhibit, an advance team should go several days ahead to set up the exhibit as soon as possible. By arriving early, you'll be able to get everything arranged ahead of time, get your labor personnel when you need them, avoid overtime charges, and have time to make alternate arrangements if there are problems—and there usually are.

You see many exhibitors setting up the evening before—or, worse yet, the morning of—the show. They are trying to keep their time commitment to the show at a minimum.

The truth is, if something goes wrong, and it will, they don't have time to fix it. We watched one exhibitor frantically trying to fix a computer for the first half-day of the show. This exhibitor was selling software and felt that the computer was essential to making a good impression. In reality, the sales reps blew off half a day's worth of visitors and seemed flustered for the rest of the day, constantly apologizing for the computer not working and looking like jerks in general for not having their act together.

If they had arrived the day before the show opened, they could have arranged for a rental computer or made other plans that would have salvaged the show.

When you're worn ragged from setting up your exhibit, you can't compete with salespeople who are well-rested and working in a perfect exhibit.

■ WORKING WITH THE SHOW MANAGEMENT SUCCESSFULLY

The show managers really want you to have a great show. They brought together the place and the people, dealing with a million details you'll never see when the job's done right. They'll be looking after 50 to 5,000 other exhibitors, and you're only one in the crowd. You're interested in getting your exhibit up—they're interested in making sure the show isn't closed down by the fire marshal. To work successfully with the show management team, treat them with dignity and respect, and be willing to work things out. You'll be amazed at what they can do for you if you give them time and treat them right.

We've seen exhibitors make a show producer so mad that they were lucky to get their exhibits up. There are 1001 ways a show producer and staff can make your life miserable, from asking the fire marshal to go through your exhibit with a fine-tooth comb (and they'll probably find something) to seeing that your power fails at the worst possible time.

When you storm up mad, producers respond mad. When you threaten them, they retreat to more important battles. Your threats are minor compared with others they have heard.

Labor, over which management usually has little control, may be difficult to work with. Remember, they're just as frustrated as you are, up late making sure everything is coming together and that all the important details are covered.

Get to know your show manager. Search him out. Introduce yourself. Don't flatter him but compliment him on a job well done. A compliment is about something the manager has done well. Flattery is about something over which the manager has no control. And give a little gift. We think a couple dozen donuts is a great gift, and the rest of the crew will appreciate your efforts, too.

Treating your show producer with respect and dignity will move you further down the road than anything else you'll do. We've seen a show manager say "Sorry, sir, you'll just have to wait your turn for labor to find your booth shipment," to one irate exhibitor who was threatening to pull out of the show. This was a dumb thing to threaten when the management already has your money and won't refund it! But the same manager then turned to us and offered us a cup of coffee, and left her post to help us find *our* exhibit.

■ WHEN TO LEAVE

Stay around for a while after the show closes. Don't be in too big of a hurry to take things down and leave. Some buyers scope out the whole show and then make their buying decisions towards the end. Sometimes they don't have a chance to see everybody's exhibit.

Wait until the next day, if you can, to dismantle your exhibit and pack up. Labor is much less hurried—and less likely to damage your exhibit. You won't get into overtime hours, which will cost you less.

Often exhibitors will begin dismantling their exhibits before the show ends, just chomping at the bit to get out of the exhibit hall. Boy, is this stupid! If buyers come along during dismantling, they aren't inclined to stop and talk; they'll think you're the installation and dismantling labor!

Tell other exhibitors who are prospective customers to come by *after* the show closes. Tell them, "We're leaving up our exhibit until the morning, so come on by and let's see how we can work together."

Sell to other exhibitors after the show closes! Bring in a cooler of beer, wine, and soft drinks, and offer them a post-show drink in your exhibit.

■ WORKING WITH UNIONS ON THE SHOW FLOOR

George, a software distributor at a show in New York City, was seen by a union steward reaching up to adjust a light. This, by the union jurisdiction, was a job for an electrician. So the steward stopped him and radioed for the laborer. After quickly making the adjustment to George's satisfaction, the electrician presented him with a bill for $200.00, including four hours of labor, the minimum order. George was shocked, surprised, and angry. "If I'm paying you for four hours," he said, "you're going to stay here for four hours. Sit!"

George's show contract said that his move-out materials would be delivered by midnight on move-out day. To retaliate, the union waited until the last minute to deliver his crates and boxes. So George sat in the middle of a deserted show floor until midnight.

Guerrillas avoid problems with unions by knowing how to successfully work with them. About half of the states don't have right-to-work laws, which means you have to use union labor in the largest convention cities.

Carpenters—uncrate, install, dismantle, and recrate exhibits, displays, and fixtures. They lay flooring and carpet. They're responsible for anything associated with building the exhibit, such as scaffolding.

Decorators—take care of anything made of material, such as drapes and fabric panels. They're responsible for hanging all signs that aren't electric.

Electricians—involved in anything that needs electrical power. They may be involved if you have a complex A/V show that requires a technician.

Plumbers—take care of all pipes, such as water, waste, gas, air, and venting.

Projectionists—sometimes are required for A/V shows. Ask the local union.

Riggers—handle all machinery.

Teamsters—handle all materials in and out of the show, except for machinery.

Here's what guerrillas do to work best with union labor.

1. Find out what you can and can't do. Since this is different from city to city and from union to union, check the exhibitor manual. If you have any questions, talk with the show management.

2. Most shows have provisions for you to install and dismantle your own exhibit if you can do so in 30 minutes (60 minutes in some cities) with one person, without using a ladder.

3. If there is any labor situation that seems like it might cause a problem, call the unions ahead of time and find out what you must do to comply with their jurisdiction rules. Sometimes jurisdictions overlap, and two unions claim the right to the work. The official contractor will settle the issue.

4. While the show management selects an official contractor for each show, you can choose your own contractor. Both of these contractors will use union labor.

5. Doing your homework will save you money. When the people on your crew show up, they're on the clock and will take scheduled breaks. Be ready for them, with everything lined up, ready to go.

6. You'll save money if the same crew installs *and* dismantles your exhibit.

7. Your workers are there to do a job, and they'll most likely do a great job. Most of your workers have installed and dismantled exhibits before, so they might take a different approach than you would. Treat them well, and they'll take care of you.

8. If you experience lazy workers, or have other problems, talk with the labor supervisor. This person is better equipped to deal with the problem. If you think you have the right to do something the union insists on doing, talk with show management.

9. Wage rates are straight time, overtime (time and a half), and double time. One of the biggest budget busters is paying for overtime labor. Know in advance when each work period starts and plan accordingly.

10. Each show has electrical standards the electricians will enforce. If you have something that doesn't comply, such as nongrounded extension cords, expect the electricians to fix it and charge you. Know the standards in advance.

11. Fortunately, the days of tipping union labor are past. Most laborers are professionals and would be insulted. If you have laborers that suggest a tip, report the incident to show management. But, like the show visitors, they'll probably appreciate getting your giveaway.

Chapter

Trade Show Peak Performance

■ HOW TO KEEP YOUR ENERGY HIGH ALL DAY LONG

"It has long been an axiom of mine that the little things are infinitely the most important."

—SIR ARTHUR CONAN DOYLE, 1925

➤ Physically Prepare for the Trade Show

Selling at a trade show is not a normal physical activity. Standing on ultrahard concrete (that gets harder by the hour) and being nice to visitors all day will strain even the most seasoned sales veteran. To feel your best and be your best, you must be in good physical condition.

Consider getting in shape for the show. Exercising lightly before hitting the show floor will give you energy and keep you in peak shape for the show. Do this, and you'll be way ahead of your competition!

Warm Up

Warming up before your shift on exhibit duty will make you much more comfortable. Do the same warm-ups you would when preparing for a walk or jog. Better yet, exercise before the show, doing warm-ups before and after your workout.

Eat

To be at your best, eat light and eat right. It's best to avoid salty foods such as hot dogs, nachos, sandwich meats, pizza, and other junk served at most trade shows. Too much salt aggravates the swelling of the joints that accompanies standing for long periods. Even if you normally like salty foods and snacks, take a break this once. You'll feel much better. At the show, stick to fruit, granola snacks, and other low-salt snacks, or take the time to eat a good meal. An army travels on its stomach, so keep your troops combat-ready by providing regular opportunities and healthy options.

Even if you don't normally like breakfast, you may not know when you'll get your next meal at a trade show. You'll need all the stamina and energy you can get for the day ahead, and breakfast is the only sure-fire way to get it. The best breakfast is a complex-carbohydrate meal: cereal, toast, potatoes, fruit. If you don't like eggs or cereal, go for the pancakes or French toast. Another benefit of eating breakfast is that it will keep you from having bad breath. If you don't eat breakfast, your body burns fat, creating bad breath. This breath comes from your lungs, not your mouth, so breath mints or sprays will only mask it temporarily. Eating breakfast also keeps your stomach from rumbling in front of your most important visitor.

Avoid heavy, greasy, protein-laden meals, and the exotic or spicy foods that could upset your stomach. This goes double if the meal is late at night. You need to sleep well when you can get it, and heavy meals jeopardize your rest. There's a real temptation to eat a big steak when you're on an expense account, but save it for the last night of the show and order the chicken or fish until then. You'll be way ahead of your competition in the morning.

Drink Up!

Before the show, stock up on low-calorie drinks, fruit drinks, and bottled water. Keep the drinks in a cooler in your exhibit. Drinking enough fluids is very important to feeling your best and preventing fatigue. Dehydration will make you feel more tired and your selling less effective.

Protect your voice by drinking water throughout your exhibit shift. You lose about a pint of water per hour when you're speaking. You'll notice that people who are on the show floor for long periods of time often lose their voice. It's because they aren't drinking enough water, and at the same time, they are usually drinking too much coffee. Voice teachers will tell you coffee and other beverages like colas and tea are hard on your voice because of the drying effects of caffeine.

Don't worry about having to go to the bathroom in the middle of your shift. That's more from the diuretic effect of caffeine than from drinking the water you need to replace the moisture you're losing through your breath.

Avoid having cups or soft-drink cans cluttering up the exhibit. Get bottled water and keep it hidden away. Be sure to drink lots of water during breaks.

Limit Your Alcohol Consumption

Better yet, don't drink at all, and *never* drink on the show floor. Shows held in hotels will often have a cash bar open for visitors. And many shows sell beer at the concession stand. Sixty percent of Americans drink at least occasionally, so some exhibitors assume it's all right to have a cocktail or beer in their exhibit as long as their visitors are drinking. This is a kiss-of-death mistake. When you have alcohol on your breath from just a sip of beer or wine, you will alienate the forty percent who don't drink. If you want to drink alcohol in your exhibit, wait until after the show closes.

Alcohol is also a diuretic, contributing to your dehydration problems. A drink packs a greater punch when its effects are augmented by fatigue and the natural dehydration that occurs at trade shows. Besides, nothing's worse than a hangover at a trade show. If you do drink, alternate alcoholic drinks with water, juice, or sodas. And drink extra water before going to bed.

Control Aches and Pains Caused by Inflammation

Consider taking the recommended dose of an over-the-counter pain remedy such as ibuprofen (sold under the brand names Motrin,® Advil,® and Nuprin®) *before* you start your shift. Naproxin,® an even more potent class of anti-inflammatory, is now available over the counter in the United States. Ask your doctor or pharmacist. If you don't want to take these drugs, ask your doctor about other options such as homeopathic inflamminoids.

These anti-inflammatory agents are reported to prevent joint tissue damage and thereby offset the normal pain, swelling, and discomfort of standing for long periods of time. You'll find it really makes a difference. You'll feel much more comfortable, and your energy will stay high. When you're uncomfortable, you're not at your best. This simple suggestion can make the difference between a bad show and a great show.

Wear Comfortable Clothes and Shoes

Make sure your clothing fits properly and that your shirt and blouse collars are loose enough to be cool and comfortable. If your weight has recently gone up or down, a quick trip for alterations is money well spent.

Exercise Your Feet

If you're standing still for a long time, remember to exercise the foot muscles that keep your circulation pumping. Stand on one foot and move the other around in figure eights. Raise up and down on your toes. Or simply wiggle your toes if you want to be inconspicuous about it.

If you've been seated for a long time (on an airplane, for example), move each foot a good deal, scrunching and stretching your toes prior to standing up. This will begin circulating the blood that has become static in the lower extremities and will reduce swelling of your feet.

Take a Walk

You need to work out your legs after standing for a long time. A quick walk around the show floor pumps fresh blood into your legs, picking up your energy level. Split the time between getting some exercise and resting. Light stretching of your legs lessens the feeling of exhaustion. Place the foot on the edge of a carpet or stair and move it back and forth. This will stimulate the muscles and circulation. The most important thing you can do is to vary the surface on which you are walking.

At the end of the day, lie down, elevate the extremities, and massage your feet and legs.

➤ How to Avoid Bad Breath

Avoid breath-killing foods during the show. The worst offenders are garlic, onions, stinky cheeses, and tuna.

Avoid coffee breath and bad breath from smoking. Please don't smoke during the show. Even if you just step out for a cigarette, the smell will be on your hands and clothes. Use an over-the-counter nicotine gum if necessary, but be especially wary about mixing smoking and stop-smoking aids. If you choose to smoke, that's your business. But we know people who won't do business with smokers on the grounds that they won't work with people who know what's best but won't do it. If you're serious about doing business with professionals, consider giving up smoking altogether.

Have you ever noticed that someone on a low-calorie diet, like the liquid diets, has a pungent breath? That's because the person's body is burning fat. When you skip a meal, your body burns fat to keep you going. The only cure for this bad breath is to eat breakfast and lunch.

To keep bad breath away, floss (the plaque between your teeth is a source of bad breath) and brush your tongue.

We know people who swear by chlorophyll tablets, available at health-food stores. Another natural remedy is to eat the parsley garnish served on your plate. You can also always use breath spray.

If you do choose to use mints, select small mints, such as Tic-Tacs.® They are less noticeable than larger, roll-type mints.

If your visitor has bad breath and it keeps you from concentrating on business, casually take out a mint for yourself and politely offer one to your visitor. If the visitor refuses, lower your voice and ask, "Are you sure?"

Chapter

Making the Connection That Creates a New Customer

Folks who never do any more than they get paid for never get paid for any more than what they do.

—Elbert Hubbard

At a trade show, you're going to meet hundreds of people, and thousands more will see your exhibit. What these people see will make a lasting impression, so you would expect all the vendors in the show to be on their best behavior. Fortunately for the guerrilla, this isn't the case. We see exhibit staffers acting out, visiting with each other, and dressing in the same casual clothes they wore for the move-in.

Guerrillas can create a competitive advantage by making sure that the exhibit staff is at its very, very best, as if making a sales call on the most important customer. Cliché, but true: You never get a second chance to make a first impression. This is the time to pull out all the stops and upgrade the staff members' dress, grooming, attitude, and customer-service skills.

Hey, anyone could overlook the importance of how you come across to others. But if you want to be part of the elite 15 percent that walks away richer than when they walked in, put your best foot forward.

■ WHAT TO WEAR

To sell yourself and your product, you need to appear likable, honest, credible, and sincere. When you are in your trade show exhibit, the best thing you can do to attract and stop prospects is be approachable, and one of the best ways to be approachable is dress like your customers. Dress for the business you want, not the business you have.

Your clothes send powerful messages about your economic class, your educational level, your social position, your level of sophistication, your trustworthiness, your hopes, your fears, your state of mind, and your sales savvy.

At the same time, overdressing can be intimidating. A good rule of thumb is to dress just a little bit better than your customer. You want your prospects to feel comfortable walking up to you and talking about your products. The last thing you want to do is shut out people by the way you look and act. With all the competition that exists in your prospects' minds, it's easy for them to say to themselves, "Skip it, they look busy," or "Nah, I don't think I want to talk to them," and keep on walking.

The old saying "Birds of a feather flock together" captures the essence of human behavior. People like people who are like themselves. People tend to distrust people who aren't like themselves. If your big buyer wears a business suit and is clean cut, you will be much more effective if you match that style. Likewise, if your typical customer wears jeans and a khaki shirt, that style of dress is appropriate, except that your jeans should be *new* and the khaki shirt *pressed.*

How you dress also affects your behavior in subtle ways. How you move in your clothes and how you wear them are a crucial element of the image you project.

You or members of your staff may be more comfortable in alternative-lifestyle clothing. That's appropriate if you're selling to the alternative-lifestyle market. Keep in mind how your costuming impacts your potential audience. At a trade show, you may have to compromise your comfort in favor of your customers'.

One of our business associates loves to hunt, and he loves to eat steak. But he's discovered that when he goes on a strictly vegetarian diet for a month before hunting season, he's much more likely to get his trophy deer. He's discovered that, by adopting the vegetarian lifestyle of his quarry, the deer are less likely to be alarmed by his scent, and he can more easily make his big kill. You, too, may find it advantageous to adjust your habits temporarily to make your big kill.

Take a close look at everything. Beards, long hair for men, unusual jewelry, casual or eccentric clothing, or unusual mannerisms could drive away your big prospect. So will big hair, big jewelry, and excessive makeup on women. If you have any doubts, err on the conservative side of classic styles. If you really want to make an impression, dress in formal wear.

➤ Consider a Uniform

A popular alternative is for the exhibit staff to dress in uniform. One of our clients, Governors Club, a golf community in Chapel Hill, NC, has perhaps the most respected sales and marketing team of any resort community in the United States. Whenever they travel to a conference or show, *everyone* from the CEO on down wears matching slacks with golf shirts and sweaters embroidered with the corporate logo. They are wearing the same merchandise that the company sells in its pro shop, so it's easy for them to create a uniform look. And it makes an impression: They *look* like they have their act together, and they do!

Your team uniform could be as simple as chinos, a matching T-shirt, and white tennis shoes, or as complex as special costumes for a theme exhibit. Uniforms make it easy for your visitor to see who's the exhibit staff and who's the visitor. Uniforms ensure the dress code you want.

If your target market is primarily business-to-business, we suggest that you not use uniforms but stick with standard business suits. When people are dressed casually, they tend to act casually; this can create a mismatch if your visitors are dressed for business.

Men's Dress Suggestions

Wear a two-piece suit that's comfortable and fits well. Remember, the business suit is a uniform. It tells people that you are a professional, and that's the only information they have to go on until they get to know you.

A suit subliminally tells prospects, "I'm proud of my products," "My company looks after the details," and "We are professionals."

Wear classic single-breasted three-button or two-button (preferred) suits. For a professional look, keep the top or middle button buttoned, and leave rest unbuttoned.

Make sure you can button the jacket comfortably. You'll look sharpest if you keep the jacket buttoned, and you don't want to look like you're about to burst your buttons. For a more relaxed look, leave your jacket unbuttoned. If you wear a double-breasted suit, button both buttons. Double breasted suits don't look as neat with the buttons undone and all that fabric flapping around.

If you have more than a one-day show, bring two suits. After 10 to 16 hours in your coat, it will need a day to air out.

When shopping for suits, get the most expensive suit you can afford. Better fabrics stand up well under wearing, perspiration, and weather. You want the suit to still look great after a long day on the show floor.

Chose medium blue, navy, beige, or camel gray. Avoid solid brown because it lacks power in the business world and signals a lower social class. Browns are acceptable in tweed and herringbone fabric, and for casual wear. Avoid them for most shows. Black is very formal and severe. It may make you less approachable.

When you buy your dress shirts, make sure they have a large enough collar to slide a finger or two between the collar and your neck. Also make sure the sleeves are long enough to reach to your wrists. If you have an unusual body build, think about custom-tailored shirts for a well-fitted, professional look.

Wear a white or light pastel blue shirt. These colors are psychologically inviting and comforting. You want a low profile in keeping with the professional image.

Take your shirts to a professional laundry and have the laundry put them in boxes. This will make sure your shirt looks pressed, even after the journey in your luggage. Do this, and you won't need to take an iron, and you'll really increase your professional image.

Wear thigh-high socks. One of the worst fashion mistakes is to show a band of leg between your socks and your pants. Ignore the fashion implications and buy several pairs of support hose socks just for the show. They'll substantially reduce leg fatigue. They really do feel good.

Wear an undershirt. An undershirt keeps you cooler throughout the day because it wicks away perspiration and keeps your shirt from getting perspiration-stained. As a bonus, it makes your shirt look better and more professional.

Wear a creative tie. This is about the only "personalization" you are allowed to make with a business suit. You can wear statement ties, such as Looney Tunes characters, clowns, or endangered species, if it fits your business image. Striped ties are out, bright colors and crazy designs are in. Bring a different tie for each day for relief of boredom. Tie your tie with enough length to reach the top of your pants or your belt buckle. Make sure your tie doesn't stick out under the buttons of your suit jacket.

Women's Dress Suggestions

Women may wear suits, dresses, or a dress and jacket combination. For businesswomen, no color is totally off limits. However, some colors do work better in smaller amounts or as accent colors. Be careful of very trendy items so that you don't appear to be in costume.

A classic and basic suit is best. This shows you're in business. You want to focus on your business image, not on being sexy. Women *shouldn't* look like floozies, unless the only differentiation your product has is "the girls in the exhibit."

You can add a creative touch to keep with the current trends. For instance, you may add a colorful scarf or a piece of ethnic jewelry.

Your hosiery color should match your skirt hem or shoe color. So don't wear dark hose with a light colored shoe. For example, black hose with red or ivory shoes is out. If you cannot match the color of your outfit, wear a neutral hose color, such as soft taupe. Avoid suntan hosiery; opt for neutral beige instead. Black, navy, and off-white or ivory hosiery are always appropriate when worn with the matching clothing colors.

Wear a natural hair color. Touch up your hair color if you have different color roots.

Wearing sexy outfits seems to attract people, especially men, to your exhibit. Unfortunately, you are then alienating a substantial portion of your potential market. And your focus is on the wrong thing, unless, or course, that's what you're selling.

Avoid plunging necklines, loud colors, very short skirts, see-through fabrics, glittery fabrics, and anything tight. There's no reason for your dress to distract visitors from doing the business you want.

Visitors can spot runs in a pair of hose from the other end of the show aisle, so bring extras.

Wear Comfortable Shoes

Aching feet and legs are the main physical complaint of both men and women at a trade show. Shoes should look new, but never be new. A show is the wrong place to break in a new pair of shoes. Cushioned-shoe makers include Jarmin Cushins, Easy Spirit,[1] Rockport[2] shoes, and other brands. You'll substantially increase the comfort of your feet and

---

[1] Call 1-800-284-9955 for the store near you.

[2] Call 1-800-343-WALK for a free catalog.

legs. These companies offer very comfortable business-style shoes for men and women.

Sneakers, tennis shoes, and running shoes are definitely out, unless they are part of a uniform or part of your product line.

Keep those shoes polished. Use the shoeshine stand at the hotel if you have to. It's amazing how scuffed shoes show up under the bright lights of an exhibit. Remember, you don't have a desk to hide your feet under.

Give your staff a daily shoeshine and laundry allowance of $5.00 to $10.00. This is a small expense that will really pay off in your company's image and staff satisfaction. Your exhibit staff will really feel pampered, and they'll look great!

Minimize Distractions

You want to keep physical distractions to a minimum. Keep the customer focused on their problem and how you can solve their problem.

It's better to wear conservative jewelry for the same reasons. Dangling earrings and jewelry such as bracelets that clang, bang, or jangle will distract your visitor.

If you decide to wear perfume or cologne, keep it light! Don't overpower people. You don't want those walking down the aisle to smell you coming. Remember, many people are allergic to perfume, so you're safest to wear little or no scent. For a trade show, no smell is the best smell!

Men, you will run the risk of losing a customer if you wear an earring. It's your choice, but you'll never see an earring worn (at least to work) by a Million Dollar Club salesman.

Get a Manicure

People notice your hands, so keep them well groomed and manicured. Nobody wants to shake hands with a hand that looks like a bird's claw. Let your staff get a manicure before the show and pick up the tab. They'll feel pampered and be more motivated.

Use lotion on your hands to keep them soft and smooth. Your hands will get dry from shaking people's hands and handling literature, so keep unscented lotion in your exhibit, and use it.

As you spend all day speaking, your lips will probably get dry and chapped. Use a lip balm to keep them moist.

➤ Wear Your Glasses

If you wear contact lenses, consider bringing your glasses along as a backup should your eyes become irritated. Your visitors won't care about you wearing glasses, and you won't have to worry about having difficulty seeing things or having your contact lenses be uncomfortable or pop out.

➤ Get Your Hair Styled

Go to a salon that knows current local hairstyle for decision makers in your field. Ask them, "What's the top executive look now?" We suggest avoiding the local haircutting chains. They know the "wannabe" and popular styles, not the image you want to portray.

➤ A Good-Quality Pen Shows Success

Use a high-quality pen for your note taking, one that shows you're really proud of your business. For many businesses, a good-looking pen is a critical dress accessory. Better still, keep a supply of Cross or Mont Blanc pens in your exhibit, and offer your best pen to your customers to use to complete the order. When they offer it back to you, respond with, "I believe that's yours." They'll say, "No, you just gave it to me." And you'll respond, "Yes. That's right." They will put it in their pocket with a smile and remember you every time they use it.

If you're not using your pen to take notes, put it down or put it away. Fidgeting with your pen is distracting and implies that you are nervous and uncertain of your product.

➤ Wear Your Name Badge Up and to the Right

Always wear a name badge. This is an easy way for you to keep your name in the prospect's vision during your conversation and identifies you as someone who can help. Because most people are right-handed, they automatically put their name badge on their left shoulder or left pocket. But the most effective location for your name badge is as high up as possible on the *right* side of your clothing. Now, when you reach out to shake your prospect's hand, you are literally putting your name in their face. Visitors with bifocals won't have to hunt for your name because it's at eye level and automatically in focus.

Get professional-looking name badges made for every member of your exhibit staff. These badges will let you control your entire image instead of leaving it up to the show producer. Some show producers get bent out of shape if you don't wear *their* name badge. Explain that you'll wear their badge to get into the exhibit hall, but you wish to wear your own during the show because it better fits your theme or image.

■ MAKING FIRST CONTACT

Making the first contact with your visitor is the first step to a potential sale. Most people at the show won't initiate a conversation with you unless they are attracted to your exhibit.

How you start the conversation is critical to getting the sales process heading in the direction you want.

➤ Why Every Visitor Is Important

Every visitor is important until proven otherwise. You need to treat each person who walks into your exhibit as if he or she is the most important person you'll meet that day.

You don't want to categorize anyone you meet until you've had a chance to ask questions and discover who buys. It's too easy to make judgments based on looks, behavior, or taste in clothes. While you can't judge your visitors, they'll judge you. You have to make sure that what you do and what you wear don't get in the way of doing business.

➤ The Top 10 Things That Drive Visitors Nuts

This data is based on surveys we've done during live training sessions. Here's what annoys visitors most in roughly the order of importance:

1. *Being ignored.* This ranges from staffers talking among themselves to staff unwilling to break away from some nonsales activity, to long-winded conversations with other visitors that prevent your staff from acknowledging the new visitor is there. Sitting, reading, and any activity other than being ready to serve visitors can lead to lost sales.

2. *A staff that doesn't know the products.* Visitors are underwhelmed when they're looking for answers and all they get is, "I don't know." Make certain your staff is trained on what you sell. If you have to bring in temporary staffers, make sure they have a basic knowledge of what you do and can refer the visitor to the right person for more details.

3. *Eating in the exhibit.* When you lunch in your exhibit, you'll drive away most visitors. This sends the message that your food is more important than making a sale, and most people are too polite to interrupt your meal.

4. *Being interrupted.* Let visitors talk! Men are the worst offenders when speaking to women, frequently interrupting the conversation. Let your visitors complete what they're saying and don't try to second guess what they'll say next. If you jump ahead of your visitor, you'll miss important information—details that could mean the difference between you making a sale and your competition getting the business. This is tough to do when you've heard the same question again and again and already know the answer. Start every conversation as though you have no idea what your visitor wants, as if you need to hear everything that is said to do business—and you do!

5. *Hands in pockets.* Make the mental picture of a salesman, hands in his pockets, jingling change, rocking back and forth on his heels. He doesn't appear very sincere, does he? Empty your pockets of keys, change, and other items. That way you're not clanking as you speak with your visitor. When you stick your hands into your empty pockets, you'll find nothing's in there and take your hands back out.

6. *Being kept around when they're ready to move on.* When they've seen and heard enough, they'll either be interested or want to move on. Keeping visitors who are not interested is a waste of your time, and it leaves them feeling uncomfortable about your company.

7. *Excessive touching.* Exhibit staffers who want to touch their visitors really put off a large number of people. Current customs permit you to shake hands, but other touching, unless that is a major part of your business, is off limits.

8. *Gum.*   It's difficult to speak clearly with the gum in your mouth, and it is an annoyance to most visitors.

9. *Continuous throat-clearing.*   Some people have a habit of clearing their throat while others are speaking or just before they speak. This is very distracting, and some people think it's rude. Ask your colleagues if you frequently clear your throat, or listen for throat-clearing when you speak to visitors. If you have this problem, see your doctor. Continuous throat-clearing is very hard on your voice, and it can indicate other problems, too.

10. *Bad breath.*   See the section on dealing with bad breath in Chapter 7.

➤ The Communication Gap between Men and Women

Men and women live in the same world, but when they try to talk together, it seems as if they're from different planets.[3] Guerrillas understand these differences and are sensitive to them.

Women make suggestions indirectly, while men make direct commands. Perhaps you've been in a situation where the woman says, "Are you hungry?" and the man responds with, "No." He interprets her question literally and responds by directly answering the question. But what she's *really* saying is, "I'm hungry. Can we please stop and eat?" but the man didn't hear it. That's why women frequently complain, "He just doesn't *listen* to me."

Men focus on *report* talk: news, sports scores, factual data. When men introduce themselves, they talk about their accomplishments and credentials. Women focus on *rapport* talk, and they are more likely to share family, relationships,

---

[3] For more on this topic, read *Men Are From Mars, Women Are From Venus,* by John Grey.

and personal matters. They tend to be more reserved about discussing personal achievements. Guerrillas use this awareness to read between the lines and pick up subtle implications when speaking with prospects.

Think about the things that exhibitors do that drive you crazy. Ask your exhibit staff to do the same, and you'll make sure that you don't drive your visitors nuts.

➤ Ready for Action

Look alert, ready, and willing to do business. Body language is very important to attracting and stopping prospects. A relaxed, comfortable stance will prevent you from feeling tired and will make you more approachable. Stand with hands at your sides or lightly clasped in front, feet several inches apart. Don't cross your arms. This action places a barrier between you and the prospect.

What if your prospect has crossed arms? Offer a business card, a piece of literature, or your giveaway. This uncrosses the arms and opens your prospect up to you.

Don't view crossed arms as necessarily negative at a show. It doesn't automatically mean your visitors are defensive. It could mean their arms are tired from carrying bags of literature all day. It could mean they are cold. It could be a comfortable stance for them when they're standing. So don't necessarily be put off by crossed arms. Just don't do it yourself!

➤ Face the Aisle

Show that you're open and ready to do business by facing your prospects as they approach. When there is slack time in your exhibit and you're having a discussion with colleagues, face towards the aisle, shoulder to shoulder. When you stand facing your colleagues with your back to the aisle, it closes out prospects, giving them the message, "I'm busy; go away."

Don't guard your exhibit when the traffic is light by standing at I-dare-you-to-enter-this-exhibit parade rest. Move slowly around the exhibit, giving you a chance to stretch, and you'll appear more approachable.

➤ Sit Only if You're Closing Business

When you're sitting down, people are inclined not to interrupt what you're doing. It is easier for a walking prospect to relate to and establish rapport with a standing staffer. If you need to sit, take a break *away* from the exhibit. Your exhibit is a place of business, not a place of rest.

When you invite your visitors to sit down with you, you limit your ability to move them on quickly. So invite a visitor to sit only if you're making real progress that you can't make later.

If you have staffers who have physical disabilities who must sit down, order tall stools or taller director's chairs. This way they are positioned at the same standing level as your visitors.

➤ Smile First

Even if you don't feel like it, smile. You'll start to feel better, and you will look and sound friendly. We're not talking about a cheese-eating, used-car-salesman's grin, but a pleasant, inviting look on your face.

A bored expression is uninviting. Do you feel inclined to seek out and to talk to bored-looking people at parties? No! You want to talk to happy-looking people. You want your expression to tell your prospect, "I'm eager to talk with you about our product."

When you smile at prospects, they'll smile back. There are exceptions to the rule, and they might have money to spend. So smile at them anyway.

Try this. Imagine that you just paid off all your bills for the month and discovered you had $500 left in your bank you didn't know about. Feel that smile? That's the kind of smile you want on your face. It's a *real* smile.

Always have a smile on your face while you're in the exhibit. Just think about all the business you're taking away from your competition!

If you're already smiling when a visitor first looks at you, the visitor gets a completely different feeling than if the visitor notices you putting on a smile when you see her coming. Since they don't know you, they don't know what you're smiling about and may turn away. If you're smiling first, the visitor tends to return the smile, giving you the instant opening you need for a greeting and getting down to business.

➤ Maintain Eye Contact

If you make eye contact with a visitor and then look away without saying anything, you've just dismissed them. Once you make eye contact, you have to do something to initiate a greeting.

Once you've greeted the visitor, maintain eye contact. This doesn't mean you have to stare the visitor in the eyes the whole time; just don't be looking around like you're looking for someone more important to speak with.

We can't recommend any of the fakey eye contact devices you may have learned, such as looking at the tip of a person's nose, forehead, or ear. People can tell, and you'll just come across as a phony.

As you first greet a visitor, observe his or her eye color. Noting eye color will make you look naturally interested, and eye contact will be *electric*. This will give you a very caring and sincere expression.

Another way to make your eye contact really connect is to think, "This is the most important person I'll probably meet today!" as you first reach out to greet the visitor.

➤ Handshakes

Guerrillas reach out to their visitors and offer a welcoming handshake. It formalizes the introduction and starts building rapport. If they don't respond, gently drop your hand to your side and carry on. The act of touching a stranger does more to establish a relationship in a few seconds than anything else you can do.

Handshakes telegraph a tremendous amount of information about the personality and intent of your visitor. In Western culture, and particularly in the business world, it's appropriate for either a man or woman to initiate a handshake.

People have been greeting one another by shaking hands since the dawn of man, and no doubt, it originally meant, "See, I'm unarmed, you can trust me." But over thousands of years it's evolved, and today it conveys a number of subtle messages, each communicated by slight differences in touch, pressure, and force. These subliminal signals are easy to decipher *if* you know the secret code. Used carefully, these microgestures can send subtle messages that will put your visitor at ease and help to neutralize differences in age, status, physical size, or gender.

Web-to-Web

A wimpy, fingertip handshake is sure to make an impression—a bad one. Make sure that you get hold of the visitor's hand correctly. Most four-finger handshakes happen accidentally because you're looking the visitor in the eye, walking, talking, and *not* paying attention to how you're clasping the visitor's outstretched hand. Extend your open hand with the palm rotated slightly counterclockwise, and then, at the moment of contact, push away gently against the fleshy part at the base of the thumb until it's made a good web-to-web contact. Then fold your fingers gently around the other person's hand. This slight delay communicates confidence and avoids the accidental dead fish slip-grip. Shake hands only for as long as it takes to exchange names and then let go. An overextended handshake is uncomfortable for most people—they feel like they've lost control.

Grip

One of the most frequent questions we're asked in our Guerrilla Selling[4] seminars is, "How hard should I squeeze the prospect's hand?"

The answer: Match the pressure offered by your visitors. They may grip your hand lightly or firmly. A firm grip is asserting dominance, and this visitor wants to ask the questions and control the interview. A light grip communicates passivity, and this visitor will appreciate your taking the initiative to guide the discussion. Excessive pressure communicates insecurity. This is the exception; never reciprocate an excessive grip, but strive to relax and make the visitor feel more comfortable.

Tilt

Differences in status are communicated by tilting the handshake. Some visitors will rotate their elbow out slightly and roll their hand over, putting their hand on top, taking the one-up position. You may feel them press the top of your hand slightly with their thumb. This tilts the handshake down slightly on your side, tipping you a tad off balance, and creating the impression of them being taller. Subconsciously, they are literally putting you down, elevating their own status at your expense.

We've observed that older men often do this when shaking hands with younger men, and high-status managers may

---

[4] Guerrilla Selling is a registered trademark of The Guerrilla Group, Inc.

shake hands this way with subordinates. Men usually take the one-up position when shaking hands with a woman, and a well-dressed sales rep may do this with a visitor dressed in a T-shirt and jeans.

You might think that an aggressive, assertive greeting communicates confidence, but this is really a kiss of death. The customer *always* has higher status, regardless of age, gender, or position. Whoever signs the check has the status.

Guerrillas do the opposite of what feels natural, reversing the tilt of the handshake and creating an advantage by relaxing their arm, gently rotating their hand underneath, and lifting their fingers slightly, tilting the handshake down on their side and up on the visitor's side. This sends the signal, "I acknowledge your higher status and I am here to serve you!"

Push/Pull

A handshake quickly sets limits of personal territory. Most people will settle into comfortable distance during the handshake. This distance can vary from visitor to visitor.

Some visitors will literally push you away when they shake hands, while others will gently draw you in as they step up to you. This indicates the visitor's comfort with intimacy and tells the guerrilla where to start the conversation.

The pusher is subliminally asking you to keep your distance. This person doesn't want to become overly friendly, and the conversation should focus strictly on business issues. Ask straightforward questions like, "Have you used this product before? What has been your experience?" Never compliment clothes, hair, or jewelry with this prospect, and do not inquire about family or personal matters, at least not right away.

The puller is literally inviting you in to the inner circle of his personal space. He'll want to get to know you person-to-person, and if you connect on a personal level, then he'll feel comfortable talking business. With this visitor, it is essential to establish common ground. You might open with, "I see you're from San Diego. My wife went to school at UCSD. Maybe you know her?"

Ancillary Touch

A simultaneous touch with the left hand denotes familiarity and acknowledges history. The most common form of ancillary touch is the two-handed handshake, which communicates intimacy. The degree of intimacy is communicated by moving the touch further up the wrist. With someone you have known a long time, you would touch higher up the forearm, at the elbow or even on the shoulder.

Guerrillas never use ancillary touch with strangers because there is no history to acknowledge. They know it will be interpreted as insincere, the "politician's handshake."

Ancillary touch can be helpful when being introduced by a mutual third party to create an atmosphere of immediate intimacy. You're bringing the history of their relationship into yours. And the farther up the arm you touch, the more familiar the message. Just a brush on the elbow is all it takes.

Stance

How you stand during your handshake is also significant. Stepping forward with the right foot is the most common form, and it communicates parity, or equality with the prospect, mirroring the forward motion of their approach. This is good, but, for a change, try stepping into the handshake with the *left* foot. Practice on a friend and you'll feel the subtle difference it makes. It makes the other person reach into your personal space with the outstretched hand and communicates a degree of warmth, acceptance, and trust, which is even better.

Special Considerations

A colleague of ours, W. Mitchell, is an effervescent fellow who always wants to shake hands, and he often offers his hand first. The problem is that Mitchell is confined to a wheelchair, and his hands are severely disfigured, with most of his fingers missing from a tragic fire.[5] What should you do? When shaking hands with people who are missing fingers or wearing a prosthesis, clasp the hand as best you can and respond as you normally would. If they offer you their hook, treat it as if it were their everyday hand; for them, it *is*. And most important, maintain your eye contact, resisting the temptation to stare at the disfigurement. These people really appreciate being treated like everyone else. The more you treat them as if they are just like you, the more likely they are to like you and do business with you.

➤ Respect Your Visitor

It's important to have respect for your visitors. In a trade show environment, it's easy to get carried away. For some reason, things can seem funnier, and you may tend to joke around more. Keep your focus on business.

Remember, men: Women prefer the word *woman* to *lady, female, gal,* and other slang.

When speaking with international visitors, you need to really focus your attention. They may speak with an unfamiliar accent or use words that you don't understand, and they could respond differently to body language than you expect. The key is to speak slowly and pronounce your words clearly. Give them time to understand what you're saying. A common mistake is to raise your voice, as if shouting would somehow make your message more intelligible. Instead, slow down, rephrase and simplify the sentence. And don't make jokes. Humor seldom translates as intended.

Use the person's name during the conversation to keep attention, increase rapport, and acknowledge the visitor's identity. That doesn't mean you use their name in every sentence. But use it two or three times during your conversation and again when you part company.

Feel free to use visitors' first names if they are your age or younger, unless local culture dictates otherwise. If your visi-

---

[5] W. Mitchell, *The Man Who Would Not Be Defeated.* WRS Publications, 1-303-425-1800.

tor is older than you, or if you're uncertain of their age, use the last name along with the courtesy title Mr. or Ms. until they invite you to use their first name.

If a name is tough to pronounce, take some time to find out exactly how to say it. Work together to make sure it's right. Ask for the correct spelling. Your visitor will be flattered. A warm, sincere smile translates into any language.

On your notes, write your visitors name phonetically. For example, if your visitor's name is Stein, you could say *STYne* or *STEEn*. So write out a phonetic version, and you'll be able to ask for the right person when you follow up after the show. Some contact management software includes a special "Say:" field for this purpose. If yours doesn't, then add one.

We have a client whose name is Düster. The umlaut makes the sound of *oo*. When someone calls him on the phone asking for a Mr. DUHster (as in *feather*), he says, "He's not here." If a call comes in for Mr. DOOster, he knows it's someone who he's met, and he'll take the call.

➤ What to Say First

A trade show is not a cocktail party. Forget the throwaway greetings and unproductive pleasantries. Avoid any opening line that doesn't move you to business. Don't comment about the weather, the show, other exhibitors, your feet being sore, or that it's been a long day. Start the conversation immediately in the direction you want it to go.

Some opening lines will work for certain shows and not for others. Brainstorm and write down opening lines you feel comfortable using. Review these before hitting the show. Test opening lines. You'll soon learn what will work for a particular show and what won't.

Visitors' activity levels range from the very aggressive to the virtually comatose. Most visitors you'll meet are either aggressive or uncertain. You won't have enough time to speak to unresponsive visitors unless the show traffic is slow. All visitors are prospective customers, regardless of activity level. Don't interpret low energy as meaning they aren't interested.

You want to match your opening line to the activity level of your visitor. Ask aggressive visitors strong, open-ended questions. Ask uncertain visitors easier, gentle questions.

"Can I help you?" just triggers the automatic response, "No, just looking." This doesn't let you tell your story or find out what the visitor wants or needs. Try asking, "Have you heard of our company before?" If no, say, "Then you'll be glad to know that we are . . ." and explain briefly what you do. If the response was a yes, say, "Then you probably already know that we are . . ." using the same opening transition. You want to achieve the "Oh? Really!" response.

➤ The WOW Factor

Your opening tells visitors the most amazing fact about your firm. The very things that you take for granted (because you hear them every day) would probably impress the socks off your prospects if they knew it. You would be amazed how little most people know about your company or your technology. Find something that makes people say "Wow!" and use that as your opening.

One of our clients offers a unique service. They bring a truck equipped with an industrial-duty shredder right to your office to destroy confidential and obsolete records by the bankers' box. A small-print line in their brochure explains that for every seven boxes of paper that they recycle, you are saving one tree. The sales reps didn't think this fact was very impressive, but now when they use it as an opener at a show, it stops people in their tracks. Wow!

➤ Active Visitors

Very active visitors walk right up and initiate the conversation or they begin inspecting the displays. They usually know something about who you are or what you do, or they have a specific agenda. They tend to have assertive personalities. When they see something of interest, either professionally or personally, they waste no time to satisfy their curiosity.

Greet them by introducing yourself, shaking hands, and saying

➤ "Thanks for coming in. What caught your interest?"

➤ "I see you're taking a closer look. Do you use our products at your company?"

➤ "You seem to know something about us already. What are you looking for?"

Active visitors are the easiest to engage in a conversation, but they will generally control the direction the conversation takes. They often start off by asking you a question. Answer the question as briefly as possible and move to your agenda, qualifying them.

➤ Uncertain Visitors

Uncertain visitors will gaze into the exhibit or enter hesitantly. Their eyes scan the displays, looking for something to catch their eye, but they are reluctant to get too close. They are curious but reluctant. They may have less aggressive and low-assertive personalities. They could feel out of their element and may be new to a job or industry.

Avoid questions with yes/no answers. Be gentle, avoiding a sales approach or a pitch. Greet visitors by introducing yourself, offering a handshake, and asking

➤ "What did you come to the show to see?"

➤ "Are you looking for something specific?"

➤ "What about the show have you found most interesting?"

Once you've established rapport, you can move on to qualifying your prospects. They need to be guided along. Don't push them too hard. They may need time to consider your question. They may even refuse to answer a question if they don't feel you need the answer.

➤ Unresponsive Visitors

Unresponsive visitors wander down the aisle with no apparent interest in anything. They may not want to be at the show. They could be tired, hung over, jet-lagged, or depressed. They usually don't stop, but they may make eye contact with you.

Use only conversational tones, and introduce yourself after you've gained rapport.

> ➤ "Have you enjoyed the show?"
> ➤ "Have the sessions been interesting?"

If they stop, you have the opportunity to qualify them *gently*.

Don't give your visitor the impression you're just about to pounce and jump into a sales pitch. It's better just to use the right opening question.

➤ How to Greet Someone You Met Last Year

When you meet an acquaintance from the year before, always shake hands and reintroduce yourself: "Hi, my name is (*Your name*). I met you last year. It's good to see you again." Don't make them guess your name. They probably won't remember it, so make it easy to get reacquainted.

If you forget your visitor's name and your visitor isn't wearing a name badge, say, "Would you please remind me of your name?" It's gentle, and you don't have to apologize for not remembering.

➤ Controlling Your Visitor's Attention

With all the distractions going on in an exhibit, it's difficult to control your visitor's attention. But controlling their attention is critical to your success. Here's how to do it:

➤ If you use something to attract attention to your exhibit, make sure it's not so attractive that the visitors or your exhibit staff could watch it for hours, because that's exactly what they'll do! You want something that's initially attention-getting but that loses its attractiveness after a few seconds. You don't want it to be your center of attention.

➤ The least number of uncontrollable distractions is in the direction of your exhibit. So direct your visitor's attention into your exhibit. Do this by standing so that when your visitor faces you, they're looking into your exhibit.

➤ By shifting your position, the visitor will unconsciously and naturally follow you to align themselves with you again. So if your visitor is standing at an angle to you, slightly shift the direction in which you're standing to bring the visitor around, facing directly towards your exhibit.

➤ Invite your visitor into your exhibit to look at something specific, get a piece of literature, or move out of the traffic so that you can talk where it's quieter.

➤ If there is a sudden distraction such as a loud noise, or if someone interesting walks by, stop and comment on it. If you ignore it, your visitor's natural curiosity will distract him and you will lose his attention. When you comment on the distraction, you acknowledge it, and you can both return to your discussion.

➤ Creating Rapport

People like people who are like them. The fastest way to create rapport is to be like your visitor. And the fastest way to do this is to match the person you're meeting.

You can initially match the intensity level, voice tone, and volume of your visitors. If they are active and outgoing, you can be active and outgoing. If they are reserved, you can be reserved. This doesn't mean that you should match outrageous or unusual behavior, but do match general energy levels.

Make people feel comfortable. This will help them to trust you. Be easy to converse with and willing to talk about their problems with ease. The quickest way to build trust is to actively *listen* to your visitor.

➤ Listening Is the Key

There are many distractions at the show: music, lights, moving displays, familiar faces. Sometimes it's very difficult keeping your visitor's attention focused on business. Focused, active listening is critical.

➤ How Well Do You Hear What People Are Saying?

When Conducting an Interview with a Visitor, Prospect, or Customer, Do You ...

	Usually	Sometimes	Seldom
1. Prepare yourself physically by facing the speaker and making sure you can hear?	☐	☐	☐
2. Maintain eye contact with the speaker?	☐	☐	☐
3. Assume what the speaker has to say is worthwhile regardless of dress or appearance?	☐	☐	☐

	Usually	Sometimes	Seldom
4. Listen primarily for ideas and underlying feelings?	☐	☐	☐
5. Encourage the speaker to continue by using verbal signals like "Uh huh," "I see," and "I understand?"	☐	☐	☐
6. Keep your mind on what the speaker is saying?	☐	☐	☐
7. Encourage the speaker to elaborate when you hear a statement that you feel is wrong?	☐	☐	☐
8. Use gestures like smiling, nodding your head, and leaning forward in your chair to encourage the speaker to elaborate?	☐	☐	☐
9. Paraphrase and demonstrate your understanding of what you've heard?	☐	☐	☐
10. Make a conscious effort to evaluate the logic and credibility of what you hear?	☐	☐	☐

Scoring

Give yourself 10 points for each answer of "usually"; 5 points for each answer of "sometimes"; and 0 points for each answer of "seldom."

90+	You're a very good listener.
75–89	Not bad, but could improve.
74 or less	You definitely need work on your listening skills.

➤ Becoming a Better Listener

Listening is a process of hearing, understanding, remembering, and observing what people are telling you.

Hearing

Hearing is the physical process of having the sound waves reach your ears with enough loudness for you to recognize what your visitor is saying. Make sure your exhibit is quiet enough and that you're close enough to your visitor to hear them clearly. If not, move the conversation to another location.

Understanding

Understanding is the mental process of grasping the ideas your visitor is trying to communicate. The key is never to assume that you know what the visitor will say. Although you may have asked the same question and heard the same answer a thousand times, you never know when it might be different. It's the same when you ask your visitors questions. You may know *your* answer, and you may have heard nine others answer the same way, but you don't know *their* answer. Don't assume anything. Repeat back what they said to make sure you understand them correctly. Ask further questions to clarify important points.

Your visitors don't *feel* understood until they *know* you understand. Demonstrate your understanding with questions that clarify what they've asked and by repeating back what you've heard in your own words.

Remembering

With all the activity going on and all the people you'll meet, remembering details can be difficult. You *intend* to remember an important detail, and then someone interesting comes along, your attention is redirected, and you forget.

It's critical to remember what your visitor says so you can make the appropriate recommendation and take the correct follow-up action. The best way to do this is to take notes. More on this later.

Observing

Observe your visitors' body-language clues that can tip you off to their internal state.

➤ Nonverbal Communication Signals

Signal	Possible Meaning
1. Folded arms	Defensive, no compromise
2. Hands covering mouth	Insecure, not sure of what is being said
3. Tugging at ear/nose/ throat	Impatient, usually wants to interrupt
4. Fingers of both hands touching	Supremely confident
5. Tightly clenched hands, wringing hands, excessive perspiration, rocking/swaying	Nervous to varying degrees
6. Feet and/or body pointing toward exit	Ready to leave
7. Hands supporting head when leaning back	Thinking, unsure of ground, stalling
8. Hands to face	Evaluating, listening
9. Clenched hands and locked ankles	Nervous or upset

10. Legs comfortable and arms open	Interested and involved
11. Avoiding eye contact	Ill at ease

➤ Take Notes

The dullest pencil works better than the sharpest memory. Look at the section on creating your own, customized lead form in Chapter 7. You don't have to take extremely detailed notes. Just a word or two will suffice to remind you of the key points.

Taking notes accomplishes five things:

1. You better focus your attention on what the visitor is saying.

2. Your visitor knows you're paying attention and listening.

3. You don't have to stare the visitor in the eye the whole time.

4. You have written details that you can use to resume the conversation after the show is over ("Looking at the notes I took during our discussion at the show . . .").

5. When you have a record of the conversation, your prospect is less likely to change his mind.

When asking qualifying questions like, "What do you want in a ——?" write down the visitor's criteria words *verbatim*. You will want to use this *exact* vocabulary later when you do your presentation (we'll cover this in detail in Chapter 9). Guerrillas understand that every prospect feels that "these ears believe most what this mouth says." When you truly understand your prospect's needs and can describe your offer in familiar terms, your offer becomes irresistible.

➤ Selling to Executive Buying Teams

The team approach to trade show selling has been around for years. An R&D team would hit the show looking for ways to complete a project. The team would return home, compare notes, and make recommendations to management on what to buy.

The emerging trend is for companies to send an integrated team of R&D, CFO, and CEO to make decisions on the spot. They'll formulate a list of objectives and spread out on the floor to gather information, including technology, operational information, merchandising strategies of competitors, and potential fusion-marketing partners. Then they'll reconvene to discuss and review their objectives and create a short list of potential vendors. Now the whole team will visit the final candidates to make a decision.

Knowing this, guerrillas are prepared to discuss all aspects of their product, from operational background to financing and delivery details. All the right players will be there to close the transaction.

For success at a trade show, you must quickly contact all the visitors you can to maximize the number of leads and prospects you get. There are three characteristics you must exhibit when connecting with your visitor—you must be *enthusiastic, approachable,* and *active.* Your attitude is critical. Remember, it's easier for a visitor to keep walking than to stop in your exhibit.

Being enthusiastic means being positive, upbeat, and happy, and you'll attract visitors.

Being approachable means open body language, appropriate clothing, and a smile on your face. Don't place any physical barriers such as tables or desks between you and your visitor.

Think of your exhibit as a party, and you're the host or hostess. Actively reach out, shake hands, and greet your visitor. Welcome them to your exhibit, and do what you can to make them feel comfortable.

Now the stage is set to find out how you can help them.

➤ How to Maximize Networking and Parties

There are often lots of networking opportunities during industry trade shows. Many companies host hospitality suites and special customer-appreciation parties. It's usually pretty easy to get invited, and, with few exceptions, no one minds if you're a well-behaved party crasher. We've certainly met people at show parties who went on to make a big difference in our business. Some we even met at competitor's parties!

Here's a winning strategy to maximize networking at show parties:

1. *Decide who you want to meet and brainstorm where these people are likely to go after the show closes.* If you are meeting someone important, call before the show and invite the person to a meal. You can usually catch breakfast or lunch. Most dinners are reserved for corporate events or VIPs. But don't let that stop you from asking the person to join you for dinner, too. If you plan to take your VIP to a popular restaurant, make reservations well in advance, even a year ahead.

2. *Target companies with which you want to get acquainted.* Assume that those companies will have a hospitality suite, and make a point of finding out where it is. The easiest way is to ask one of the exhibit staffers. If the person doesn't know or won't tell you, ask another staffer later in the day.

3. *Target the parties that will attract the people you want to meet.* Some parties have the reputation of "must go." You'll know them for your industry, or ask the old-timers where the VIPs hang out.

4. *Make a schedule of the events you must visit, leaving the less important events for later in the evening in case you don't make it to them.* Ideally, go to four parties every night with a goal of meeting two people of real interest at each party.

5. *Limit your alcohol consumption.* There will be people at the party who aren't drinking alcohol, and it won't hurt to be one of them when you're out creating your new network.

6. *Give and get leads whenever appropriate.* You want your part of the relationship to carry its weight and be viewed as a valuable resource.

7. *If you only know someone by name, ask the person who's greeting at the front door to point that person out to you.* Ask the greeter to introduce you.

8. *Follow up immediately after the show.* Send interesting people a thank-you note. If you made any specific promises, keep them. When you run across information that is valuable to your new contacts, phone them or send it to them.

We recommend Bob Berg's excellent book *Endless Referrals* for a sure-fire method of meeting and making unforgettable impressions. He recommends these ten questions to ask when meeting people at a function:[6]

1. How did you get started?

2. What do you enjoy most about your profession?

3. What separates you from your competition?

4. What advice would you give someone going into this business?

5. What one thing would you do with your business if you knew you could not fail?

6. What significant changes have you seen take place in your profession through the years?

7. What's the strangest or funniest incident you've experienced in your business?

8. What ways have you found to be the most effective in your business?

9. What one sentence would you like people to use in describing the way you do business?

10. How can I know if someone with whom I'm talking is a good prospect for you?

---

[6] Berg, Robert. *Endless Referrals*. McGraw-Hill. 1994.

■ HOW TO CONNECT QUICK

There are five steps involved in a trade show sales call. The five steps spell out the acronym QUICK. You can't skip a step and still be successful. One or two of the steps may fly by in just a few words, but you must take all five steps to win.

1. The Q of QUICK stands for *qualify*. You must understand what your visitor does or is responsible for. This gives you the information you need for the next question. The questions you ask a CEO will be different from the questions you direct to a technical expert.

   The best question in the world for discovering a visitor's needs is the "tell me about" question.

   ➤ "Tell me about what you are doing at your company."

   ➤ "Tell me about your current project."

   ➤ "Tell me about the responsibilities you have."

2. The U of QUICK stands for *understand*. Why is this person at the show? What is he looking for? What problem does he want to solve? What need does he want to fill? Having this information helps you understand how you can help.

   ➤ "Tell me about the problems you've encountered."

   ➤ "Tell me about the steps you've taken to solve this problem."

   Take notes. Even if it's a single word. This shows you're interested in the visitor and will help you recall the key topics of your conversation later. During the listening process, highlight the visitor's needs your products can meet.

   Restate and clarify the visitor's needs. This lets the visitor know you're listening, and it will identify which of your products and their specific features to discuss with the visitor. You will then demonstrate how the product meets those needs.

   If the conversation is wandering away from your main point, restart with "Earlier, you said . . ." and get back on track. It's critical to stay focused on business.

Your visitor's busy, and you have lots of other visitors to speak with, too.

3. The I of QUICK stands for *identify*. Identify how you can help. All you really need to do is isolate one or two key points. If you determine that you can't help, that's good, too. It means you won't waste your time or theirs.

   The visitor is looking for a 15- to 30-second overview of what your company can do to solve the problem. Write out and rehearse beforehand the first 25 words. People buy benefits. The benefits could be practical (your product gets a specific job done) or psychological (the customer feels better having the product). Product benefits that satisfy a visitor's specific needs motivate your visitor to become a customer.

4. The C of QUICK stands for *create an action plan*. You and your visitor should decide what to do next, write up a purchase order, get information from a credit card, watch a demonstration, set up a meeting, mail literature, or—nothing! This step lets your visitor buy or move to the next step of the sales process.

5. The K of QUICK stands for *kick 'em out!* Once you've agreed to the action plan, restate your plan, shake your visitor's hand, and thank them for stopping by. Move them on gracefully with this process, and you'll be free to meet your next visitor. We'll show you how to move visitors along in Chapter 9.

➤ Qualifying in Seconds

Be Enthusiastic

You're excited about what you sell! Your job is to translate your excitement to your visitor.

If you're not excited about your product, how can your visitor be excited about it? You want your enthusiasm to rub off on your visitor. Yes, there is such a thing as too much enthusiasm, usually called fanaticism. But too little enthusiasm is much worse than too much.

The Guerrilla's Secret

Most exhibit staffers use questions suitable for a half-hour sales call. Guerrillas know you don't have half an hour, so they seek to *disqualify* their visitors. The instant they realize that the visitor isn't likely to buy, they say, "Based on what you've told me, I don't think I can help you right now. What should *we* do next?" Let them respond by confirming the mismatch. You can also politely move a visitor along by offering another handshake. This second handshake means good-bye, and will gently terminate the conversation.

What information do you need in order to decide whether to spend time with a visitor? It is critical to know your visitor's responsibilities. This knowledge lets you tailor your questions to that level. You need to know if your visitors have a need or desire for what you have to offer. You also need to know what they plan to spend, when they plan to buy, and whether you can meet their needs. Write these questions down and rehearse them until they are second nature.

Always find out the visitor's company before starting your presentation. You may be able to leverage previous sales to their organization. Or you may find your five-minute pitch was wasted because the visitor had just one, simple question.

Maximizing Your Prospects

Effective lead management begins before the show opens. Decide what kind of inquiries you're expecting and what you're going to do with those inquiries after the show.

➤ What will you send in response?

➤ Do you need different follow-up packages for decision makers, end users, and resellers?

➤ What information do you need to move your show visitor to the next step of the sales process?

➤ How will you send the information?

➤ What do you want your sales force to do with the information?

Once you know what information you need to gather and how you'll react, create a lead form that helps you get that information.

Create Your Customized Lead Form

Decide what qualifying questions you want to ask your visitor and create a small, pocket-sized lead form to guide your exhibit staff through these questions. This will keep the sales process on track and give you lots of details for a successful follow-up call.

Your own lead form is more complete and less expensive than the forms available from the show management. Design a form that reminds you what information you need from your visitor to follow up successfully after the show. For a sample lead form, see the Appendix.

There's a number of ways to approach your lead form:

➤ You can ask prospects open-ended questions, like, "Why did you stop by our exhibit?" and record their answers.

➤ Have a list of products you can check off when you find out what they are interested in.

➤ Ask specific questions and record the answers: Which products are you interested in purchasing? Who is your current supplier? What is the timing for your purchase? Have you settled on the funding methods? Who are the key contacts and decision makers? What are the important issues?

➤ You can design a general lead form so that the sales staff can check a box or circle something for common responses. This way, your people don't have to write down as much. Be careful with these types of lead forms. They tend to limit the information you take to those questions you've thought about. You may be missing critical feedback.

➤ If you have specialized product lines, create a lead form for each of the product lines you have at the show. Change the lead form whenever you add new products or enter new markets or when you want to focus on a specific type of product.

➤ Some savvy companies go as far as creating a new lead form for each show they attend, tailoring the information gathered to the visitor profile expected at the show.

➤ One of the most important pieces of information is how to reach the visitor after the show. Ask, "What's the best way for me to reach you to follow up?" You'll discover their favored way, whether through phone, voice mail, fax, mail, or E-mail.

➤ Get your visitor's fax number and ask permission to fax occasional updates. Most people have fax machines in their offices, giving you another way to stay in touch. You can write on the fax header, "Here's the update you asked me to fax to you," cutting through the piles of mail most professionals get every day.

If your lead form uses carbons to make multiple copies, guard the carbons from your competition. They can pick up a copy of all of your leads if they raid your trash can.

Most larger shows use a credit-card-type visitor badge, with name, title, address, and phone numbers embossed on the card so that it can be run through a credit-card-type imprinter[7] or scanned for electronic data capture. Check to see if your target show offers this type of visitor badge. You can rent card imprinters from the show. It's cheaper to buy your own if you plan on doing more than one show.

---

[7] Call NHC Registration Systems (1-314-334-5171), or NewBold Corporation (1-800-577-8347) for a free brochure.

Is Automated Lead Entry Ready for You?

Larger shows and conventions now offer magnetically and optically coded visitor badges, giving exhibitors the option of capturing this information electronically. This means you don't have to key in the information. You will capture the data more accurately, giving you an edge in getting the after-show packages in the mail and speeding the leads to your sales force, but you will get better data when your sales staff takes the information personally.

Automated lead capture systems have their drawbacks. They are very slow. The tape will run out when you're very busy, and the system uses additional electricity, which is expensive, and puts power-cord holes in your carpet.

While many of the systems let you check off what to send to the visitor, you are very limited in the number of products you can list.

Automated systems don't allow you to easily attach your custom lead form to the electronically captured demographic data. The systems that use a serial-number-encoding scheme are even more difficult to use. You have to match your written visitor information with the coded demographic information after the show. This defeats most of the advantages of the system.

The number of different lead-capture systems in use by show management increases the challenge. Since each show deals with a different technology supplier, the systems aren't standardized. If you have the capture software customized for one show, you'll have to start from scratch for the next show.

Another option is to create your own automated data-entry system with portable computers. With the increasing availability and reliability of business-card scanners, you can ask a person for a business card, scan the data on the spot, and get it into your database.

One issue with using portable computers is the human interaction. Most visitors want to know what you're writing about them. It's difficult for them to see an LCD computer screen. But it's easy for a visitor to glance at your notes, making corrections or confirmations as necessary.

Ask for E-mail addresses. People read their E-mail. Send your visitors an E-mail each evening after the show closes, saying, "Thank you for stopping by to see us! I'm looking forward to working with you to meet your needs."

What Your Visitors Must Get from You

Visitors need four things from you, and you need four things from them. Without this exchange, it's as if they never stopped by. If you don't do these four things, you're throwing away your trade show budget.

When visitors enter your exhibit, they need—

1. *Your name.* Always introduce yourself and the company you represent. Offer a handshake to the visitor.

2. *Your business card.* This puts your visitors in the position of owing you something, whether it's a name or a card in return, or more.

3. *An understanding of what your company can offer.* Practice your company overview until it's clear in your mind. If the visitor leaves without understanding the benefit of doing business with your company, you've lost a potential customer or referral.

4. *A plan for what to do next.* Your visitor needs to understand what the next step will be. Will they be receiving literature? A sales call? A quotation?

Keep your business cards in your left pocket. This way you can easily take a card out without tying up your handshaking hand. Keep the cards you collect in your right pocket. You can smoothly take the card from the visitor with your right hand, and, after looking at the card for several seconds (important), slip it into your right pocket.

It's amazing how many business cards get passed around back at the office. Have an ample supply on hand to pass out everywhere. It's the cheapest form of advertising you can buy.

What You Must Get from Your Visitors

You need—

1. *Their vital statistics.* Get their name, address, and phone number along with the same information for anyone else they know who may be interested in your product. It's always best to double check visitor information for follow-up. Visitors will borrow badges from others, especially for competitive snooping. Larger companies will sometimes have their headquarters address and main telephone number listed on visitor badges, making follow-up difficult.

2. *An understanding of what they need and when they need it.* This will allow you to sort out the best prospects for immediate follow up.

3. *Notes on your conversation.* It makes a good impression when you follow up by picking up the conversation right where you left off at the show. Simple notes are best, and any notes are better than none at all. Without good notes, your trade show dollars are wasted. Get into the habit of taking good notes and following up after the show is over.

4. *A plan to follow through.* Are you going to send literature, create a quotation or proposal, or schedule a visit? Make clear notes of your action items. Don't disappoint your new visitor by failing to follow up.

How to Increase the After-Show Contact to Near 100 Percent

Ask this magic question: "Is this the best phone number to reach you?" Most of the time your visitor will say yes. But one out of five will say, "No, my direct dial number is . . ." or "I'm more often at this number," or "Here is my pager/mobile/home number."

Ask for a fax number and ask permission to fax occasional updates. Most companies have fax machines, giving you another chance to stay in touch. You can write on the fax header, "Here's the update you asked me to fax to you," cutting through the piles of mail most customers get every day.

The One Thing You Can Do That Will Improve Your Lead Quality by over 1,000 Percent

Use a quality-assurance approach to make sure you get the information you want. Have your team manager (the person who is responsible for the actions of the people working on the floor) review the leads as they are generated. After a salesperson is finished with two or three leads, review the information gathered for completeness.

If the lead forms are not complete, coach that salesperson on the spot. It's critical that you gather the right information from your visitors every time.

Grade your sales staff at the end of the first day. By that time you will have already reviewed the leads, and have everybody get with the program.

You're gathering more than leads. The information you get from show visitors has real, timely value. Sensitize your exhibit staff to watch and listen for issues that need immediate attention.

If it appears your visitor has a hot issue with your company—positive or negative—make a note of it and immediately make plans to follow up. For example, if somebody comes by and says, "Yeah, we have one of those, and we don't like it," find out what that person doesn't like about it, make a note, and plan to fix the problem.

Although it appears that you're simply generating leads, often those leads can serve double duty as market-analysis tools. Keep track of how many people expressed an interest in something. For example, given the option of three items on the list, which one do they look at the most?

With Whom Should You Spend Time?

"Seldom does a visitor stop into an exhibit to see a salesperson out of courtesy." Some professional buyers tend to give you more time for a detailed presentation at the exhibit. They will sit down and make sure it's something that they really want before giving you their contact information. They will tell you exactly when to call if they're interested. Value the time you spend with these people! You will have to work much harder to make customers of the other prospects at a trade show.

When you select the right show, the management puts a good selection of people in the aisles that could do business with you. The fact that these folks are even at the show makes them all *suspects.* You can safely suspect that they will be interested in what you sell.

If a visitor meets any of the following criteria, this person is worth the time to talk with and gets upgraded to a *prospect*— a prospective customer. It's up to you to separate the prospects from the suspects attending the show.

A prospect—

➤ Can be convinced he has a problem or need that you can solve (hard work)

➤ Knows he has a need or a problem but doesn't know how to solve it (good prospect)

➤ Wants to solve a problem or need and thinks your company may be able to do the job (better prospect)

➤ Knows he needs what you sell (best prospect)

A *warm* prospect has these characteristics and—

➤ Has money available to buy what you sell

➤ Has the authority to recommend (good), influence (better), or buy (best) what you sell

A *hot* prospect has these characteristics and—

➤ Has the motivation to act. This prospect wants to solve the problem right now.

➤ How to Double Your Trade Show Leads

Every visitor can potentially buy or suggest someone who will buy your product. Every visitor with whom you speak is a source of leads or business. You'll never know the business potential until you talk with the visitor.

Even if they can't do business with you, ask the saving question, "Who else do you know that could use a product like this?"

Write the information down and call the referral after the show. When you call say, "I'm (*Your name*) with (*Your company*). I met (*Your visitor*) at the (*Trade show*). (*He/She*) asked me to give you a call, and I promised that I would."

You now have a few minutes to investigate the referral's situation and determine if you can be of service.[8]

➤ How to Avoid Questions That Are Traps

You must control the discussion of certain dangerous topics. You need to know how to avoid these topics tactfully and how to answer sensitive questions consistently.

How Much Does It Cost?

This is a common question, often asked early on in the conversation. When and how should you answer this question? If your visitor doesn't understand *what* you sell and the *value*

---

[8] For an outstanding audiotape program on rapidly growing your business with referrals, call David Garfinkel (1-415-564-4475) and ask for his Referral Magic program.

you give them, you'll *always* sound too expensive. So your first job is to meet their needs and build up the value of what you sell.

If price is the key benefit or differentiates your product, then answer right away with a question, "That's the best part about our product. What quantities were you looking to buy?"

If price is competitive or needs some explanation, the answer to this question depends on when it is asked.

Always control *when* price is discussed. If your visitor asks it as the first question, put them off.

> ➤ "That depends on what you want. What features do you need?"

> ➤ "I'll be glad to answer that. But first, what do you know about what we do?"

> ➤ "Before I quote a price, I need to understand what you need. That way, I can offer you just the right thing. What are you looking for?"

> ➤ "I'll be glad to give you our prices, but unless I can meet your needs, the price I give you won't make any sense. Can we discuss what you're looking for first?"

If the prospect insists on a price, quote your least expensive product, saying, "Our entry level product, which includes (*List all the important features*), only costs x dollars. Is this within your budget?"

It's very important that your prospects understand what is included for the price and how much money they can save because they buy your product. Summarize the product features and benefits before quoting the price.

So, Why Are You Better than Your Competition?

Questions about your competition should always be treated with care. Unless you know who the visitor is, why he's asking the question, and what he's really looking for, any response could backfire.

Many visitors will feel uncomfortable about competition bashing. One of the biggest credibility busters is for you to talk about something your competition has changed recently or now does better than you. Guerrilla responses include—

➤ "Our competition is a *fine* company. But our customers tell us we better meet their needs. Tell me what you're looking for specifically."

➤ "That's a hard question to answer. Obviously *their* customers think *they* do a good job, and *our* customers love *us*. What do they offer that you think is critical to you?"

➤ "I'm not an expert about our competition. We have people in our company that study them extensively, but I'm focused on how my customers benefit from what we can do. What are you looking for?"

A well-known software company ran ads against its competition in a magazine. In the same issue, the magazine editors reviewed the respective products and declared the competitor's to be superior. Sure, the ads made us think and check out the situation, but in the process, the advertiser lost credibility.

How to Handle Sensitive Topics and Subjects That Will Get Asked

It's imperative that all staffers have a single message when asked sensitive questions. These answers are your party line. This list will give you an overview of some of these topics. Preshow training by management on the company platform will help keep the message consistent and help fend off bad press. Feel free to use this list of out-of-bounds topics for your company.

➤ *Financial projections.* Forecasts of orders, shipments, earnings, and related internal data should never be disclosed at a trade show. (When asked, "How's business?" the response should be, "Business is great!")

➤ *Operating results.* Don't divulge any sales or profit figures (past or projected) for the company, a product line, or a specific product.

➤ *Market share.* Don't estimate market share. Obvious generalizations are all right ("Our technology positions us as the leader in the marketplace . . ."), but avoid dollar estimates, percentages, or expressions such as "We dominate the market," unless you have irrefutable proof.

➤ *Marketing strategy.* This includes projected marketing plans and expenditures, sales force information, advertising plans, and other information that could aid competitors.

➤ *Legal matters.* Patent information, tax matters, and any other legal matters shouldn't be given comment.

➤ *Impending changes.* This means changes in structure, expansion, staffing levels, and the like. It's often tempting to build your ego by dropping hints or leaking information if you're in the know. It's better to play dumb and suggest that the person talk to a corporate officer. Your ego may suffer, but the company won't.

➤ *Products under development.* Until a product is officially introduced, it shouldn't be discussed—either directly or by implication. Any discussion should be covered by a written nondisclosure agreement, and then only with a bona fide customer or prospect. If necessary, keep copies of your nondisclosure agreements on hand.

Here are some deflecting replies to these questions—

➤ "I'm sorry, but I don't have the authority to discuss that with you." Refer the questioner to the right person in your organization.

➤ "That's a good question. What makes you ask?"

➤ "Our company considers that to be company-private. What makes you ask?"

➤ "Good question. Is that important to us doing business?"

➤ Create Your Own Training Programs

There are a number of experts available who can train your sales staff at trade show selling. Expert preshow training is always a worthwhile investment, and you'll see it paying off show after show. But you can also create your own training program. Here are some ideas as to how to structure a program for your sales staff.

1. Set clear instructional objectives. What's your goal for the training? What skills do you want your trainees to learn? What behaviors do you want them to change?

2. Assemble information that supports your goals. Eighty-five percent of trade show exhibitors don't have a clear selling plan. So be careful about using training sources that just report what the majority of exhibitors do. Focus on those sources that recommend new ideas that will work for you.

3. A great way to change negative selling behavior is to ask your sales staff to think back to the last show and comment on exhibitor behaviors that they wouldn't want to see in their own exhibit. All the no-nos will come out. Write down the answers. Get the staff to commit to avoid doing these things. Since the list of what is and is not acceptable came from the sales staff, personal pride and peer pressure will help to change behavior.

4. After introducing new trade show sales tools, have your staff role-play trade show scenarios. Write an imaginary visitor's name and company on the front of standard sticky-label name badges. On the back, briefly sketch the personality and buying style of the "visitor." Be sure to include some brief information about needs and wants and so on. Create a variety of buyers, competitors, buying styles, and so forth. Hand these badges out at random, and have your people role-play visitors and sales staff in round-robin fashion. After the role-play, ask for comments on what went well and what could improve.

5. Better still, videotape the role-plays and then review them as a group, using the remote control to freeze the tape and point out every time you see a member of the sales staff doing something *right*. You need not comment on the negatives; people will pick them out for themselves.

6. Wire your stars. Have your most effective salespeople wear a wireless microphone or carry a microcassette recorder so you can record their conversations as they're working the exhibit. Have these tapes transcribed into a word processor, and then edit the resulting files into scripts. Train your new hires to use the same effective phrases and questions that your superstars use.

Guerrilla Presentations They'll Never Forget

It was a simple exhibit, a standard eight-by-ten, consisting of the draped table provided by the decorator, positioned against the back of the booth. On the table rested a half-dozen small canisters, each about the size of a can of styling mousse, and the sales rep's Samsonite briefcase. As he squirted lighter fluid onto the briefcase, he said, "Now imagine you're frying something in the kitchen," and he gestured for his prospect to step back, "and it suddenly catches fire." He ignited the briefcase with a cigarette lighter, WHOOOISH, picked up one of the tiny canisters, and backed out into the aisle. "Now watch." From ten feet away, he pointed the nozzle at the briefcase and pulled the trigger. In a blink of an eye, the fire was out, the briefcase unharmed. All without leaving a discernible trace of chemicals, foam, or fumes. I bought two.

A dramatic and effective presentation is by far the most effective way to sell your product at a show. Every product or service is a *combination* of tangible and intangible features and benefits, so guerrillas strive to demonstrate *both*. If you're selling a tangible product (like kitchen fire extinguishers), the guerrilla tactic is to demonstrate the *intangible* benefits (ease of use, efficacy, easy cleanup, and peace of mind). Likewise, if you're selling an intangible product or service, look for ways to demonstrate its *tangible* aspects. One exhibitor we saw had a transparent plastic box containing the shredded remains of one million dollars, representing the money his typical industrial customer was saving by using the company's engineering services.

Offer a presentation only after you know that your visitor is able to buy. Most trade show presentations will be given to a group of people. If you expect to demonstrate to more than five at a time, resist the urge to shout above the noise. Use a small public-address system with a lapel or head-boom microphone. You will sound more relaxed and, as a result, more credible; your visitors will hear your message more clearly; and you'll avoid blowing out your voice.

Rehearse your presentation and demonstration in advance. After all, this is a *show*. Sometimes you'll be asked to try something with your product that you haven't practiced. Don't do it! You're risking failure. Decline by asking, "How do you see yourself using it that way?" or "It's not designed or rated in that mode. How important is that to you?" Or delay by being honest, "Yes, the product will do what you're asking, but we're not prepared to demonstrate that here at the show. Would you like to schedule a private demonstration?"

■ NINE WAYS TO MAKE YOUR PRESENTATION IRRESISTIBLE

1. *Show specific benefits your visitors would gain that would allow them to meet the individual needs they discussed with you.* Customers do things for their reasons, not yours. You might have a hundred good reasons for them to buy from you; their decision will hinge on the three or four reasons that *they* think are important. Present proof that you can fulfill these few criteria and you can safely ignore everything else.

2. *Show exclusive or superior features.* Don't waste time on basics. Demonstrate what your competition can't do, but only if it's important to your visitor. Use the magic word *only*. "We are the *only* supplier that has a warehouse within same-day shipping radius of your plant."

3. *Project the idea that your company is a reliable vendor.* You do this with your professionalism and a positive approach to selling. Negative remarks about your competition imply you don't have a better product and suggest that all you can do is knock your competition.

4. *Position what you sell as having the right price.* Make sure your visitor understands the value you provide for the price you ask.

5. *Demonstrate that the time to buy is right now.* Do this through special trade show pricing or promotions, or by immediately solving one of your visitor's problems.

On the basis of your notes, match your product's benefits to the visitors' needs using—

6. *Proof statements.* "With this new technology, our product takes less time to do the job than you're taking now, saving you hundreds of dollars."

7. *Visuals.* "This chart shows your savings over the next three months."

8. *Dramatization and success stories.* These are especially effective when they're from your visitor's industry or location. "Widgets Inc. has slashed its production costs by 10 percent with this product."

9. *Demonstration.* If a picture's worth a thousand words, then a demonstration's worth a thousand pictures.

■ WHEN DO YOU DO A DEMO?

It's less often than you think. You should resist doing demonstrations.

Unless your product is dead-easy to demonstrate with no possible chance of confusion, then you must carefully choose who will see a demo.

The first thing most exhibit staffers want to do is demonstrate their products. And this is logical. The company has spent lots of money to be at the show, and the product is everywhere. But jumping into a demo before qualifying the visitor isn't smart.

Only give a demonstration if the visitor asks for one, and then think again. Ask yourself, "Will I move this visitor closer to buying my product if I do a demonstration now?"

It may be better to say, "In the interest of time, let me give you a quick overview, highlighting the areas you said were most important to you. And then, let's schedule a complete demonstration at your office as soon as possible. This will allow all the right people to see it." This will free you up for other visitors as quickly as possible.

➤ Doing Verbal Demos

If you're explaining processes or procedures, use a poster or chart to preview what you'll demonstrate. For some visitors, this verbal description will be enough.

There are three parts to a quick verbal overview—

1. Review the basic operations, highlighting the areas that are of most benefit to your visitor.
2. Stop after each major point to check and make sure your visitor is satisfied with what they've seen so far.
3. Make a trial close after pointing out the key features.

If the customer agrees that the product is attractive, schedule a follow-up visit to do a complete demonstration in the office. Better still, take the order or get a commitment and schedule a time to take the order.

There are three exceptions to the no-demo rule—

1. Demonstrate the product if the visitor will never see the product again and the visitor needs to see it to buy it.

2. If the prospect will buy *now* only if they see it.

3. If you can't follow up with a demonstration at their office.

➤ Demonstrate Success, Not Failure

Only show the exclusive or superior features, explaining why these are important to your visitors in terms of benefits to them.

Make sure to get the visitors involved in the demo. Let them convince themselves how easy it is to use your product by doing it themselves. Let them experience what you sell through touch, taste, smell. Let them operate it, make it work.

Keep your demonstration simple. Show just the portion of the product that will solve the visitor's problem. Remember, the trade show floor is a distracting environment. Don't run the risk of having a complicated demo that could confuse your visitor.

You can show too much. If you show much more than the visitor needs, the prospect may perceive your product as being too hard to use.

➤ How to Do Demonstrations That Set You Apart

Long ago, when one of the authors worked for a major electronics company, his sales manager told him, "Never do a demonstration. Let the customers do all the work. Just point out how they should do it." This was profitable advice. When the visitors pushed the buttons, understanding exactly what was going on, they became convinced that they could operate the complex equipment by themselves. His closing ratio increased substantially.

Since then, we've noticed that when a salesperson flies through a demonstration, leaving us confused and uncertain of the operation, we're less likely to buy. They've done more to convince us that what they sell is difficult to use and hard to learn.

We've asked salespeople, "How long did it take for you to learn how to do that?" And their reply has been something like, "I've been working here for years." We don't want them to brag about their abilities, but you do want them to reassure prospects that what they sell is easy to operate.

What do your buyers want to see when they're making the decision to do business with you? Their key criteria may be as simple as short manuals and a product that's easy to operate. Concentrate your demonstration on these key points and ignore the rest unless you're asked.

➤ How to Work with Over-the-Shoulder Demo Viewers

If a new visitor joins you in the middle of a demonstration that requires a specific sequence to be effective, stop the demo. Say to the audience, "Just a second." Then say to the new visitor, "Hello, I'm (*Your name*) from (*Your company*). I'm just completing a demonstration, and I'll be with you in a moment." Or, call over a fellow staffer. "Mary, can you help Mr. (*Visitor's name*)?"

In these cases, it's the duty of the other staffers to help to qualify visitors and get them involved in a demo, if it's appropriate.

➤ Using Samples for Your Success

If you have samples out in your display for people to see, touch, and handle, put out only one or people will think that they're *free* samples and take them. In any case, expect a few to disappear.

■ WRAP UP THE SALE AND MOVE 'EM ON

➤ Trial Close

Now that the visitors understand how you can solve their problem, do a trial close to see if they are ready to buy.

> ➤ "From what you've seen so far, is this a product you would be interested in owning?"
> ➤ "Based on what we've discussed, how do you see this service working for your company?"
> ➤ "What do you like best about this?"

If the answer is negative, ask:

> ➤ "What other questions do you have?"
> ➤ "What are you uncertain of?"

Now, ask questions to identify where you missed their needs.

A negative response means the selling process isn't over yet. It doesn't necessarily mean that the visitors don't want your product. It may be that your prospects don't fully understand the benefits your product offers them.

If the answer is positive, go for the close.

➤ Closing on the Show Floor

If you've done a good job of qualifying your visitors, determining their needs, and demonstrating how you can satisfy those needs, your visitors are just a whisper away from becoming your customers.

To close, make a closing statement and shut up!

There are a number of closing statements you can use at a trade show—

➤ *Assumption.* "It seems that this meets your needs. How do we go about getting it into your company?"

➤ *Recommendation.* "Based on what you've told me, I recommend that you buy our *x* model. How long would it take for you to get an order through your purchasing department?"

➤ *Alternate choice.* "I think our company can solve your problem. Would you prefer model *x* or model *y*?"

➤ *Summary of benefits.* "To summarize, (*Refer to your notes*). How do you see this product fitting into your company?"

➤ *Today.* "You can take advantage of our show special. How would you like to proceed?"

Any of these closes will work for trade shows. But, because of time considerations, the summary of benefits and alternate choice seem to work best.

After you have made a closing statement, shut up. Don't say a word. Even though you may be tempted to add something, don't say another word until the visitor has spoken.

After the visitor agrees, do *not* continue to sell. You run the risk of confusing the visitor and losing the sale. Besides, it's time to move to the next visitor.

Create your action plan, such as taking the order on the spot, arranging a date and time for a salesperson to follow up, or arranging for a quotation to be faxed. Thank the prospect and move them out of the exhibit.

➤ Acceptable Behavior on Giveaways

We discussed premiums and giveaways in Chapter 4. Your exhibit staff must be trained as to who should receive gifts and how to give them away. For example, if you're giving away premiums that can be worn, tell your staff to *hand* the giveaway to your visitors and *not* to put the item on for them.

At one show, a vendor gave away stick-on embroidered bees, a giveaway popular with show-goers. (By the way, this vendor used them as a way to indicate to whom he had spoken during a multiday industry conference.) One woman came up and requested two bees and asked that they be placed on strategic locations of her body. The exhibitor refused, instead handing them to her, and quickly moved her along. Soon after, another vendor came up and pointed out that the woman was the wife of a local competitor, and she had arranged for show management and security to watch what happened with the bees. She was baiting them with sexual harassment charges to have them thrown out of the show!

➤ Powerful Parting Gifts

We think that the best way to use good premiums is to give them as a parting gift. "Here, I'd like for you to take this with you. I think you'll find it useful."

This has your visitor walking away from your exhibit with a good feeling about stopping by. This has the same effect as a fine restaurant giving you a mint after your meal. You leave the restaurant with a good taste in you mouth.

As a bonus, you'll be able to follow up after the show, asking them how they're using your parting gift.

➤ How to Move Visitors Along

Getting rid of visitors is just as important as attracting them. Calculate how much you have paid for each minute that the show is open. This will show you how much it costs you to spend time with the wrong person.

If you spend too much time with a visitor, you're wasting money and missing opportunities to meet and qualify others. It's not rude to disconnect and move on to another visitor.

Shake hands and say, "Thanks for stopping by." Or give the visitor a piece of your literature and say, "Why not take this with you. We'll call you next week." Think of other ways you can move your visitor along, and have them practiced and ready.

When you've completed the sales process, move the visitor out of your exhibit. This is just as important as attracting the visitor. Guests who overstay their welcome cost you money. Use their body language to let you know what they have in mind.

When it's time to move them on, offer your hand and say, "Please feel free to look around the rest of the exhibit," if your exhibit is big enough.

Otherwise say, "Thanks for stopping by. I hope you enjoy the rest of the show."

➤ Dealing with Your Competition

Count on it: Your competitors will be at the show. Probably as fellow exhibitors; if not, at least as visitors.

A guerrilla always treats the competition with respect and dignity. It's an amazingly small world. Your competitor's salespeople might be working for you next year (or you might be working for them). We've seen tooth and nail competitors merge companies, and the most combatant participants on both sides lose out. Compete in front of your customer, but work together to increase the size of the market.[1]

If your competition is abusive, we suggest that you meet after the show to discuss how you could work together. Oftentimes you'll find that there is a history of personal conflict that prevents the relationship from being one of friendly competition.

---

[1] For an outstanding discussion of how to understand and effectively work with your competition, call Billie Lee and Company (1-800-468-1110) and order their *Get Savvy: Success Skills for the 90s* audiotape.

We feel that competition is healthy. You'll come out on top when you supply your customers with what they want, not by attacking the competition. At trade shows, visitors want to find out how you can help them. If you follow the advice of this book, you'll do substantially better than your competition at your next trade show.

Often your competition will borrow a badge to visit your exhibit incognito. If you don't know who your competitors are, what their people look like, who sells their products, and what questions they're dying to answer, you're a sitting duck.

Your exhibit staff needs to know who your competition is. If they sell through other companies, they need to know which ones. Your staff needs to be alert to probing questions that your competition may ask.

This doesn't mean you should be paranoid when visitors ask probing questions. If they are serious buyers, they *should* ask probing questions. Just know who you're talking to and why they're asking the questions. Have them sign a nondisclosure agreement if necessary.

We saw a company president extensively discuss the intricate details of a new product with the key designer for his competition before an officer of the company finally ended the conversation.

The president had no idea that the man who was so interested in what he created was from the competition. He virtually gave away the store, seriously damaging his firm's competitive advantage, since the competition knew, at product introduction, how to sell against the new product.

An effective guerrilla tactic is to send one of your team out on the floor armed with a telephoto lens to shoot close-ups of the competitors' exhibit staff from a discreet distance. Have the film developed at a quick-print shop, and make a set of *Wanted* posters for your staff.[2]

---

[2] Kodak makes a line of digital cameras ideal for this purpose. You can load the images right into a computer and enlarge, crop, and print them on the spot. Call 1-800-23KODAK for a free brochure.

➤ Dealing with Magazine Editors

Magazine editors roam industry trade shows. Knowing how to work with editors can make a lot of difference in your media coverage.

> ➤ *Nothing you say is ever "off the record"—so don't say anything to an editor you wouldn't want to see in print.* Refer questions on topics that you don't feel comfortable answering to the right person in your company. Remember, editors are professional brain-pickers. If you're willing to give them juicy copy, they'll print it.

> ➤ *Prepare for the interview.* If an interview is arranged, try to get the questions ahead of time, if possible. If an editor asks you for a comment, don't just start answering questions. Ask for the topic, intent (is it for an article on your company or for a competitor), publication date, and a list of questions. Then say you'll be in touch. No matter how urgent the editor says the interview is, any editor worth talking to can wait an hour for your well-thought-out replies.

> ➤ *Let your marketing department know when you talk to an editor.* You have little control over what magazines print, so you must manage what information is given to the press.

> ➤ *Don't compromise yourself or your company.* If you feel that you'll be misquoted or misunderstood, stop talking until the situation is cleared up. A follow-up correction is never given the same emphasis as the original story.

> ➤ *Know what you can and can't talk about.* Refer to the list of topics that may cause trouble in Chapter 8. There are very good reasons for not giving out this information.

> ➤ *Don't expect to clear a story before it's published.* Except for articles you write, you won't get a second look. Make sure you think carefully about what you say, say it clearly, and make sure the editor understands you.

➤ Twelve Ways to Deal with Angry Visitors

You might have angry visitors stop for a variety of reasons. Some people may have had a bad experience in the past with you, your company, or with what you sell. Others may have heard bad things about you. Some people may object to what you sell based on their belief system. And there are a few people who want to pick fights and you have been selected as their next victim.

Beware of competition that attempts to sabotage your sales by provoking your exhibit staff. We've seen exhibitors so steamed about what their competition is doing that they forgot why they came to the show.

Watch Wednesdays! People tend to be easier to provoke on this, the furthest day from the stress-relieving weekend. Be aware of your reaction to Wednesdays, and understand that others will be more likely to get angry, too.

Here are 12 ways to deal quickly and effectively with angry visitors:

1. *Listen carefully.* Immediately begin taking notes. Taking notes shows the visitor you're willing to listen and trying to resolve the problem—whether you actually can or not.

2. *Assume nothing.* Behave as if you are completely ignorant about the situation. Sometimes your knowledge and your visitor's knowledge about the same thing are different. Allow for that difference. Say, "I want to understand the problem from your viewpoint. Let's start at the beginning, and tell me what happened." Ask questions to clarify points you don't understand.

3. *Stay positive.* Don't respond negatively to emotional language. A visitor's anger usually isn't personal.

4. *Empathize.* Do your best to understand your visitors' feelings.

5. *Agree to agree.* Make a commitment to work toward an agreeable solution. Say, "I'm sure we can work something out here."

6. *Ask for suggestions.* If your visitor continues to complain, ask, "What would you like for us to do?" This moves them to consider a resolution of the issue. Don't say, "What do you want me to do about it?" That sounds like you don't care.

7. *Adopt their point of view.* Listen to what your visitor says, even though you might not agree with it. This isn't the time to get into an argument. Who's right or wrong isn't the point. Other visitors assume the angry visitor is right, and they're watching to see how you might handle them if they were mad.

8. *Never dextify.* Do not attempt to *de*fend, *ex*plain, or jus*tify* what has happened. People don't want to hear you defend yourself. They want to be heard and to have their feelings recognized and acknowledged, even if you think they are wrong and crazy.

9. *Never say "I'm sorry."* Don't apologize until the visitor is prepared to accept your apology. Then say, "I apologize." "I'm sorry" is what you say when you bump into someone.

10. *Work toward solutions.* Focus on what you *can* do. If the visitor asks for something impossible, instead of saying, "I can't do that," make a counteroffer: "I understand your request. What I *can* do is . . .".

11. *Offer hospitality.* If you can't calm a visitor immediately, invite them to join you for a cup of coffee or a soft drink to get them out of your exhibit. You don't want their anger to influence your other visitors or your exhibit staff.

12. *Let go of your anger.* If you hang on to the smallest bit of anger, you'll immediately have an impact on the next visitor you meet, possibly causing you to blow the sale. Most visitors don't care what just happened to you, so don't pass along the bad experience.

Calm yourself rapidly after encountering an angry visitor. Here's how—take four quick deep breaths, flooding your brain with oxygen. Next, inhale while you count slowly to seven, and then exhale while you continue the count to 15. Anger changes your breathing pattern, and this exercise resets it to normal breathing.

Real-Life Success Story

One of the authors stopped late at night at a restaurant for a quick meal before facing a two-hour drive. While enjoying his sandwich, a man who appeared drunk came into the restaurant. He sat, ordered a cup of coffee, and began to harass the customers. The waitress warned him to stop and then finally physically threw him out of the restaurant while the author was standing at the counter, waiting to pay.

The instant that she had finished with that piece of dirty work, she turned to the author, smiled sweetly, and, with no trace of anger or resentment, said, "Did you enjoy your meal?" The author was truly surprised at her ability to let go of the situation immediately and insulate him from the experience he had just witnessed.

Can you let go of your anger and resentment instantly after dealing with an angry visitor or your competition?

➤ Dealing with Abusive Visitors

If your visitor is abusive, quietly ask the person to leave the exhibit. The team leader should immediately come over to manage the situation. If a visitor continues to be abusive, immediately contact show management and security. Never let your exhibit staff become involved in a physical altercation at the show.

You may have visitors who will use foul language and four-letter words in their conversation. Don't fall into the trap of using the same language yourself to gain rapport. It's easy to do, especially when others are doing it and you sometimes express yourself that way. Other visitors will overhear the conversation, and you will alienate them and drive them away.

➤ Know When to Call It Quits

Sometimes you have to know when to call it quits at a trade show. A saleswoman for the Denver Home Decorating Show said, "Many people exhibiting are strong on the front end and weak on the back end. We know a man who builds espresso carts. If he gets more than ten orders, it will kill him. So when he accepts ten orders, he has to put up a sign that says SOLD OUT."

Know your production or service limits, and be prepared to hang up a SOLD OUT sign on your exhibit. It's better to quit while you're ahead and satisfy the customers you can serve than to overcommit and make everyone mad! You'll be the talk of the show, and you can come back next year, ready to do expanded business—if you want to.

Chapter

Inside Secrets Trade Show Pros Know and Use

Lots of things can go wrong at a show. This chapter outlines strategies and resources so you can cope with the unexpected and keep a minor snafu from becoming a major disaster.

■ TRAVEL HELP

Here are seven sources of help when travel trouble strikes.

1. Ask for your travel agent's toll-free number for making itinerary changes or seeking alternative routes during travel delays. Ask if there is an emergency after-hours service available.

2. Check the back of your credit card for the toll-free number. Most executive credit cards, such as American Express and Diners Club, offer emergency help services, including cash advances, travel arrangements, and medical referrals.

3. The Aviation Consumer Action Project (ACAP) offers a booklet called "Facts and Advice for Airline Passengers," with information on lost luggage compensation, canceled flights, and filing complaints.[1]

---

[1] Write ACAP, PO Box 19029, Washington, DC 20036.

4. The Air Transport Association (ATA) offers free brochures, including *Air Travel for the Handicapped, Think Before You Pack,* and *How Safe is Flying?*[2]

5. The Centers for Disease Control's International Traveler's Hot Line provides medical information for foreign destinations, including eating precautions and immunization requirements.[3]

6. The Department of State's Citizens' Emergency Center offers advisories and updates from U.S. embassies on travel conditions in foreign countries.[4]

7. If you need anything, and we mean anything *legal,* call LesConcierges. For a modest fee, this company will track down equipment, entertainment, show tickets, travel, lodging, gifts, and hard-to-find items. This is a guerrilla firm that offers truly amazing service.[5]

➤ Surviving on the Road

Dress in business attire for your flights—We have found that the airlines treat well-dressed passengers more favorably and tend to overlook excess baggage.

Find out who your seatmate is—More than one deal has been closed on the flight to the show.

Don't discuss proprietary information on the flight—Your competition or people friendly to your competition may be sitting within earshot. During one flight, a guerrilla noticed that his competitor's sales manager was sitting one row back. By leaning his seat back and

---

[2] Write ATA, Public Relations, 1301 Pennsylvania Ave. NW, Washington, DC 20004.

[3] Call The Centers for Disease Control's International Traveler's Hot Line at 1-404-332-4559.

[4] Call The Department of State's Citizens' Emergency Center at 1-202-647-5225.

[5] Call LesConcierges at 1-800-362-5500.

pretending to snooze, he learned all about a new product launch as the manager and sales rep naïvely chatted away.

Eat before the flight—Many airlines don't offer meal service. The last thing you want is to arrive hungry, tired, and burnt out.

Beat jet lag by drinking water, and lots of it—This is not the time for a cocktail.

Reset your watch to local time—You'll avoid the risk of missing appointments.

➤ Protecting Yourself from Crime

Portable computers are frequent targets of thieves worldwide. What would happen if your competition got hold of your customer database, internal documents, and memos? Are the files password-protected? Encrypted? Backed up? And did you pack the backup disks in your suitcase or in the carry-on bag with the computer? Guard it at the exhibit, and keep it out of sight in your hotel room.

Be especially careful at airports. In a widespread airport hustle, a thief cuts in front of you just after you've placed your computer bag on the X-ray machine belt. The thief purposely sets off the metal detector. While the thief fumbles around with pockets full of coins and keys, your computer rides through the X-ray machine, where an accomplice makes off with it before you ever get through security.

The solution to this is to empty your pockets of metal, remove your belt, and place all these items in your briefcase. Wait until it's your turn before putting your computer on the X-ray belt, and make an "Excuse me!" fuss if someone steps in front of you. You'll pass right through the metal detector before your computer gets through the X-ray. Or have a colleague clear the metal detector first and then catch all the bags as they exit the conveyor.

Avoid packing your laptop in one of the fancy purpose-made bags that screams "Steal me!" Carry it in a battered carry-on or even a Jet Pac envelope to divert attention.

Ship your valuable equipment and samples in lockable containers. Or hand-carry them.

When shipping boxes, mark the outside with your name and address and a box number. Labeling the contents of the box is an invitation to a thief. Guerrillas have been known to *mis*label boxes to discourage thefts. Use an inventory sheet listing the contents of each box.

Watch your product samples carefully. Unscrupulous competitors could ruin your show if they steal them. You are most susceptible to this kind of sabotage during move-in, move-out, and after hours. Lock your samples away if your exhibit has locking drawers. Ask show management if an overnight safe storage area is available. Take your valuables with you at night, or hire a security guard or off-duty police officer.

Guard your personal belongings, purses, and briefcases. Most exhibitors just stash them under a table or behind the exhibit. It's too easy for them to be taken while your attention is diverted. One method is to hide belongings in an empty box, close it up, and put it under a skirted table. Or use a length of security cable and combination lock to chain them to a fixture. Give the show team the combination.

Your name badge marks you as a target for muggers. Take it off the instant you leave the show floor.

Be a little paranoid when visiting a convention town. Use your own good judgment about where and when to walk.

If your wallet is lost or stolen, your credit cards can allow the thieves to instantly open other credit lines. Immediately notify the credit bureaus, and they'll call you before approving any new accounts in your name.[6]

Know how to contact your fellow travelers at all times. Have a standard way to leave messages in case of travel problems. For example, have an executive assistant be the message-clearing house, or perhaps have a spouse at home field messages after hours. This will prevent problems when planes are delayed or traffic is going slow.

---

[6] Contact Equifax (1-800-685-1111), TransUnion (1-312-408-1050), and TRW (1-800-392-1122) for details.

■ ADJUSTING INSTANTLY TO PROBLEMS THAT ARISE

Meet the vendors in adjacent exhibits. You'll be staring them in the eye for the next several days. They can help you in the event you've forgotten something or they can watch your exhibit if you have to dash off to the bathroom. Who knows? They might need your product, or they might buy you a drink at the end of the show.

When problems arise, take a positive attitude on the outcome. At trade shows, expect the best, and you'll get the best. Expect the worst, and you won't believe how bad it can get. Here's a checklist to use when problems arise.

1. *Assess the problem.* What exactly isn't going right?

2. *Determine the impact on the success of your show.* Is this a show-stopper or an inconvenience? (By the way, the only real show-stopper is loss of your exhibit staff. You can improvise everything else and still make lots of sales. We've seen improvised exhibits with excited staff outpull gorgeous exhibits with lazy staff.)

3. *Look for alternate ways to get the problem solved.* Solutions range from doing nothing to taking everything down and leaving. Keep in mind that the only people who know when you don't do something, such as a fancy demo, are your exhibit staff, unless you've done a promotion that brings people to your exhibit for that, specifically.

4. *Decide exactly what you want to have happen.* Write down a list of events or steps you need to get the problem resolved.

5. *Decide to whom you can assign this list of tasks so you can move on to other things that have to be done before the show opens.* Your master show guide should be invaluable, since you've already located alternate vendors and sources of help before you left for the show.

6. *Don't complain.* Your visitors don't care about your problem. All they want to know is how you'll solve their problem.

7. *Learn what you can do to prevent this problem from arising next time.* Add your wisdom to your master show guide.

A small local antique show was scheduled in August at a large hotel. The exhibition producer didn't have extensive experience at producing shows and left an important clause out of the hotel contract (no meeting-room substitutions allowed). The hotel got a better offer and moved the show out into the parking lot under a big tent.

In the 110° heat, valuable antique wax dolls began to melt and disfigure. One savvy exhibitor foresaw the problem, called the closest rental company and ordered an air conditioner for immediate delivery. This exhibitor placed the wax dolls in the cold air stream and salvaged both the show and the valuable inventory of antiques.

Chapter

How to Make Your Show Really Pay Off Big

Trade shows will get the people to you so you can meet them. But it's up to you to complete the process and close the sale. You'll generally close most of your business after the show is over. Guerrilla trade show selling is getting agreement on the next step—scheduling a sales call, demonstration, or evaluation; sending literature; or writing a proposal.

Your visitors won't always remember your impressive exhibit—there's too much going on at the show. It's the after-show follow-up that makes a lasting impression. They'll certainly forget you if you send them photocopies of your data sheet, compared with the four-color data sheet of your competitor. When you follow up, you'll close sales and be way ahead of many exhibitors.

In this chapter, you'll learn the magic five-step sequence that turns your leads to sales, six guerrilla ways to get visitors to open your information package, and how to make money from your trade show leads. You'll also learn the five reasons why most companies waste their leads, how to avoid these pitfalls, and why proper lead management is your best investment.

➤ Why Trade Show Leads Are Hot

Your trade show leads are very different from any other lead you'll get. If you're like many salespeople, you get most of your leads from advertising. Prospects call or write for information, or they send in a literature-request card. They might pick up the phone and call, or they could just show up at your showroom. Beyond reading, seeing, or listening to your ad, these people don't know much about you, and you know nothing about them. So with leads from these sources, you have to educate them, qualify them, and move them into the sales process. You must make a number of favorable impressions in order to build their confidence in you.

An impression is anything that makes your prospect think about your company. This could be advertising, mail, your business card, or a sales call. Remember, only four percent of all sales are made after the first call. Eighty percent of sales are made after the *eighth* call. You've got to commit to a long-term investment in those leads if you want to make them pay! It takes an average of *nine* impressions to move your prospects from total apathy to purchase readiness, the point at which they are psychologically ready to buy. How fast you follow up definitely makes an impression.

Trade show leads, on the other hand, are much better. Surveys done by the Center for Exhibition Industry Research indicate that it will take less than one sales call on average to close the business!

Four Reasons Why Trade Show Leads Are Hot

1. Prospects from trade shows are better buyers. They are smarter than most prospects you'll meet. Since they, and their companies, are willing to spend money and time to go to the show, they tend to be more familiar with the industry. They know what they want, so offer it to them in terms they understand and they'll buy if they're ready.

2. Trade show prospects are much more receptive to your offers. You or a member of your company has had a chance to build a face-to-face, person-to-person relationship with them. They walked into your exhibit by

choice, interested in what you had to offer. When they met with you, they were probably in a receptive frame of mind. This gives you an enormous advantage over the competitor who must start the sales cycle from square one.

3. Trade show prospects already have some degree of trust in your company. After all, you made the commitment to be at the show. They were able to compare you with the competition and see firsthand what your company offers.

4. Trade show prospects in general are ready to buy. A recent study released by Continental Exhibitions found that trade show visitors outspend those who stay at home by substantial amounts, thousands of percent more in some industries.

All four of these factors mean that your trade show leads are more valuable than any other lead you have. And a lead follow-up system lets you capitalize on them.

■ SO WHAT DO WE DO WITH ALL THESE LEADS?

So, what will be your follow-up program? What sequence of events will the trade show lead trigger? What series of letters, cards, phone calls, and sales calls will your visitor receive? The leads you've collected at your show are valuable, and you've paid a lot to get them. Stop now and calculate what you're paying for each lead at the show. Take your show budget and throw in what it's costing you for your exhibit staff and what it will cost for you to complete the sales process for each lead you take at the show. Divide that by the number of qualified leads you collected. That's your cost per lead. You'll find the cost ranges from $50 to $300 per qualified lead.

Most organizations will take their very expensive lead and spend just a few dollars sending out literature, and that's it! This view of lead management is narrow-minded and extremely wasteful. If that's all you'll do with your leads, stay home and take very good care of the customers you already have.

➤ Effective Lead Management

Most companies miss incredible opportunities with their leads. Studies show that 80 percent of exhibitors do not follow up on their leads from trade shows.[1] According to a survey conducted by the University of Massachusetts Center for Marketing Communications, 43 percent of prospective buyers receive material they request after they have already made a buying decision. Another 18 percent never receive the material *at all*. Unfortunately, the longer you wait, the less likely you are to close (see Figure 11.1).

The good news is that just five simple steps turn your trade show leads into sales. No doubt, you're doing one of two of these steps now, but do the rest, and you'll clobber your competition.

Most of the sales leads generated by trade shows are never adequately followed up, and there are five perfectly good reasons why:

The Surge Overloads the Capacity

At one show, a company may get as many leads as they'll typically get in a month, maybe even a quarter. There are just too many leads to handle promptly. And the one poor person in data processing who is responsible for entering the information gets overloaded.

The surge overwhelms other departments, too. They may not have enough demo units, samples, or literature. Making

---

[1] *How to Improve Your Sales Success at Trade Shows,* a Center for Exhibition Industry Research publication.

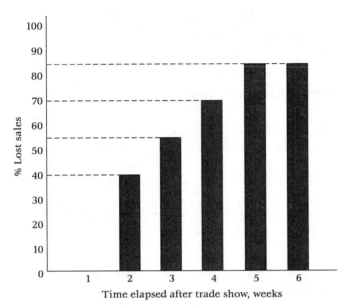

FIGURE 11.1 Lost sales opportunity. SOURCE: Express Lead Response, LLC, 39159 Paseo Padre Pkwy., Suite 252, Fremont, CA 94538, 1-800-644-1116, sales@elr.com, http://www.elr.com.

sure you have adequate supplies should be part of your success checklist.

Poor-Quality Leads Cause the Sales Force to Ignore the Lot

If your salespeople call on ten leads from the show and they're all dead ends, they'll dump the rest into a bottom drawer.

Some companies measure their show success by the number of leads taken. When the people on the exhibit staff know this, they take unqualified leads just to boost the numbers. Their behavior would be different if they knew they'd have to follow up.

Use self-selecting contests and promotional items to guarantee top-quality leads as discussed in Chapter 4. Train your exhibit staff to qualify buyers and record information on the lead forms that will move the sale to a close.

Dealing with the Aftershow Backlog

When your people return home, there's all the things that were postponed while getting ready for the show and all the things that stacked up while they were at the show. They feel overwhelmed and focus on daily activities to avoid the show follow-up.

Schedule time after the show to follow up, refusing to let other activities degrade your show investment.

No Follow-Up Budget

Companies routinely spend $50 on advertising to acquire a sales lead, then are loath to spend $5 following it up. Put your money where your leads are. When budgeting for a show, put as much money into postshow follow-up as you did into preshow promotion.

No One Was Accountable

Someone had to be responsible for getting the show up, breaking it down, and shipping it back, but no one has responsibility to make the show pay off. Assign a designated guerrilla who has cradle-to-grave responsibility for the show and accountability for sales results after the show is over.

➤ Follow-Up Planning

You've already spent a bunch of money to get their attention and interest. Now, what will you do to get them to buy? And just as you scheduled time before the show for planning and preparation, reserve time immediately after the show to manage your new leads. As we have previously mentioned, a common excuse is that people are too busy catching up after the show to do anything with the leads. It's your company's responsibility to keep the promises your exhibit staff made to visitors. Send visitors what you promised, when you promised. Call them. Visit them. Don't ignore them! Follow up your hot leads within two or three days, and tend to the rest within a week.

Once you have a lead, spend what you need to develop that person into a customer. Never skimp on your follow-up program. At least one-third of your trade show budget and staffing should be assigned to follow-up sales activity for after the show.

A computerized follow-up system lets you get the most out of your trade show leads. A good follow-up system provides reports that measure the effectiveness of the show and lets you target which shows to continue and which shows to rethink.

If you don't have a system to follow up trade show leads, purchase a software package designed specifically for contact management, forecasting, and follow-up (like ACT!, Sales Maximizer, or GoldMine), or consider creating an in-house department, or use an outside lead-management service.[2]

➤ Sort Leads for the Winners

During the show, review and code your leads for *when* the prospect plans to buy and their long-term potential. You can code them 1, 2, 3 or A, B, C; it doesn't make any difference. Your goal is to separate the hot and soon-hot leads from the literature collectors. Whatever coding system you've used, work first on the prospects who have the most immediate need.

---

[2] See Appendix for a listing of lead-management services.

➤ Process Leads Immediately

Next, get the information your exhibit staff promised to visitors and send the leads to the sales force as quickly as possible. If you have a small exhibit, get those leads off to the main office the same day, by courier, overnight mail, or enter them into a computer and have them transmitted to the office via modem or E-mail.

If you're expecting lots of visitors, consider hiring local help to enter the lead data into a portable computer on the spot. This means the leads will be ready for you when you are ready for them!

Card Scanners

Business-card scanners can help you increase your productivity in entering address data. These devices use optical character recognition software to read the information on the card and process it into data that can then be sent to a database or other application. We recommend doing the card scanning after the show or off-site instead of having the equipment where visitors can see it. Your company should be the star of the show, not the scanner. See the Appendix for a listing of card-scanning systems.

Send an Overview

If your information packages are expensive, you may prefer to send out an overview piece instead. Send a note to your contact that says it was nice meeting at the show and that someone will be following up shortly. Have your salesperson make the contact personally, and leave literature or samples as necessary.

If you are overloaded and can't respond quickly, at least send a postcard that reads, "We were overwhelmed! You will receive the material you requested at the show in two weeks. If you have a more immediate need, call Christina at 800. . . ."

Get help! Hire temporary staff to enter the data and stuff the follow-up packages. Or consider using a lead management or fulfillment company to help.[3] These companies stock your literature and samples. You just send them the leads, and they'll send out what's requested and will even follow up with a phone call. For a price they can work with you to manage your leads efficiently.

➤ Your Sales Letter

Have your troops poised for a quick aftershow attack by having literature packages preassembled and sales letters prewritten, preferably by a professional direct-mail copywriter.[4] Since your letter is the next sales contact you'll make, it needs to work hard, moving your prospective customer to make the next step. You'll be better off when you pay your copywriter and printer more than you pay the post office. Take a close look at your investment in the sales collateral. It's key to completing the sales process you started at the show. You'll probably spend thousands on literature, printing, postage, and assembly, so invest in help from a specialist. Ideally, your aftershow letter should be personalized, at least with the person's name, and, better yet, a reminder of what the prospect was interested in and why.

There are four types of letters you can send to your visitor: a form letter, a personalized letter, a customized letter, and an individually written letter.

Form letters open with "Dear friend" or some such bland and impersonal greeting. Most of the time, they are printed on company letterhead, although sometimes you see photocopies on cheap paper.

Personalized letters have the recipient's name in the greeting. This is the minimum acceptable letter that we recom-

---

[3] Call Inquiry Handling Service Inc. (1-800-847-5323) and ask for their free newsletter.

[4] Call David Garfinkle, coauthor of *Guerrilla Direct Mail*, at Overnight Marketing (1-415-564-4475).

mend for a trade show. Personalization is well worth the extra expense, and it gives an image that your company is one with the personal touch. You can do a mail merge with a laser printer, creating personalized letters very inexpensively.

If you have the database to handle it, customize the letters. Customized letters are assembled from prewritten sentences and paragraphs that are selected depending on the information on the person in the database. This is a very effective way to have high impact, but it requires a well-designed database and a skilled letter writer.

Individually written letters should go to hot prospects and VIPs who visit your exhibit. Take the time to write or dictate a letter to these people. Have the letter remind them of what they saw and the commitments they made at the show.

➤ Get Your Fulfillment Package Out Immediately

This greatly increases your odds of closing sales. Lead management consultant Mac McIntosh says, "If your literature is already on your prospects' desks when they get back from the show, they'll be very impressed with your service—impressed enough that they'll want to do business with you. You are showing your responsiveness. People perceive that you do business that way, and people like to do business with companies that are responsive. According to TARP, a government-funded study, when service is perceived to be immediate, 95 percent of customers will do business with you again."[5]

➤ The Five-Step Magic Sequence That Turns Leads into Sales

Recontact your visitors immediately. Immediate response to visitor requests gives you an edge over your competition.

---

[5] You can reach Mac at 1-800-944-5553.

1. *Your next contact with the visitor has to happen immediately.* You want the prospect to recall your at-show conversation. This substantially increases the likelihood of the literature package being opened. You could send a postcard, thank-you note, E-mail, or fax saying, "Thank you for stopping by to see us at the show. Expect your information package to arrive Tuesday. I'll call to make sure you have everything you want." One guerrilla sends a fax sequence starting with that message. Then, on the day the package is expected, she faxes, "You should be getting the information package you asked for today. I'll call you tomorrow."

2. *Send out the literature requested by a predictable carrier, such as UPS or Federal Express.* This way you will know when the package will arrive.

3. *Follow up with a phone call.* "Have you received the information you asked for? What did you like best about it? What should we do next?"

4. *Initiate a series of mailings.* If you featured a show special, send a sequence of offers with escalating urgency.

   First offer—"Here's a special offer . . ."

   Second offer—"Don't miss our special offer . . ."

   Third offer—"The deadline is near for the offer . . ."

   Fourth offer—"Act now or you'll miss out . . ."

   Guerrillas know that most business is won because the competition gave up.

5. *Mail to them forever.* Send anything that visitors would find valuable. Send media releases, articles, seminar schedules, case studies, newsletters, brochures, samples, trade show invitations, and special offers.

➤ Get Your Package Delivered

Keep your mailing list clean. Business mailing lists go bad at the rate of one percent per week. Half the people in our sales seminars have a business card that's different from the one they had a year before. People change jobs and companies. Request address correction by printing in the lower right-hand corner of the envelope *Address Correction Requested*. The post office will then send you address change information.

Send out postcards asking, "Do you still wish to be on our mailing list? Who else do you know who we should know about?"

Always use at least first class mail. While bulk-mail rates are attractive, they can be a kiss of death. There are three reasons why.

1. Some larger mailrooms refuse to accept bulk-mail items.

2. The post office doesn't consistently deliver bulk-rate mail in a timely fashion. There are lots of documented instances where it wasn't delivered at all.

3. Bulk rate sends a negative message to the receiver. "You're one of thousands who have gotten this piece."

Better still, send it by Priority Mail. You can use the U.S. Post Office's bright, colorful Priority Mail envelopes that clearly stand out in a stack of mail. At the time of this writing, it costs you $3.00 for postage, and the envelopes are free. Just order them in bulk from your local postal marketing center.

➤ Six Ways to Make Sure Your Information Package Gets Opened

1. *Sensitize your visitors to expect your mailing. Reader's Digest* sends out a postcard that says, "Watch the mail for your sweepstakes entry form." People only look at it for seconds, but that short impression increases response rates. Leave after-hours voicemail or send a fax announcing that the mailing is on its way. Have your exhibit staff promise exactly when the package will arrive.

Now, when the package shows up, your prospect recognizes it and perceives you as one who keeps promises—a trait not found enough in business.

2. *Prioritize the information.* Use Express Mail, Federal Express, UPS Red, Airborne, or other expediter to give your packet a feeling of urgency. Or send your packet by certified mail. For just an extra dollar you get that little green sticker attached to the package; the one that says, "Hey! This is an important document!" Someone will have to sign for it, which usually gets the package—unopened by the executive assistant— not just on the top of the mail, but on top of the buyer's desk. We would advise against using this tactic with consumers. If they have to run to the post office to sign for a certified letter and then find out it's literature, they're bound to feel frustrated.

3. *Personalize everything!* Today, people reject anything that is not perceived as personal communication. You probably sort your mail over the trash can. If it doesn't appear to be personal or important, you don't even open it.

No form letters! With computers and laser printers, there is no excuse for "Dear COMDEX visitor" form letters. Letter shops can help you if you're overloaded. Check the yellow pages of your phone book under the heading "Mailing Services."

Your sales letter is usually the first thing your visitor will see after the show. Don't be cheap. Most companies spend more on postage to deliver the information package than they do for the contents of the envelope. Sending photocopies of a form letter in your follow-up package won't make the strong impression you need.

Sign the letter in blue ink. Use a pen that is water-based, such as a Flair product. You want the signature to pass the smudge test. We've found that some people wet their finger and try to smudge the signature to see if it's real, a personal communication, or just a mass mailing.

Sign the letters in mass while watching TV. Or have staff members forge your signature, since your reader doesn't know what your signature really looks like. Just make sure that the signature your staff signs is similar to your personality. It wouldn't do for a flowery, high-school style signature to appear over a prestige-position title. Another option is to use a letter shop with bonded letter signers. These people are actually skilled forgers who, with your permission, will duplicate your handwriting and signature.

In longhand, write on the envelope, "Here's the information you requested."

4. *Surprise and delight your letter reader.* Send a gift, such as a companion premium to the one handed out at the show.

You can use stock cartoons,[6] or you can create custom cartoons around the theme of your exhibit (see Figure 11.2).[7] Since you have to run the envelope through the laser printer to address it anyway, it's easy to add the customized caption, merging the name from the database. These mail pieces get opened when slick, four-color pieces end up in the trash.

When your competition is sending out their stuff in an express envelope, you can stand out by sending a box. Or better still, send materials in unusual containers—boxes, tubes, Chinese food containers, and so on. Just make sure that the container is appropriate for what you sell and appropriate for your company image.

One guerrilla sent a box with a picture of a large aspirin tablet and the caption, "Headache Relief Kit." Inside were three different types of pain reliever and

---

[6] Available on CD-ROM from T/Maker (1-415-962-0195). Call for a free brochure.

[7] Contact Stu Heinecke, the creator of the cartoon (1-206-286-8668), and ask for a free brochure.

Mark S. A. Smith
3530 Cranswood Way
Colorado Springs, CO 80918

"Have you seen the latest issue of
the *Journal*? It's all *Mark Smith this* and
Mark Smith that, and nothing about *us!*"

FIGURE 11.2   A good example of personalization is this envelope.

the requested brochures. When this box arrived with all the other FedEx envelopes, it was opened first. When the follow-up call came, 100 percent of the prospects remembered getting the box, and 94 percent asked for a salesperson to call.

5. *Merchandise your mailings.*   Send special reports, flash bulletins, media releases, books, audiocassettes, CDs, videocassettes, CD-ROM, software, games, and gifts.

6. *Serialize your mailings.*   Send the information in a series over a period of time, such as newsletters, multipart training programs, and case studies.

➤ Call to Confirm Receipt

Within a day or two of the prospect's receipt of your packet, call and confirm, "Did you receive the material we sent you?" If no, offer to send another at once, or offer to fax the information immediately. If yes, ask, "Have you had a chance to look it over?" The likely response will be no. Then ask, "Well, then, how soon should I follow up," and schedule a *telephone appointment*. If the prospect has looked at the literature, simply ask, "Well, what do you think?" A certain percentage of your prospects will close *themselves* then and there. Others will ask questions before ordering. Still others will want you to make a face-to-face appointment. A few will decline, having decided that they don't have a need after all.

Check their buying temperature, and find out if the facts gathered at the show still stand. McIntosh points out, "Sometimes visitors tell you what they think you want to hear so they'll quickly get what they want. Or, they'll tell you they aren't that hot to keep you from 'attacking.' Based on what they've told you about their purchasing intentions, ask permission to call them back when they plan to buy to see if anything has changed. Tell them, 'We're ready when you're ready.' "

➤ Motivating Your Sales Force to Sell

You would think that your salespeople would be so cranked up after the show that they would just jump on all these new red-hot leads. Unfortunately, this isn't the case. They will be road-weary and peopled out and may not work as hard as usual. How can you ensure that your sales force follows up the leads? Have each salesperson fill out a call report tracking the ultimate outcome of every single lead. Did it result in an appointment? A presentation? What happened at the customer's location? For example, ask, did you meet the person who gave us the lead? Did you do the presentation to them and others? Did you do a quotation? Did you take an order? For how much? Did you leave a reason to come back? You will need this data to measure the effectiveness of the show, and what gets measured gets done.

A guerrilla management tactic is to *sell* the leads to your sales force. That's right: Charge your people for every lead you give them. For example, you may want to charge them $25 for each lead and then give them a rebate after they close so many sales.

You've paid a lot of money to get a name, qualify the prospect, send out literature, or have a salesperson visit.

Make all this investment pay off with continuous attention to—and improvement of—your lead management strategy.

➤ Keep in Touch

Set up and execute an automatic mailing cycle for your prospective customers. Send them your press releases, trade show invitations, brochures that they would find interesting, newsletters and bulletins, and special offers. McIntosh says, "Sending lots of stuff on a regular basis is better than sending a work of art once."

You need to be there when your prospective customer is ready to buy and automatic mailings are the least expensive way to keep in touch. Send customers your message in bite-size chunks, so that when they're ready to buy, you're the vendor of choice.

Continue to do this until they buy, die, or leave the industry, or it gets too expensive to keep them on your list. The modern wisdom is a prospect is a prospect for life unless they leave the industry or are no longer involved in the purchase of your product.

■ FOLLOW-UP STRATEGIES

Keep sending reminders to your visitors. You've invested a lot of money to meet them. You've had personal contact with them at the show, and you know something about them personally. Here's some follow-up strategies that you can use to increase your impact.

➤ Thank-You Notes

When you meet a particularly interesting person, hand write a follow-up note. Let your prospect know that more information will follow in the mail or that you'll be in touch soon.

The extra, personal contact that a note gives will take you miles ahead of your competition.

Use our THANKS approach—

T—Today!—Write your thank-you letter the same day, if at all possible, and get it in the mail. The only thing worse than receiving a late thank-you note is receiving none at all.

H—Handwritten—In today's world of word-processed everything, a handwritten note especially stands out in a stack of mail. It will probably be the first piece read.

A—Active—Make your note active. Don't start out, "Dear John"; say, "It was great, John, to meet with you today. I'm really looking forward to seeing you next week. Thank you for stopping by our exhibit. Sincerely, Mary."

N—Next Step—In the previous example, the note outlined what would happen next. Make sure your reader knows what to anticipate, what date to check, and when to expect action.

K—Keep It Short—You only need 25 to 50 words. A few sentences are enough to make the point and get the impact.

S—Specific—Be very specific on why you're writing the note. For example, "I kept thinking about what you need and I believe I have an answer. I'll call you Monday with my idea." You can be certain that your call will be taken.

➤ **Audiotapes**

Record an aftershow program reviewing the show and the hot ideas that came up, both from the competition and from your customers. Record it with your own tape recorder, and get a local company to duplicate them (look in the phonebook Yellow Pages under the headings "Audio Duplication" or

"Audio Production"). Use a typed-look label, and, in the cover letter, tell your visitor that you wanted to rush this out while the information was still hot, so you didn't have time to print your regular labels.

➤ Videotapes

You can get great looking videotapes produced for less money today than ever before. Reasonable-quality, low-cost production systems are available everywhere. Video production equipment, like the Video Toaster, provides effects that at one time required $250,000 machines. Now you can get these same effects at a fraction of the price. You can put together a great aftershow videotape for a few thousand dollars and make copies for several dollars each, and you'll have a promotion piece that gets passed around and shown in meetings.

➤ Newsletters

Newsletters are the cheapest way to reach people on a regular basis. One of the authors was once responsible for a monthly four-page two-color newsletter (circulation 28,000) that was 60 percent must-read industry news and educational columns and 40 percent sales. This newsletter generated 80 percent of the in-bound telephone calls to the sales department.[8]

➤ Fax on Demand

FOD (Fax on Demand) is an even stronger promotion medium. This is a system that lets your visitor dial into your computer for more information, 24 hours a day. Statistics on

---

[8] For information on creating your own in-house newsletter, contact Bob Kelly of Kelly Communications, Inc., 1-303-681-2123.

FOD close rates are stunning, with some companies reporting a 40 percent close-to-inquiry ratio.[9]

➤ Software and Computer Programs

If your customers are computer-literate, think about creating a demonstration disk for their computers, or a computer-based catalog and price list. This works very well when people who buy what you sell like computers. Most people who are computer enthusiasts can't resist popping a new disk into their machine and satisfying their curiosity.

ComputersAmerica, a microcomputer products distributor in northern California, provides the entire company catalog on disk to its customers. To place an order, customers simply select the items they want on-screen, and the system dials into headquarters and places the order while simultaneously updating the customers' online catalog.

➤ Four Ways to Follow Up by Phone

Just pick up the phone and call. Let your prospect know you're calling based on your meeting with them at the trade show. You know, the only follow-up calls we usually get from the trade show are from vacuum-cleaner salespeople. So we've used this line successfully: "Hello, this is Susanna Smith with The Guerrilla Group. We met at the trade show. I'll bet the only follow-up call you were expecting was the one from the vacuum-cleaner salesman." This almost always gets a laugh and positions us immediately in the prospect's mind against the rest of the competition.

---

[9] If you would like to try a FOD system and get free information on systems available, call Dan Poynter's system at Para Publishing. Dial 1-805-968-8947 from a phone handset that is attached to a fax machine and follow the voice prompts.

When your call is answered by a gatekeeper, such as a secretary, assistant, or spouse, get this person involved in the process. Say something like this: "We met at the show, and he asked me to call and follow up on our conversation. When is the best time for me to reach him when we could speak for about 15 minutes?"

If the contact isn't currently available, schedule a telephone appointment.

If you get an answering machine or voicemail, leave a message that makes the prospect want to get back to you. For example, say, "Hello, this is Harrison Smith with The Guerrilla Group. I'm glad you stopped by our exhibit at the trade show, and I'm following up like you requested. Unfortunately, the notes from the show are kind of sketchy. All I need is a minute to get the information you requested off to you. Call me at . . ."

If you offer a premium or giveaway, say something like, "As soon as we speak, we can drop your gift into the mail."

Remember to always leave your phone number, even if you think your contact has it. The person getting the message could be away from the office, and may not be able to call you back unless your number is available.

If you have the fax number or E-mail address of your visitor, use this to follow up. So few companies are using these communications tools, you'll cut right through.

What if the person isn't interested? Salvage the call by asking for a referral. You have a five-times better chance of closing paid-on business from a referral than from any other lead from any other source. Many times, prospects who turn you down flat will give you excellent referrals. Ask, "We understand that this offer isn't right for you. But I was wondering if you would do me a favor. Who do you know that would be interested?" After the contact gives you a name and phone number, ask, "Why do you think this person would be interested?" Then call the referral. Say, "I was just speaking to John, and he suggested that I speak with you. Why do you think he suggested your name?" Now you have a way to find out if the referral needs what you sell.

➤ On-Site Sales Calls after a Show

Your prospects will really appreciate that you respect their time and keep your promises, so do everything possible to prepare yourself for the presentation meeting. Recruit the person who initially visited you as the champion. Do your homework and let this person help you get ready for the visit.

If you're preparing for an on-site meeting, fax the written agenda to your prospect in advance. Include details on who you would like to be there, why, and what will be covered. Bring along a copy of the agenda. This lets everyone know what's going on and why you're there, and it makes sure that you deliver what they want.

When you get to the meeting, know why each person is attending and what you can do to meet each of their needs. One of our favorite questions is, "What is your motivation for coming to this meeting? What do you want to get out of this discussion?" This will allow you to make adjustments to your agenda if necessary.

One of the most powerful ways to open an aftershow sales call is to let members of the prospect's team who were at the show give a short presentation on what they saw. This gives them a chance to be the expert and the hero in front of their coworkers. You'll win, because you have an ally on your side.

Do everything you can to make this person look good. Don't interrupt or correct minor inconsistencies. Just make a note of it and let the presenter know later. If there are major misunderstandings, it's appropriate to raise your hand and say, "I just want to make sure that everyone understands," and restate the information as clearly as possible.

During your meeting, if you hit the time limit, stop, and ask permission to continue. Say something like, "At the beginning of the meeting, we agreed to end at 11:30. It's that time now. We can stop now, or, if you wish, we can continue for another 15 minutes. Which will it be?"

➤ Five Ways to Make Money from Your Trade Show Leads

1. *Sell the leads to your sales force.* We've discussed this option in a previous chapter. All you do is calculate your actual cost per lead by dividing the number of leads by the total cost of the show. Then, instead of just handing them out for free, say, "These leads have already cost us more than $20 each. We know that your closing ratio on trade show leads is 25 percent. We'll sell the leads to you at $25.00 each, and when you close a sale, we'll buy that lead back from you for $100, plus your regular commission." Buy the closed leads back at a premium that covers the cost of the leads they don't close. This increases the incentive to follow up the leads and gives you the incentive to make sure the leads are of the best possible quality.

2. *Sell the leads to others.* Find other companies that don't compete directly with you that sell to your prospects and customers, and sell them your leads. A list broker can help you with this process.

3. *Endorsed mailings.* Find someone who has influence with your prime prospects. Have this person write an endorsing cover letter for your sales materials to give them additional credibility and impact.

4. *Cross-sell other products and services.* What else can you offer your prospects? What else do they buy that you can supply?

5. *Upsell.* Offer the prospect a trade-in on old equipment with a generous allowance on the purchase of the next better model. Sell a higher level service contract.

How to Measure
Your Show Success

Depending on how many of the ideas and techniques you have put to work in this book, your trade show success will increase by 30 to 300 percent. That's measured in either sales volume or super-qualified leads, depending on how you use the show to grow your business. In this chapter, you'll learn how to measure this success, and duplicate it at will.

➤ Why Proper Lead Management Is Your Best Investment

The value of your business isn't your manufacturing ability, intellectual property, land, assets, or technology. It is the willingness of your customers to spend money with you time and again that keeps your company healthy. For example, Microsoft has a higher stock value than General Motors, and the reason is that 95 percent of the salespeople we've polled use Windows software. They willingly upgrade their software suite annually and individual applications quarterly. Microsoft's value is in the long-term, lifetime value of their customers.

Two good reasons to exhibit at trade shows are to build that customer base and to keep current customers loyal for life. If a customer requests information, materials, or a catalog, and you fail to respond, the customer will assume you don't really care about the business and will switch vendors. They may assume that you conduct *all* your business in such a shoddy fashion. That's why guerrillas must manage their leads.

➤ Calculate Your Customer's Lifetime Value

Think about your average customer. How much does he spend with you each time he buys? How often does he buy from you? How many years will he do business with you? Multiply out these numbers, and you'll know how much money the average customer will contribute to your business over his lifetime. This is the *lifetime value* (LTV). Another way to determine the LTV of a customer is to take your annual sales divided by the number of *active* accounts in Accounts Receivable and multiply by five.

$$\frac{\text{Sales}}{\text{Active accounts}} \times 5$$

For example, a gift boutique's corporate client purchases an average of $1,000 per quarter. Their average customer buys from them for five years. So the LTV is $1,000 × 4 × 5, or $20,000.

The true business value of that customer is even greater. If that boutique can get just one referral per year from that corporate client, the client will direct 5 × $20,000, or $100,000 worth, of additional business their way. Pretty amazing for a $1,000-a-quarter customer.

Your assignment is to research these numbers for your firm, calculate the LTV of your customers, and make sure everyone knows what the numbers are.

For example, a major hotel in Minneapolis housed the Warner Bros. film crew during the location shoot of the film *Grumpier Old Men*. The hotel management posted an internal memo at the front desk for all the staff that said, "This client is buying 3,830 room nights from us, worth over $250,000. Be nice."

➤ Calculate Your Return on Investment

As with any investment, knowing what kind of return your trade show effort is producing is critical to your management of resources. Total all the expenses associated with your show and divide this sum by the number of leads you brought back. This could work out to anywhere from several dollars to several thousand dollars per lead.

Now consider how much it will cost for you to manage that lead. Let's assume that you send a five-step mailing sequence after the show, and the first package goes out express. You make several follow-up phone calls. You put the prospect on your newsletter mailing list, and you invest in database management. Add up these costs. For most companies, the cost to thoroughly manage a lead is *less* than the cost of obtaining the lead.

Now divide the LTV by the cost to acquire and manage that lead multiplied by your closing ratio.

$$\text{Trade show ROI} = \frac{\% \text{ Close} \times \text{LTV}}{\$ \text{ Lead acquisition} + \$ \text{ Lead management}}$$

➤ Measure the Show Results

Review what you've accomplished for both completion and effectiveness. Did you get what you expected from this show? Did you get your target number of contacts, leads, and demonstrations done? How many new visitors did you get to know? How many sales have you closed from contacts at the show?

➤ Postshow Survey

Aftershow surveys can help you measure how well the show went for you and how well it attracted the buyers you wanted to reach. Six months after the show, select a cross section of the leads you gathered and call until you've talked to 100 visitors. Ask these questions:

"You stopped by our exhibit at the *x* show. Do you have a quick minute so we can find out how the show went for you? Have you bought yet?"

1. *If no:* "Are you still in the market?"
   A. *If yes:* "Would you like a salesperson to contact you?"
2. *If yes:* "From whom did you buy, and what did you buy?"
   A. *If they bought from a competitor:* "Because we want to serve our customers better, what was it that caused you to select them instead of us?"

Tabulate the results, and see how well you did and how well your competition did at the show. Use this information to decide whether to go back next year.

➤ Conduct a Mail Survey

1. *Decide upon the goal of the survey.* What outcome do you want? What do you want to improve? Do you want to improve exhibit appeal, appearance, attendance, participation, publicity? How will you know when this goal is achieved?
2. *Determine your budget for this survey.* Include tabulation and possible phone follow-up expenses.
3. *Based on your goal and budget, decide what you will do.* We recommend a one-page self-mailing return survey (with business reply postage-paid) that goes out in your company envelope with a message typed or stamped on the cover that says, "We really need your opinion." These are inexpensive to produce and easy for the respondent to complete and mail.

4. *Choose a premium to help boost returns.* Premiums that work well are drawings for merchandise or discount certificates for what you sell. One of our clients enclosed a dollar bill and a note that said, "We recognize your time is valuable. Would you please take a minute to complete the enclosed." The response rate was nearly 100 percent.

5. *Choose about five questions, depending on your goals.* Reinforce that the questionnaire is confidential and that no numbers will be reported individually. Include an optional blank for name and address. Consider number-coding the pieces for tracking.

Questions could include—

➤ What did you find most exciting about the show?

➤ Did you go to make a specific purchase decision?

➤ Did you make that decision yet?

➤ What other shows do you find worth your while to attend?

➤ What was your impression of our exhibit?

➤ What do you remember best about the exhibit?

➤ What could we do differently at the show to better serve you?

You can also ask respondents to rate your performance on a five-point scale ranging from "strongly disagree" to "strongly agree." Ask them to rate variables like—

➤ The sales staff was knowledgeable.

➤ Your exhibit was easy to find.

➤ I got the information I was looking for.

➤ I want to do business with your company.

If response is poor three weeks after the mailing, do a telephone follow-up and survey a sample on the phone.

➤ Plan for Next Year's Show

Review everything about this year's show. Decide what you did well and what you will do again, and consider what needs review and planning for next year.

With solid, defined results, a good lead-tracking program, and proper attention to the people you meet at your exhibit, you can determine the return on your trade show investment and budget for the right size exhibit at next year's show.

■ NOW, IT'S UP TO YOU

We've given you hundreds of ideas that you can use to increase your trade show sales substantially. But just knowing about these ideas won't do the job. Trade shows are a lot of work. And they can be incredibly rewarding when done right. So take the ideas that you believe will work for you and use them.

We're always looking for interesting and effective ideas for the next edition of this book and real-world success stories to include in our seminars. Please keep in touch and share your successes.

Bibliography

■ RECOMMENDED READING, LISTENING, AND VIEWING FOR GUERRILLAS

➤ Books

Abelson, Norman. *Trade Show Basics,* South Holland, IL: Commerce Communications, Inc., 1986.

Albrecht, Karl and Ron Zemke. *Service America!* Homewood, IL: Dow Jones-Irwin, 1985.

Alles. *Exhibitions: A Key to Effective Marketing.* London: Cassell, 1989.

Allwood, Montgomery. *Exhibition Planning and Design: A Guide for Exhibitors, Designers and Contractors.* London: B.T Batsford, Ltd., 1989.

Alt, M. B. and R. S. Miles. *The Design of Educational Exhibits,* 2d ed. Winchester, MA: Unwin Hyman, 1987.

ASAE. *Association Meeting Trends.* Washington, DC: American Society of Association Executives, 1-202-626-2723.

ASAE. *Making Your Convention More Effective.* Washington, DC: American Society of Association Executives, 1972, 1-202-626-2723.

ASAE. *Principles of Association Management,* 2d ed. Washington, DC: American Society of Association Executives, 1988, 1-202-626-2723.

Astroff, Abbey. *Convention Sales and Service.* 3d ed. New Jersey: Waterbury Press, 1991.

Axtell, Roger E. *Do's and Taboos Around the World,* 2d ed. New York, NY: John Wiley & Sons, 1990.

Axtell, Roger E. *Do's and Taboos of Hosting International Visitors.* New York, NY: John Wiley & Sons, 1990.

Axtell, Roger E. *The Do's and Taboos of International Trade.* New York, NY: John Wiley & Sons.

Bandler, Richard and John Grinder. *Reframing.* Boulder, CO: Real People Press, 1979.

Belasco, James A. *Teaching the Elephant to Dance.* New York: Crown, 1990.

Berne, Eric. *Games People Play.* New York: Ballantine, 1964.

Bettger, Frank. *How I Raised Myself From Failure To Success In Selling.* Engelwood Cliffs, NJ: Prentice Hall, 1975.

Blackwell, Turner, & Wolfe. *Fundamentals of Association Management: Conventions.* Washington DC: American Society of Association Executives, 1985.

Bly, Robert. *Recession-Proof Strategies: 14 Winning Methods To Sell Any Product Or Service in A Down Economy.* New Milford, NJ, 1-201-559-2277.

Booth, Emily. *Emily Booth's Goof Proof Truth For Boothing Success.* Woodland Hills, CA: Exhibit Builder Inc., 1990, 1-818-888-5288.

Cates, Bill. *Unlimited Referrals.* Wheaton, MD: Thunder Hill Press, 1996.

Cathcart, Jim. *Relationship Selling.* New York: Perigee Books, 1990.

CEIR. *Trade Show Bureau Research—Ten Years of TSB Reports in Ten Minutes.* Bethesda, MD: Center for Exhibition Industry Research, 1991, 1-301-907-7626.

CEIR. *Center for Exhibition Industry Research Publications Catalog.* Bethesda, MD: Center for Exhibition Industry Research, 1-301-907-7626. This catalog is published annually and distributed for free.

Chapman, Edward A. Jr. *Exhibit Marketing: A Survival Guide for Managers.* New York, NY: McGraw-Hill Publishing Co., 1987.

Christman, Christine. *The Complete Handbook of Profitable Trade Show Exhibiting.* West Nyack, NY: Prentice Hall, 1991.

Coleman, Lee, and Finkel. *Powerhouse Conferences: Eliminating Audience Boredom.* Educational Institute of American Hotel & Motel Association, 1991.

Communiqué Exhibitor Education Inc. *Exhibit Management.* Marco Island, FL, 1-813-394-3333. This series available in booklets, videos, and cassettes.

Confederation of German Trade Fair and Exhibition Industries. *Successful Participation in Trade Fairs.* AUMA, Lindenstrasse 8, D-5000 Köln 1, Germany. This publication is free.

Convention Liaison Council. *Convention Liaison Council Glossary.* Washington, DC, 1-202-626-2764.

Convention Liaison Council. *Convention Liaison Council Manual.* 4th ed. Washington, DC, 1-202-626-2764.

Covey, Stephen R. *The Seven Habits of Highly Effective People.* New York: Simon & Schuster, 1989.

Davidow, William H and Buro Uttal. *Total Customer Service: The Ultimate Weapon.* New York: Harper & Row, 1989.

Dotson. *Introduction to Meeting Management.* Professional Convention Management Association Publishers, 1-205-823-7262.

Ecroyd, Lawrence G. *Exposition Management.* Mississauga, Ontario: Canadian Association of Exposition Managers, 1989, 1-416-678-9377.

ED&PA. *International Standards for Exhibit Production,* parts 1 and 2. Milwaukee, WI: Exhibit Designers & Producers Association, 1-414-276-3372.

ED&PA. *Labor Relations Manual.* Milwaukee, WI: Exhibit Designers & Producers Association, 1-414-276-3372.

Exhibition Industry Federation. *UK Exhibition Industry: The Facts.* London, England, 044-81-878-9130.

Exhibitor Publications Inc. *Exhibit Management Annual Salary Survey.* Rochester, MN, 1-888-235-6155.

Exhibitor Publications Inc. *Exhibit Planning Guide.* Rochester, MN, 1-888-235-6155.

Exhibitor Publications Inc. *Handbook of Trade Show Marketing: A Compilation of Relevant Industry Articles and Case Studies.* Rochester, MN, 1989, 1-888-235-6155.

Exhibitor Publications Inc. *The Illustrated Buyers Guide: An Exhibitor's Guide to Trade Show Displays and Accessories.* Rochester, MN, 1-507-289-6556.

Fojtik, Carol A. and Michael S. Muribi. *Marketing by Exhibiting in the Global Market.* Lombard, IL: Expressions International, Inc., 1993, 1-708-495-8740.

Friedman, Susan. *Exhibiting At Trade Shows: Tips and Techniques for Success.* Los Altos, CA: Crisp Publications, Inc., 1992, 1-800-442-7477.

Gartrell, Richard. *Destination Marketing for Convention & Visitors Bureaus.* Kendall Hunt Publications, 1994.

Gerber, Michael E. *The E Myth.* Cambridge, MA: Ballinger, 1986.

Gilles, Jerry. *MoneyLove.* New York: Warner, 1978.

Girard, Joe and Stanley H. Brown. *How To Sell Anything To Anybody.* New York: Warner, 1977.

Gitomer, Jeffrey. *The Sales Bible.* New York: William Morrow, 1994.

Goldblatt, Dr. Joe Jeff. *Special Events: The Art & Science of Celebration.* Van Nostrand Reinhold, 1990.

Groome, James J. *How to Make the Perfect Hotel Deal.* Princeton, NJ: Groome Marketing Associates, 1992.

Groome, James J. *Marketing the Annual Convention.* Princeton, NJ: Groome Marketing Associates, 1989.

Groome, James J. *The Essentials of Meeting Management.* Englewood Cliffs, NJ: Prentice Hall, 1990.

HCEA. *Conventional Wisdom.* Atlanta, GA: Healthcare Convention & Exhibitors Association, 1987, 1-404-252-3663.

HCEA. *Guidelines for Healthcare Conventions.* Atlanta, GA: Healthcare Convention & Exhibitors Association, 1-404-252-3663.

Henderson, Richard L. *Voo Doo Economics of Public Assembly Facility.* Bethesda, MD: Center for Exhibition Industry Research, 1-301-907-7626.

Higgins, J. M. *The Trade Show Selling Guidebook.* Billings, MT: Lewis & Lewis Marketing Services, 1988, 1-213-758-8406.

Hornor, Jody. *Power Marketing for Small Business: How to Get Customers, Keep Customers and Increase Profits.* Pilot Hill, CA: Market Power, 1993, 1-916-933-4490.

Hoyle, Dorf, & Jones. *Management of Conventions and Groups.* Educational Institute of American Hotel & Motel Association, 1989.

Hutt, Michael D. *Business Marketing Management,* 4th ed. Troy, MO: Holt, Reinhart & Winston, 1992. See Chapter 16.

IAAM. *Convention Center/Exhibit Hall Survey.* Irving, TX: International Association of Auditorium Managers, 1-214-255-8020.

Iacocca, Lee with Sonny Kleinfield. *Lee Iacocca's Talking Straight.* New York: Bantam Books, 1988.

IAEM. *Checklist for Hall Contracts.* Indianapolis, IN: International Association for Exposition Management, 5001 L. B. J. Freeway, Suite 350, Dallas, TX 75244, 1-214-458-8002.

IAEM. *Exhibitor Handbook.* Indianapolis, IN: International Association for Exposition Management, 5001 L. B. J. Freeway, Suite 350, Dallas, TX 75244, 1-214-458-8002. This booklet describes various logistics requirements and display regulations.

IAEM. *Exhibitor Space Charges Survey Results.* Indianapolis, IN: International Association for Exposition Management, 1-214-458-8002.

IAEM. *Guidelines for Displays, Rules & Regulations.* Indianapolis, IN: International Association for Exposition Management, 1-214-458-8002.

IAEM. *Guidelines for Life/Safety in the Exposition Industry.* Indianapolis, IN: International Association for Exposition Management, 1-214-458-8002.

IAEM. *Guidelines for Writing Exhibitor Contracts and Exposition Rules.* Indianapolis, IN: International Association for Exposition Management, 1-214-458-8002.

IAEM. *Hotel/Client Agreement Guidelines and Information.* Indianapolis, IN: International Association for Exposition Management, 1-214-458-8002.

IAEM. *National Fairgrounds Facility Study.* Indianapolis, IN: International Association for Exposition Management, 1-214-458-8002.

IAPCO. *Planning for a Conference Hotel, and Planning a Conference Center.* Brussels, Belgium: International Association of Professional Congress Organizers.

International Trade Center. *Exhibition Stand Design.* 06.10, EXH-I.D.#ITC/004/C5/87-I, Palais des Nations, 1211 Geneva 10, Switzerland. Handbook on design and construction of stands for trade fairs and exhibitions with emphasis on national stands. Free to developing countries. UNCTAD/GATT.

ISMP. *Dictionary of Terms for Travel Agents & Meeting Planners.* Scottsdale AZ: International Society of Meeting Planners.

Jedrziewski. *The Complete Guide for the Meeting Planner.* Southwestern, 1991.

Jones. *Meeting Management: A Professional Approach,* 2d ed. Stamford, CT: Bayard Publishing, 1984.

Jutkins, Ray. *Direct Marketing: How You Can Really Do it Right.* Costa Mesa, CA: HDL, 1989.

Kennedy, Dan S. *Ultimate Sales Letter.* Adams Media, 1990.

Kennedy, Dan S. *Ultimate Marketing Plan.* Adams Media, 1991.

Kennedy, Dan S. *No B.S. Sales Success.* Self-Counsel Press, 1994.

Kennedy, Dan S. *No B.S. Time Management.* Self-Counsel Press, 1996.

Kennedy, Dan S. *How to Make Millions with Your Ideas.* Penguin/Plume, 1996.

Klein, Larry. *Exhibits: Planning and Design.* New York, NY: Madison Square Press, 1986.

Konikow, Robert B. *Design in Motion: Exhibits.* Glen Cove, NY: PBC International, Inc., 1989, 1-800-527-2826.

Konikow, Robert B. *Exhibit Design,* books 1–5. Glen Cove, NY: PBC International, Inc., 1-800-527-2826.

Konikow, Robert B. *How to Participate Profitably in Trade Shows,* 3d ed. Santa Barbara, CA: Dartnell Corporate, 1987.

Laborde, Gene Z. *Influencing With Integrity.* New York: Sintony, Inc. 1984.

LeBoeuf, Michael, Ph.D. *The Greatest Management Principle in the World.* New York: Berkley Books, 1985.

Levinson, Jay Conrad. *Guerrilla Marketing Attack.* Boston: Houghton Mifflin, 1987.

Levinson, Jay Conrad. *Guerrilla Marketing for the 90's.* Boston: Houghton Mifflin, 1995.

Levinson, Jay Conrad. *Guerrilla Marketing Weapons.* New York: Plume, 1990.

Levinson, Jay Conrad, Bill Gallagher, Ph.D., and Orvel Ray Wilson. *Guerrilla Selling—Unconventional Weapons and Tactics for Increasing Your Sales.* Boston: Houghton Mifflin, 1992.

Mackay, Harvey. *Beware the Naked Man Who Offers You His Shirt.* New York: Ivy Books, 1990.

Mackay, Harvey. *Swim With The Sharks Without Being Eaten Alive.* New York: Ivy Books, 1988.

Maltz, Dr. Maxwell. *Psychocybernetics.* New York: Pocket Books, 1960.

Manitoba Industry, Trade and Tourism. *Researching and Preparing for a Foreign Market—Making Trade Fairs Work For You.* Winnipeg, Manitoba, Canada, 1990.

Marketech. *The Basics of Exhibit Marketing.* Tulsa, OK, 1-918-481-0607.

Marketech. *The Exhibit Managers Companion.* Tulsa, OK, 1992, 1-918-481-0607.

Marketing Catalysts. *Guidelines, Standards & Techniques Toward Significantly Improved Trade Show Results.* Evanston, IL, 1987.

Maslow, Abraham. *Motivation and Personality.* New York: Harper and Row, 1954.

MediaMap. *Trade Show Exhibitor's Handbook.* Bedford, MA, 1992, 1-617-275-5560.

Mercer, Laurie J. and Jennifer Singer. *Opportunity Knocks: Using PR.* Radnor, PA: Chilton Book Company, 1989.

Miller, Steve. *How To Get the Most out of Trade Shows.* Lincolnwood, IL: NTC Business Books, 1990, 1-708-679-2494.

Montgomery and Strick. *Meetings, Conventions and Expositions.* Van Nostrand Reinhold, 1994.

Murray, Cindy C. *How to Organize and Manage a Seminar.* Englewood Cliffs, NJ: Spectrum Books/Prentice Hall, 1983.

Murray, Cindy C. *Planning a Trade Show from Z to A.* Poway, CA: Murray Associates.

Nadler, Leonard. *The Comprehensive Guide to Successful Conferences & Meetings.* San Francisco: Jossey-Bass Pub, 1987.

Naisbet, John and Patricia Aburdene. *Megatrends 2000.* New York: William Morrow and Co., 1990.

Nichols (ed.). *Professional Meeting Management.* Professional Convention Management Association Publishers.

Office des Publicitions Officielles des Communautes Europeannes. *Congress Terminology.* Service Vente, L-2985, Luxembourg, 1986. Glossary in English, German, Spanish, and Italian.

Parinello, Anthony. *Selling to VITO the Very Important Top Officer.* Hollbrook, MA: Bob Adams Inc., 1994.

PCMA. *Enjoy Your Meeting . . . Safely!* Birmingham, AL: Professional Convention Management Association, 1-205-823-7262.

PCMA. *Professional Meeting Management.* Birmingham, AL: Professional Convention Management Association, 1-205-823-7262.

Peoples, David. *Presentations Plus: David Peoples' Proven Techniques.* New York, NY: John Wiley & Sons, 1988.

Peters, Tom and Robert Waterman. *In Search of Excellence.* New York: Warner, 1982.

Peterson. *Convention Centers, Stadiums and Arenas.* Washington, DC: Urban Land Institute, 1989.

Price. *The AMA Guide for Meetings & Event Planners.* Washington, DC: American Management Association, 1989.

Rackham, Neil. *Spin Selling.* New York: McGraw-Hill, 1988.

Ramacitti, David F. *Do-It Yourself Publicity.* New York, NY: American Management Association, 1990.

Rinke, Wolf J. *The 6 Success Strategies for Winning at Life, Love and Business.* Deerfield, IL: Health Communications, 1996.

Riso, Don Richard. *Personality Types.* Boston: Houghton Mifflin, 1987.

Rowland, Diana. *International Herald Tribune's Guide to Business Travel in Europe.* New York, NY: Warner, 1985.

Rudman, Jack. *Exhibits Technician.* Syosset, NY: National Learning Corporation.

Rutherford. *Introduction to the Conventions, Expositions and Meetings Industry.* Van Nostrand Reinhold, 1990.

Schoonmaker, Alan N. *Negotiate to Win: Gaining the Psychological Edge.* Engelwood Cliffs, NJ: Prentice Hall, 1989.

Schwartz, David. *The Magic of Thinking Big.* New York: Prentice Hall, 1965.

Seekings, David. *How to Organize Effective Conferences and Meetings,* 4th ed., New York, NY: Nicholas Publishing, 1989.

Shaw. *Convention Sales: A Book of Readings.* Educational Institute of the American Hotel & Motel Association, 1990.

Siskind, Barry. *The Successful Exhibitor.* Toronto, Ontario: International Training & Management Company, 1989.

Slutsky, Jeff. *Streetfighting.* Englewood Cliffs, NJ: Prentice Hall, 1984.

Stutts. *The Travel Safety Handbook.* Van Nostrand Reinhold.

Surbeck. *Creating Special Events.* Master Publications, 1991.

Talbot. *Meeting Management.* McLean, VA: EPM, 1990.

Toffler, Alvin. *Future Shock.* New York: Random House, 1970.

Toffler, Alvin. *Powershift.* New York: Bantam, 1990.

Trisler, Hank. *No Bull Sales Management.* New York: Bantam, 1985.

Trisler, Hank. *No Bull Selling.* New York: Frederick Fell, 1983.

TSEA. *Exhibit Industry Glossary of Terms.* Springfield, VA: Trade Show Exhibitors Association, 1-703-941-3725.

TSEA. *IEA Position Statements.* Springfield, VA: Trade Show Exhibitors Association, 1-703-941-3725. This publication outlines the Association's official opinion on industry issues.

TWI International Exhibition Logistics. *Exhibition Management Guide for the International Aerospace, Defense and Space Industries.* San Mateo, CA, 1-415-573-6900. This publication is free.

Voso, Michael. *The Convention and Meeting Planners Handbook.* Lexington Books, 1990.

Walther, George. *Phone Power.* New York: Putnam, 1986.

WARF/GWSAE. *The International Meetings Guide.* Washington, DC: Washington Association Research Foundation/Greater Washington Society of Association Executives, Braddock Communications, 1987.

Washington Association Research Foundation. *Bibliography of Association Management Literature.* Washington, DC, 1-202-429-9370.

Weintraub, Diane K. *Trade Show Exhibiting: An Insider's Guide for Entrepreneurs.* Boston: Liberty Press, McGraw-Hill, 1991.

Weirich. *Meetings and Conventions Management.* New York: Delmar, 1992.

Weiss, Alan, Ph.D., *Million Dollar Consulting.* New York: McGraw-Hill, 1992.

Weissinger. *A Guide to Successful Meeting Planning,* New York: Wiley, 1991.

Wigger. *Catering to Every Whim: A Complete Guide to Catering Sales.* Englewood Cliffs, NJ: Prentice Hall, 1991.

Willingham, Ron. *Integrity Selling.* New York: Doubleday, 1987.

Witteborg, Lothar P. *Expositions, Exhibits, Industrial & Good Show! A Practical Guide for Temporary Exhibitions.* Washington, DC: Smithsonian Institution Press, 1-202-287-3738.

Wright, Nancy. *The Trade Show: Putting Its Selling Power to Work.* Hurley, NY: Nancy Wright & Associates, 1989, 1-914-338-7717.

Wright. *The Meeting Spectrum.* San Diego: Rockwood Enterprises, 1988.

Zigler, Zig. *Secrets of Closing the Sale.* New York: Berkley Books, 1984.

Zinsser, William. *On Writing Well.* New York: Harper & Row, 1988.

Zunin, Leonard. *Contact: The First Four Minutes.* New York: Ballantine, 1988.

➤ Audiotapes[1]

Battles, Brian. *How to Listen Powerfully.* Boulder, CO: CareerTrack Publications, 1988.

Bliss, Edwin. *Getting Things Done.* Boulder, CO: CareerTrack Publications, 1985.

Brinkman, Rick and Rick Kirschner. *How to Deal With Difficult People.* Boulder, CO: CareerTrack Publications, 1987.

---

[1] To order audio and video materials, call CareerTrack Publications (1-800-334-1018, or, in Colorado, 1-303-447-2323), Nightingale-Conant Corporation (1-800-323-5552), or the Guerilla Group (1-800-247-9145).

Canfield, Jack. *Self Esteem and Peak Performance.* Boulder, CO: CareerTrack Publications, 1987.

Cathcart, Jim and Anthony Alessandra. *Relationship Strategies.* Chicago: Nightingale-Conant, 1985.

Dolan, John Patrick. *Negotiate Like the Pros.* Boulder, CO, CareerTrack Publications, 1990.

Executive-Management Renewal Programs. *How to Sell At A Trade Show.* Harrisburg, PA, 1-800-535-3633.

Friedman, Susan. *Power Exhibiting.* Diadem.

Garfield, Charles. *Peak Performers.* Chicago: Nightingale-Conant Corporation, 1986.

Merrill, Douglas. *The New Time Management.* Chicago: Nightingale-Conant Corporation, 1983.

Miller, Steve. *Stand Out in the Crowd: Your Guide to Successful Exhibit Marketing.* Federal Way, WA: The Adventure of Trade Shows, 1-206-874-9665. Series of four cassettes.

Moidel, Steve. *Memory Power.* Boulder, CO: CareerTrack Publications, 1989.

Parinello, Anthony. *Selling to Vito: The Very Important Top Officer.* San Diego, CA, 1-800-777-VITO. Six-hour audiocassette series.

Peters, Tom. *The New Masters of Excellence.* Chicago: Nightingale-Conant Corporation, 1988.

Peters, Tom. *Thriving on Chaos.* Chicago: Nightingale-Conant Corporation, 1988.

Petrina, Nancy. *Trade Show Tips.* Harrisburg, PA: Executive Management Renewal Programs, 1-800-535-3633.

R D International. *Trade Show Learning Systems.* Los Angeles, CA, 1985, 1-213-876-5690.

Robbins, Anthony. *Unlimited Power.* Chicago: Nightingale-Conant, 1989.

Smith, Debra. *Telephone Skills.* Boulder, CO: CareerTrack Publications, 1987.

Smith, Mark S. A. *Guerrilla Trade Show Selling.* Boulder, CO: The Guerrilla Group, Inc., 1997.

Sommer, Bobbe. *How to Set And Achieve Goals.* Boulder, CO: CareerTrack Publications, 1987.

Tracy, Brian. *The Psychology of Achievement.* Chicago: Nightingale-Conant, 1988.

TSEA. *Step by Step . . . How to Make Every Trade Show a Marketing Success.* Springfield, VA: Trade Show Exhibitors Association, 1-703-941-3725.

Wilson, Orvel Ray. *Guerrilla Selling—Live!* Boulder, CO: The Guerrilla Group, Inc, 1996.

Wilson, Orvel Ray. *Guerrilla Selling in Action.* Boulder, CO: The Guerrilla Group, Inc., 1996.

Wilson, Orvel Ray. *Sell Like The Pros.* Boulder, CO: CareerTrack Publications, 1990.

➤ Video Training Materials

Abelson, Norm. *Trade Shows: Successful Sales Techniques.* Portland, OR: Creative Media Development, Inc., 1-503-223-6910. Set of 200 color slides in three carousel trays and six cassette tapes pulse-keyed to the slides, plus handbook.

CEIR. *Preshow Promotions: Basic Steps.* Bethesda, MD: Center for Exhibition Industry Research, 1991, 1-301-907-7626.

CEIR. *Trade Show: The Bottom Line.* Bethesda, MD: Center for Exhibition Industry Research, 1983, 1-301-907-7626.

Continental Film Productions Corp. *The Exhibitionist.* Chattanooga, TN.

Executive-Management Renewal Programs. *How to Sell At A Trade Show.* Harrisburg, PA, 1-800-535-3633.

Fox, Fred. *Power Selling for Exhibitors.* Springfield, VA: Trade Show Exhibitors Association, 1-703-941-3725.

Gudea, Darlene and Irene Sperling-Orseck. *Ten Significant Trends Affecting The Exposition Industry.* Recorded session from IAEM Winter Meeting, Indianapolis, IN: International Association for Exposition Management, 1991, 1-214-458-8002.

Hannover Fairs USA, Inc. *Hannover Fair '92,* Gateway to Global Markets, Princeton, NJ, 1-609-987-1202.

Konopacki, Allen. *The Dynamics of Trade Show Selling.* Chicago, IL: Incomm Center for Trade Show Research, 1-312-642-9377.

Konopacki, Allen. *7 Tips for Exhibiting Success: Best Tips for Boosting Success at Trade Shows.* Incomm Chicago, IL: Center for Trade Show Research, 1-312-642-9377. VHS videotape and manual.

Konopacki, Allen. *Successful International Selling Tips: Ideas and Methods to Increase Results from International Visitors.* Chicago, IL: Incomm Center for Trade Show Research, 1-312-642-9377.

Konopacki, Allen. *Watch Out For Changing Attitudes At Trade Shows.* Indianapolis, IN: International Association for Exposition Management, 1991, 1-214-458-8002. Recorded session from the IAEM Winter Meeting.

Marketech. *The Focus Is On You.* Tulsa, OK, 1-918-481-0607. VHS and training manual. Use as a standalone source or as a reinforcement to preshow meeting training.

Miller, Steve. *Recession Proof Trade Show Marketing for the 90's.* The Adventure of Trade Shows, 1-206-874-9665. Four VHS videotapes designed to teach the exhibitor the keys to proper trade show marketing.

Sanborn, Mark. *Team Building,* vols. 1 and 2. Boulder, CO: CareerTrack Publications, 1989.

Skyline Displays, Inc. *Exhibit Selling.* Burnsville, MN, 1-800-328-2725. VHS and audiocassette with workbook.

Skyline Displays, Inc. *The Guide to Profitable Trade Shows.* Burnsville, MN, 1-800-328-2725. VHS, audiocassette, and workbooks. A series of modular learning tools.

Smith, Debra. *Professional Telephone Skills.* Boulder, CO: CareerTrack Publications, 1989.

Smith, Mark S. A. *Guerrilla Trade Show Selling.* Boulder, CO: The Guerrilla Group, Inc., 1997.

Smith, Mark S. A. *How to Get the Most Leads From Your Trade Show.* Boulder, CO: The Guerrilla Group, Inc., 1996.

Smith, Mark S. A. *The Ten Most Common Mistakes People Make at Trade Shows and How to Correct Them.* Boulder, CO: The Guerrilla Group, Inc., 1996.

TASE. *Trade Show Selling*. Springfield, VA: Trade Show Exhibitors Association, 1-703-941-3725.

Ten Years of Trade Show Bureau Reports in Ten Minutes, vols. I and II. Bethesda, MD: Center for Exhibition Industry Research, 1-301-907-7626. 35-mm color slides.

Video Arts, Inc. *It'll Be OK on the Day: The Importance of Planning Effective Exhibit Participation*. Northbrook, IL, 1-800-553-0091.

Video Arts, Inc. *That's Show Business*. Springfield VA: Trade Show Exhibitors Association, 1-703-941-3725. A new version of *How Not to Exhibit Yourself* on VHS with booklets.

Wilson, Orvel Ray. *Guerrilla Selling—Live!* Boulder, CO: The Guerrilla Group, Inc., 1996.

Wilson, Orvel Ray. *The 10 Characteristics of a Guerrilla*. Boulder, CO: The Guerrilla Group, Inc., 1996.

➤ Industry Periodicals

Exhibitor Times. Virgo Publishing, Inc., 3300 N. Central Ave. Suite 2500, Phoenix, AZ 85012. Valerie A. M. Demetros, Editor-in-Chief, 1-602-990-1101, Fax 1-602-990-0819, E-mail etmag@vpico.com.

Tradeshow Week. Tradeshow Week, 5700 Wilshire Blvd., Suite 120, Los Angeles, CA 90036-5804, 1-213-965-5300.

Appendix

■ EXHIBITION INDUSTRY ASSOCIATIONS

American Hotel & Motel Association (AH&MA)
Ken Hine, Kirk Postmanteur
1201 New York Ave. NW
Washington, DC 20005-3917
1-202-289-3100, Fax 1-202-289-3199.

American Society of Association Executives (ASAE)
1575 Eye Street NW
Washington, DC 20005
1-202-626-2723.

Association for Convention Operations Management (ACOM)
Association for Convention Marketing Executives (ACME),
William Just, Tom Salvo
819 Peachtree Street Suite 560
Atlanta, GA 30309
1-404-351-3220.

Center for Exhibition Industry Research (CSAE)
Stephen Sind
4350 East West Highway Suite 401
Bethesda, MD 20814
1-301-907-7627, Fax 1-301-907-0277.

Computer Event Marketing Association (CEMA)
Melissa Bachelder, Association Manager, Danieli & O'Keefe
1-508-443-3330, Fax 1-508-443-4715
E-mail CEMA.DOK@Notes.compuserve.com.

Convention Liaison Council (CLC)
LaRue Fry, Barbara Koch Silversmith
1575 Eye Street NW
Washington, DC 20005
1-202-676-2764.

Council on Hotel, Restaurant & Institutional Education (CHRIE)
Doug Adair
1200 17th Street NW 7th Floor
Washington, DC 20036
1-202-331-5990, Fax 1-202-331-2429.

Educational Institute (EI of AH&MA)
Ray Swann
1407 S. Harrison Rd. Suite 310, E.
Lansing, MI 48823
1-517-353-5500.

Exhibit Design & Producers Association (EDPA)
611 East Wells St.
Milwaukee, WI 53202
1-414-276-3372.

Exposition Service Contractors Association (ESCA)
Randy Bauler
1516 South Pontius Ave.
Los Angeles, CA 90025
1-213-478-0215.

Hotel Sales & Marketing Association International (HSMAI)
1300 L Street NW Suite 800
Washington, DC 20005.

Institute of Association Management Companies (IAMC)
Glen Anderson, Exec. VP
104 Wilmot Rd., Suite 201
Deerfield, IL 60015-5195
1-708-940-4646, Fax 1-708-940-7218.

International Association of Auditorium Managers (IAAM)
John Swinburn
4425 W. Airport Freeway #590
Irving, TX 75022
1-214-255-8020.

International Association of Conference Centers (IACC)
Tom Bolman
243 Lindbergh Blvd.
St. Louis, MO 63141-7851.

International Association of Convention & Visitors Bureaus (IACVB)
Richard Newman
P.O. Box 758
Champaign, IL 61824
1-217-359-8881.

International Association for Exposition Management (IAEM)
Steven Hacker
P.O. Box 802425
Dallas, TX 75380
1-214-458-8002.

International Special Events Society (ISES)
Sharon Gorup, Executive Director
8335 Allison Pointe Trail #100
Indianapolis, IN 46250
1-800-688-4737.

Meeting Professionals International
Ed Griffin, Executive Director
4455 LBJ Parkway, Suite 1200
Dallas, TX 75207
1-972-702-3000

National Association of Catering Executives (NACE)
Vickie Zombolo
60 Revere Drive, Suite 500
Northbrook, IL 60062
1-708-480-9080, Fax 1-708-480-9282.

National Association of Consumer Shows (NACS)
Michael A. Fisher
825 NE 20th Suite 120
Portland, OR 97232.

National Coalition of Black Meeting Planners (NCBMP)
Ozzie Jenkins
50 F Street NW, Suite 1040
Washington, DC 20001
1-202-628-3952.

Professional Convention Management Association (PCMA)
Roy Evans, Ed Polivka
100 Vestavia Office Park Suite 220
Birmingham, AL 35216
1-205-823-7262, Fax 1-205-822-3891.

Religious Conference Management Association (RCMA)
DeWayne Woodring
One Hoosier Dome, Suite 120
Indianapolis, IN 46225
1-317-632-1888.

Society of Corporate Meeting Professionals (SCMP)
Bob Massaro
2600 Garden Road, Suite 208
Monterey, CA 93940
1-408-649-6544.

Society of Government Meeting Planners (SGMP)
219 E. Main
Mechanicsburg, PA 17055
1-717-795-SGMP.

Society of Independent Show Organizers (SISO)
Steve Schuldenfrei, Executive Director
Framingham Corporate Center, 3d Floor
492 Old Connecticut Path
Framingham, MA 01701
1-508-270-2640, Fax 1-508-270-2642.

Trade Show Exhibitors Association
Peter Mangelli
5501 Backlick Road #105
Springfield, VA 22151
1-703-941-3725.

Union Des Foires Internationales (UFI)
Gerda Marquardt, Secretary-General
35bis, rue Jouffroy-d'Abbans, F-75017
Paris, FRANCE
033-1-42679912, Fax 033-1-42271929.

World Trade Centers Association (WTCA)
Tom Kearney
One World Trade Center, Suite 7701
New York, NY 10048
1-212-432-2640, Fax 1-212-488-0064.

■ DISPLAY MANUFACTURERS

Call the Exhibit Designers & Producers Association, Milwaukee, WI, 1-414-276-3372, for a list of members and information on how to select an exhibit designer and producer. Then call each of the vendors listed below and ask for a free brochure.

Channel-Kor Systems, Inc.	1-800-242-6567
ExhibitgroupGiltspur	1-800-424-6224
Exposure Display Systems	1-800-537-0231
Exposystems	1-800-367-3976
Laarhoven Design	1-800-666-4436
Leitner USA, Inc.	1-800-544-5872
Moss	1-800-341-1557
Nomadic Displays	1-800-336-5019
Professional Displays, Inc.	1-800-222-6838
Skyline	1-800-328-2725

■ ON-LINE SOURCES OF TRADE-SHOW INFORMATION

➤ http://www.guerrillagroup.com

The Guerrilla Group, Inc., 947 Walnut Street, Boulder, CO 80302, 1-800-247-9145, Fax 1-303-938-8476.

The Guerrilla Group site provides weekly sales tips, the latest weapons and tactics for sales and marketing, the ability to send and receive E-mail from the authors, ask questions, and order training and study resources online. The site also has access to hundreds of links to other sales, marketing, and trade-show resources.

➤ http://www.gmarketing.com

Guerrilla Marketing Online Magazine

➤ http://www.exhibitornet.com

The Exhibitor Network. Exhibitor magazine's online resource for trade show and event marketing professionals.
Offerings include industry research, case studies, salary survey, guidelines on Exhibitor Show's professional certification
program (Certified Trade Show Marketer), and information
on upcoming exhibitor shows around the world. The address
is Exhibitor Magazine Group, 206 South Broadway, Suite 745,
Rochester, MN 55904, 1-507-289-6556, Fax 1-507-289-5253.

➤ http://www.ceir.org

The Center for Exhibition Industry Research, 4350 East West
Highway, Suite 401, Bethesda, MD 20814, 1-301-907-7626, Fax
1-301-907-0277. Formerly The Trade Show Bureau, CEIR's
mission is to be the advocate for promoting the value, benefits, and growth of exhibitions as a primary component in an
integrated marketing program through research, information, and communication. CEIR has the world's largest and
most specific database covering the exhibition industry.
They are a membership organization representing the entire
exhibition industry worldwide. They have served the industry for 18 years in providing valuable marketing and research report to thousands who have improved and grown
their businesses. CEIR helps you help yourselves and your
customers. Includes publications catalog, member benefits,
industry press releases, membership directory, and brochure.
CEIR's Research Reports include "The Power of Exhibitions"
(significant research about decision makers' perceptions
of the value of exhibitions in the purchasing cycle and
strategies for effective trade-show and exhibit marketing),
"Sales/Measuring Return" (specific exhibition-related objectives analyzed and compared to other marketing media),
"Attendee/Exhibitor Characteristics," "International Issues,"
"Industry Trends," and "Industry Resources." Special listings

are compiled for quick reference to members and sources of information. Also available are audiovisual presentations, facts and figures from around the industry, special reports series, and custom consulting and reports.

➤ http://www.kweb.com

The Computer Events Directory, Knowledge Web, Inc., PO Box 150331, San Rafael, CA 94915, 1-415-485-5508, Fax 1-415-721-2471. Established in 1994, the focus of this group is computers, communications, and technology events, including conferences, exhibitions, trade shows, and seminars that serve regional, national, and international markets. This site offers a comprehensive listing of over 1,000 computer industry events and shows by date, place, name, industry, and keyword. An excellent search engine makes locating complete information quick and easy.

➤ http://www.expoguide.com

ExpoGuide. This is an *excellent* listing of exhibition events in the United States and Canada. Allows for searching by date, location, topic, or keyword. Definitely a guerrilla weapon.

➤ http://www.travelweb.com

TravelWeb. The TravelWeb database contains detailed information for thousands of hotel properties to make it easier to identify and select an individual property or properties based upon criteria selected by the user. The search program takes the user's preferences into account in several categories: by city, favorite chain, type of lodging, desired amenities, and price range. A great resource for locating alternative hotels in the vicinity of a show.

➤ http://www.tsnn.com

The Trade Show News Network, with show updates, vendors, ideas, and suggestions. A one-stop, integrated resource on the Internet for the trade-show industry designed to promote trade-show attendance, exhibit sales, and supplier services.

➤ http://ciber.bus.msu.edu/busres/tradshow.htm

Links to shows all around the world.

➤ http://www.tradegroup.com

The Trade Group's "Trade Shows, Expositions & Conferences" site provides comprehensive, frequently update content for exhibitors, attendees, planners and vendors.

➤ http://www.tsea.org

Trade Show Exhibitors Association, 703-941-3725.

➤ http://www.tradefair.de

Dusseldorf Trade Fairs Exhibition site.

■ TRADE-SHOW DIRECTORIES

➤ United States

The Exhibit Review. Exhibit Review, 3800 SW Cedar Hills Blvd., Suite 251, Beaverton OR 97005, 1-800-235-3324.

Health Care Industry Trade Show Directory. Paradata Research, 2 Summer St., Suite 14, Natick, MA 01760, 1-508-655-7922.

Media Map: The Definitive Guide to Computer Industry Trade Shows. Media Map, 130 Great Road, Bedford, MA 01730, 1-617-275-5560.

Tradeshow Week Data Book. Tradeshow Week, 5700 Wilshire Blvd., Suite 120, Los Angeles, CA, 90036-5804, 1-213-965-5300.

Tradeshows & Exhibits Schedule. Successful Meetings DataBank, 633 Third Ave., New York, NY 10164, 1-800-253-6708.

➤ International

Calendar of International Events. World Access Corporation, 15 Bemis Rd., Wellesley, MA 02181, 1-617-235-8095.

Calendar of International Tradeshows and Exhibitions. TWI International Exhibition Logistics, 3190 Clearview Way, San Mateo, CA 94402, 1-415-573-6900.

Canadian Trade Show Directories. Salons Congres, Editions Info Presse Inc., 4316 Boulevard St-Lauren, Suite 400, Montreal, Quebec H2W 1Z3, 1-800-363-8725.

Exhibition Bulletin. 44-181-778-2288, Fax 44-181-659-8495. Monthly publication from England.

Shows and Exhibitions. Maclean Hunter Ltd., 777 Bay St., Toronto, Ontario M5W 1A7, 1-416-596-6035.

Trade Shows Worldwide. Gale Research, Inc., 835 Penobscot Building, Detroit, MI 48226, 1-800-347-4253.

Tradeshow Week Data Book International, Tradeshow Week, 5700 Wilshire Blvd., Suite 120, Los Angeles, CA 90036-5804, 1-213-965-5300.

Also contact your State Economic Development and Export Promotion Offices, commercial sections of foreign embassies and consulates, and foreign chambers of commerce.

The U.S. Department of Commerce offers many trade-show related services and publications, including *Business America* and foreign exhibition information.

■ INQUIRY-HANDLING COMPANIES

ADTrack
Ceder Rapids, IA, 1-800-735-3237

Creative Professional Services
Woburn, MA, 1-617-935-5007 Ext. 52

DBM Group
Palo Alto, CA, 1-800-858-1820

Express Lead Response
Fremont, CA, 1-800-644-1116

Harte-Hanks
Austin, TX, 1-800-333-3383

Hibbert West
Denver, CO, 1-800-433-1601

InnoTrac
Norcross, GA, 1-800-827-4666

Inquiry Handling Service
San Fernando, CA, 1-818-365-8131

Inquiry Intelligence Systems
Bridgeton, MO, 1-800-467-2329

Inquiry Systems Company
Athol, MA, 1-508-249-5303

MarketPro
Grass Valley, CA, 1-916-477-0248

Output Technologies
Mt. Prospect, IL, 1-708-635-3600

Rachlin Enterprises
Deer Park, NY, 1-516-243-0505

Sales Support Services
Fort Worth, TX, 1-817-685-5600

Saligent
Colorado Springs, CO, 1-800-325-7818

Techmar Communications
Canton, MA, 1-617-821-8324

Towne Advertising Mailing Service
Santa Ana, CA, 1-714-540-3095

■ BUSINESS-CARD SCANNERS

CardGrabber
Pacific Crest Technologies, Inc.
4000 MacArthur Blvd., Suite 6800
Newport Beach, CA 93660
1-714-261-6444.

CypherScan
CypherTech, Inc.
250 Caribbean Dr.
Sunnyvale, CA 94089
1-800-294-7226.

Scan-in-Dex
Microtek Lab, Inc.
680 Knox St.
Torrance, CA 90502.

■ SOFTWARE LISTINGS

Sales & Marketing Magazine's Annual Sales & Marketing Software Directory
Bill Communications
355 Park Avenue South
New York, NY 10010-1789
1-212-592-6203.

Telemarketing Magazine's Annual "Buyers Guide"
Technology Marketing Corp.
1 Technology Plaza
Norwalk, CT 06854
1-203-852-6800, Fax 1-203-852-6800.

■ YOUR SUCCESS CHECKLIST

Take a look at this checklist. This is a list of things you will have to prepare for the show and budget for. Look at each category. Some will need lots of attention from you, some of them you'll want to delegate to others, some you'll want to bring in outside experts to help you, and some of them won't apply to your show.

- ☐ Preshow promotion
  - ☐ Planning expense
  - ☐ Design
  - ☐ Printing
  - ☐ Mailing
    - ☐ Assembly
    - ☐ Postage
  - ☐ Telemarketing
  - ☐ Gifts
  - ☐ Advertising
  - ☐ PR and media relations

- ☐ Exhibit floor-space charges

- ☐ Exhibit
  - ☐ Purchase, lease, rental
  - ☐ Storage, if purchased
  - ☐ Refurbishing, if purchased
  - ☐ Tool and survival kit

- ☐ Signs and graphics
  - ☐ Show-specific
  - ☐ Refurbishing

- ☐ Exhibit furniture
  - ☐ Tables
  - ☐ Special displays
  - ☐ Garbage cans
  - ☐ Carpeting and pad

- ☐ Freight and shipping
  - ☐ Exhibit
  - ☐ Furnishings

- ☐ Sample products
- ☐ Premiums, literature, etc.
- ☐ Drayage
- ☐ Overnight services for things you forgot

☐ Install and dismantle
- ☐ Labor
- ☐ Labor supervision
- ☐ Utilities
  - ☐ Electricity
  - ☐ Water
  - ☐ Air
  - ☐ Phone lines
- ☐ Exhibit cleaning
- ☐ Additional decorating
  - ☐ Plants, flowers
  - ☐ Balloons, etc.
- ☐ Security

☐ Exhibit Staff
- ☐ Hotel
- ☐ Meals
- ☐ Entertainment
- ☐ Travel
  - ☐ Air
  - ☐ Ground
- ☐ Conference registrations
- ☐ Uniform, special clothing
- ☐ Other expenses

☐ Sales
- ☐ Lead form
- ☐ Lead capture system
- ☐ Staff training program
- ☐ Premiums
- ☐ Nondisclosure agreements
- ☐ Lead management services

☐ Other promotional activities
- ☐ Educational presentations
- ☐ Meetings expense

- ☐ Special events
  - ☐ Staff dinners
  - ☐ Customer parties
  - ☐ Hospitality suite

☐ On-site promotion
  - ☐ Signs
  - ☐ Flyers
  - ☐ Advertising
  - ☐ Premiums
  - ☐ Show-specific literature
  - ☐ Sales staff incentive programs
  - ☐ Live presenters, actors
  - ☐ Audio and video equipment

☐ Aftershow promotion
  - ☐ Design
  - ☐ Letter writing
  - ☐ Literature
  - ☐ Printing
  - ☐ Assembly
  - ☐ Postage
  - ☐ Telemarketing
  - ☐ Sales force calls
  - ☐ Premiums
  - ☐ Sales force incentive programs
  - ☐ Aftershow survey

■ SHOW SURVIVAL-KIT CHECKLIST

Here's a list of things you'll likely use in your exhibit or really wish you had. Decide which ones you plan to bring with you and which you will buy, if necessary, on the spot.

☐ Credit card with a high spending limit

☐ Spare light bulbs for your lighting fixtures

☐ Cooler with bottled water and beverages

☐ Software disks for computers

☐ Spare parts for your modular exhibit

☐ Lint brush

☐ Small vacuum cleaner

☐ Tool kit
　☐ Hammer
　☐ Adjustable wrench
　☐ Screwdrivers
　　☐ Standard
　　☐ Phillips
　☐ Needlenose pliers
　☐ Standard pliers
　☐ Hex wrench (if used in your exhibit)
　☐ Measuring tape

☐ Scissors

☐ Stapler and staples

☐ Posting notes

☐ Message pads

☐ Pens

☐ Permanent felt-tip pens

☐ Sticky labels (for shipping, cartons, labeling)

☐ Tape

- ☐ Cellophane tape and dispenser
- ☐ Masking tape
- ☐ Carton tape
- ☐ Strapping tape
- ☐ Duct tape or gaffers tape
- ☐ Double-sided tape

☐ Velcro®

☐ Glue
- ☐ Super-adhesive glue
- ☐ White glue
- ☐ Duco® cement
- ☐ Contact cement

☐ Wire

☐ Cleaners
- ☐ Glass cleaner
- ☐ General-purpose spray cleaner
- ☐ Acetone
- ☐ Mineral spirits
- ☐ Furniture polish
- ☐ Carpet spot cleaner

☐ Clean cloth rags

☐ Paper towels

☐ Utility knife and spare blades

☐ Sandpaper

☐ Assorted nails (if appropriate for your exhibit)

☐ Thumb tacks, push pins

☐ First-aid kit
- ☐ Ibuprofen
- ☐ Antacid
- ☐ Plastic bandages
- ☐ Moleskin (for foot blisters)

☐ Extension cords

☐ Power outlet strips

■ SAMPLE LEAD FORM

┌─────────────┤ **VISITOR ACTION PLAN** ├─────────────┐

Date _____ Initials _____ Other _____ Special _____
Responsibility? _____

Most pressing problem/need? _____
_____
_____
_____
_____
_____
_____
_____

Who's involved in the decision? _____

When will you decide? _____

Budget? _____

Follow-up plan _____
_____
_____

Best phone number _____
Visitor Information _____
_____
_____
_____
_____

■ CONTINUE BEING A GUERRILLA

Call The Guerrilla Group toll-free at 1-800-247-9145 for free information about:

- ➤ Guerrilla selling
- ➤ Guerrilla trade-show selling
- ➤ Guerrilla TeleSelling
- ➤ Guerrilla marketing
- ➤ Customer service excellence
- ➤ Managing multiple demands

Customized on-site training programs and seminars are available, in formats ranging from a 30-minute keynote to a multiday boot camp. We also offer books, audiotapes, videotapes, newsletters, seminars, lectures, workshops, and other professional services. Sales and marketing consulting is available to groups and individuals.

The Guerrilla Group, Inc.
947 Walnut Street
Boulder, CO 80302
1-800-247-9145
http://www.guerrillagroup.com
postmaster@guerrillagroup.com

Index

More Rave Reviews for *Guerrilla Trade Show Selling*

"Great guide for the beginner. Covers trade show planning and implementation from A to Z. Also a good resource for companies who want to step up their efforts at trade shows. Very comprehensive."

Kristin Troff Pavek
Associate Editor, *Exhibitor Magazine*

"Trade shows remain a very powerful tool for promoting international sales, and *Guerrilla Trade Show Selling* contains many useful tips on how to maximize an exhibit's effectiveness."

Thomas J. Kearney
Executive Vice President, World Trade Centers Association, Inc.

"The Guerrilla Group has done it again. Loaded with street-smart how-to's. Anyone who ever does trade shows must read this book!"

Bill Brooks
President, The Brooks Group

"*Guerrilla Trade Show Selling* is to trade shows as gasoline is to a car—if you have a fancy car and no gas, you go no place. If you have a fancy exhibit booth and no *Guerrilla Trade Show Selling*, you go no place—and sell nothing." **Jeffrey Gitomer**
Author, *The Sales Bible* and syndicated column *Sales Moves*

"*Guerrilla Trade Show Selling* is a must-read for anybody who is serious about getting more bang for their exhibiting dollar! I've been a trade show consultant and author for over 12 years and am thrilled to see such a great resource hit the trade show industry. I'm going to tell all my corporate clients to get a copy and devour *every* word."

Steve Miller
Author, *How to Get the Most Out of Trade Shows*

"This book reveals the greatest trade show secrets in the world. Follow the ideas the Guerrillas lay out, and your competition won't know what hit them." **Dr. Michael LeBoeuf**
Author, *The Perfect Business* and
How to Win Customers and Keep Them for Life

"This is an incredibly powerful book. Easy to read, written with clarity, packed with powerful ideas, and guaranteed to help anyone who wants to excel in today's ever-changing marketplace. I recommend it unreservedly."   **Nido R. Qubein**
Chairman, Creative Services, Inc.

"I'm crazy about books that are a complete resource on a particular subject and chock full of useful and creative ideas. That's why I love *Guerrilla Trade Show Selling*. If you want to absolutely maximize your trade show selling, this thorough guide is for you."
Mark Sanborn, CSP, CPAE

"This book is the best resource ever to make trade show selling fun and profitable."   **Roger Dawson**
Author, *Roger Dawson's Secrets of Power Negotiating* and
13 Secrets of Power Performance

"This is a must-read for any sales and marketing organization that hopes to *sell* at trade shows."   **Dennis E. Mannering**, CSP
Options Unlimited, Inc.

"The secrets are out! *Guerrilla Trade Show Selling* levels the playing field and gives solo entrepreneurs the inside track on how to compete with larger firms—and win!"
Terri Lonier
Small Business Expert and Author, *Working Solo*

"*Guerrilla Trade Show Selling* furnishes your mind with smart techniques to save you money and hassles while generating more business through the medium of tradeshows. Chock full of great tips to help you become a savvy exhibitor or attendee. An important addition to your reference library. Pray your competitors don't get a hold of this book!"
Joseph Ciprut
Managing Director, Tradex Associates

"Finally you can extract every dime possible out of your trade show efforts. This book is a must for anyone who participates in trade shows or is thinking about it. You will discover numerous unconventional ideas that will dramatically increase your sales and save you a ton of money on your marketing. Buy this book now!"
Jeff Slutsky, Author
Street Fighter Marketing and *How To Get Clients*